D1279087

THE RATIONALISTS

THEORY AND DESIGN IN THE MODERN MOVEMENT

THE RATIO

THEORY AND DESIGN IN THE MODERN MOVEMEN

ONALISTS

EDITED BY DENNIS SHARP

ARCHITECTURAL BOOK PUBLISHING COMPANY, NEW YORK

First published in book form in 1978
by The Architectural Press Ltd

First published in the USA by
The Architectural Book Publishing Co. Inc. 1979

ISBN 0-8038-0219-6

Printed in Great Britain by
BAS Printers Limited, Over Wallop, Hampshire

Photographic acknowledgements

Unless otherwise stated, illustrations are reproduced by courtesy of *The Architectural Review* or have been supplied by individual authors. In a few cases, copyright owners could not be traced, and acknowledgement will be gladly made in future editions if appropriate.
Peter Behrens 4 from *Die Baukunst der neuesten Zeit* by Gustav Platz
Auguste Perret 1 Lucien Hervé; 21 Hugo P. Herdeg
Adolf Loos: Ornament and Crime Portrait Bildarchiv Preussischer Kulturbeisitz; 1 Gerlach
Frank Lloyd Wright 1 Bill Engdahl, Hedrich-Blessing; 3 Doeser Fotos; 5 Chicago Architectural Photo Company
Mies van der Rohe 3a, 6a, b, c Hedrich Blessing, 4a Hube Henry, Hedrich Blessing, 5 Ezra Stoller, 9 Reinhard Friedrich
Marcel Breuer Portrait Bauhaus-Archiv
J. M. Richards 12, 15 from *The New Vision* by L. Moholy-Nagy
Rationality in Architecture and in the Design Process Frontispiece (photograph of skyscrapers) Standard Oil Company, New York
Mannerism and Modern Architecture 4 from *Adolf Loos* by Heinrich Kulka; 5 from *Internationale Architektur* by Walter Gropius; 8, 9 Lucia Moholy
A Master Plan for London Frontispiece Topical Press Agency
Irrational Rationalism: The Rats since 1960 Illustrations are by courtesy of individual architects mentioned in the captions and as follows: Frontispiece, 1 National Monuments Board; 3 *Controspazio*; 7 *The Japan Architect*; 9 *Lotus*; 17a, b Ezra Stoller; 23 John Donat; 5, 25, 26 *A + U*

Contents

Preface

This book was originally conceived as a complement—and a contrast—to J. M. Richards' and Sir Nikolaus Pevsner's book *The Anti-Rationalists* (Architectural Press 1973) which set out to explore 'the curious bridges' linking Art Nouveau and Expressionism in the early years of this century. The emphasis of that book was on the well-furrowed line of study of individual Art Nouveau and Expressionist designers who supported an historical view somewhat different from that of the 'Rationalists'. It provided a contrast to what was referred to as the 'austere rationality of the Modern Movement', which the editors claimed was 'losing out' in the face of the renewed interest in the so-called 'Anti-rationalists'. The distinction was in many ways obscure but not without its usefulness in an art historical sense in defining attitudes and positions of architects to their work.

I reviewed *The Anti-Rationalists* for the British *Design* magazine under the title 'Anti-what?' in a furious disbelief that anyone could imply that the rich decorative architecture of the turn of the century as well as the work of the brilliant German Expressionist architects could be considered anything other than rational in terms of its approach to architecture, at least insofar as its interpretation of the problems posed by architecture within the *Zeitgeist* allowed. I would concede now that this may have been a somewhat impulsive response but it did lead to the commissioning of this volume! With that commission the difficulties of definition and interpretation were compounded. How can one talk of 'anti-rational' and 'rational' architects? Because of the historical development of the term 'rationalist' certain freedoms in its use have to be accepted.

In this book I have, as cogently as is possible in an anthology, selected a number of articles on architects whose ideas and work correspond most closely with a logical and reasoning approach to design problems and have added to this selection a number of newly commissioned items. Of necessity the designers and architects chosen would be referred to as 'Functionalists' or 'Modern Movement' pioneers or adherents. The names will be familiar. What on earth one does with architects such as Frank Lloyd Wright and Lutyens I am not sure. Clearly they were neither anti-rational nor irrational, nor indeed perverse in any sense in their views about architecture. Probably it is their uniqueness that makes them difficult to deal with in an age obsessed with classification and labelling. In any case I could not resist placing Sir Nikolaus Pevsner's essay (originally published in *The Architects' Journal* in 1939) on Frank Lloyd Wright's peaceful penetration of Europe in this collection as it illuminates so clearly one of the basic tendencies of the subject under review. Wright's logical approach to architectural form-giving was readily appreciated by so-called Rationalists such as Berlage, Gropius and Oud.

On the whole, as readers will soon appreciate, this anthology is as much concerned with the idea of Rationalism as it is with the work of individual architects. J. M. Richards' text on the Rational Aesthetic, somewhat late in its appearance in 1935 in relation to Continental trends, is a basic manifesto of Rationalist principles. It summarizes in a way I have not been able to find elsewhere the aspirations of the whole modern generation of English architects. Its republication is not without curiosity value.

By inviting Geoffrey Broadbent to contribute a new article on the 'Functional versus Rational' debate, the contextual significance of the earlier pieces, particularly Richards', is made clearer. In rather a different vein, Henryk

Skolimowski broadens the investigation into Rationalism and general philosophical attitudes and offers some provocative remarks on the operational bases of present-day rationalistic attitudes. Charles Jencks, prompted by more recent tendencies that have been labelled Rationalist, provides a survey of this current phase. He discusses the work and writings of a new generation of architects, critics and historians, and the Modern Movement's eclectic revival on the East Coast of the United States where the term Rationalism is now bandied about with renewed confidence. The British architect Peter Carter confines his contribution to a detailed examination of Mies van der Rohe's development. The other stone in the wide spanning arch of opinion especially commissioned for this publication is Bruno Zevi's article on the 'Italian Rationalists'. Here the term is definitive. Professor Zevi, in providing the essential *voussoir* of the whole survey, reveals the curious logic of those who invented and used it. For me the conclusions in his article underline the problems of dealing with such a parturient subject. Less need be said about the republished material as this obviously stands or falls on its own terms and is reprinted here with minimal editorial revision. It is largely drawn from the pages of *The Architectural Review* and its republication, it is hoped, will once again provide access to material that will be of interest to architects, historians and students alike.

There is unfortunately a paucity of contemporary photographs, and much of the original archive material has been lost or was destroyed in the war. This has led to a problem in selecting illustrations for the book, and some of the photographs are of a quality which is far from ideal. Photographs taken from the AR articles have not reproduced as clearly as in the original articles, but have been re-used none the less because of their intrinsic interest.

Dennis Sharp
London 1977

Acknowledgements

I am greatly indebted to Professor Henryk Skolimowski whose patient exposition of the principles of philosophical Rationalism has proved of great value to me personally. He and John James, to whom I am equally indebted, were also kind enough to comment on the drafts of my introduction. I also acknowledge the advice and help, both in discussions and through their respective publications, of Geoffrey Broadbent and Charles Jencks. Other colleagues, too numerous to mention individually, have also sparked off many investigations into the confusing literature on the rather imprecise subject of rationalism in architecture; to them I extend my thanks which are conveyed with the knowledge that they too may well have enjoyed the drinks and discussions as much as I did. Lastly, but by no means as a mere afterthought, I acknowledge the early help provided by Wendy Aldhous, Librarian, DPU, University College London, with her patient research into past issues of *The Architectural Review*; to the Librarian of the Architectural Association who was as usual courteous and patient in coping with my infinitely extensible loans from the Library. Lastly my thanks go to Alexandra Artley, the responsible editor at Architectural Press, who was involved both in the composition of the book and in the photographic research for it.

A number of the chapters in this book originally appeared in *The Architectural Review*, as follows: Peter Behrens, September 1934; Auguste Perret, August 1953; Adolf Loos: Ornament and Crime, February 1957; Walter Gropius, August 1924; Programme for the establishment of a Company for the provision of housing on aesthetically consistent principles by Walter Gropius, July 1961; Where do we stand? April 1935; Wells Coates, 1893–1958, December 1958; Lubetkin, July 1955; Towards a rational aesthetic, December 1935; Mannerism and modern architecture, May 1950; A master plan for London by the MARS group, June 1942. Frank Lloyd Wright's peaceful penetration of Europe first appeared in *The Architects' Journal* on May 4, 1939. The remaining chapters have been specially written and appear here for the first time as follows: Mies van der Rohe by Peter Carter; The Italian Rationalists by Bruno Zevi; The Rational and the Functional by Geoffrey Broadbent; Irrational Rationalism, which appears by courtesy of Charles Jencks. Rationality in Architecture and in the Design Process by Henryk Skolimowski is based on a paper given to the RIBA, and has been revised and extended for this publication. Twentieth-century Living and Twentieth-century Architecture by Le Corbusier first appeared in *Decorative Art 1930: 'The Studio' Year Book* and If I Had to Teach You Architecture in *Focus* No 1, 1938.

Introduction

by Dennis Sharp

'Architecture is the art above all others which achieves a state of platonic grandeur, mathematical order, speculation, the perception of harmony which lies in emotional relationships. This is the aim *of architecture'*

Le Corbusier

In its philosophical usage the term rationalist can be readily defined: agreeable to reason, reasonable, sensible, not foolish, absurd or extravagant. In the philosophical sense the word has historical continuity. Its definitive use relates to the modern world view of Descartes (1596–1650) who argued for the unity of thinking and for fundamental belief in the facts of existence, without the necessity of confirmation of the senses. This view is often abbreviated to the epithet: truth through knowledge. The opposite view, in philosophy—the empiricism of Locke and his followers—argued for the evidence of the senses to be taken into account in any discussion of knowledge. This, of course, is a gross simplification of two indelible strands of thought that have had a profound relevance on twentieth-century ideas and I refer to it because an appeal to Cartesian values is often to be found in modern architectural writing. Using the word Rationalist to describe the work and aims of modern architects has produced much confusion. Rationalism is often used as a synonym for Functionalism. However, architecture is not produced by a *process* of rational thinking, although in the design of a building there are often logical sequences that have to be followed. There is often a rationale for the way a design emerges through a methodological design process. But at the end the resulting artefact will be judged largely in aesthetic terms through criteria of judgement that are only very loosely attributable to rational ideas.

Rationalism in architecture is an elusive concept. It is a bit like Arthur Korn's description of the transparent glass wall: it is there, yet it is not there! There are numerous variations on the rational theme in architectural literature, many of which add further confusion to an already problematic issue. Emil Kaufmann, in his *Architecture in the Age of Reason*, which one would view as an historical period concerned with Rationalist attitudes, actually has no text references to the word at all. The index entry for Rationalism indicates you should look up Functionalism and then directs you back to Ledoux. Banham in his *Theory and Design in the First Machine Age* takes it seriously as part of the academic (largely Beaux Arts) tradition. He distinguishes the 'predisposing causes' in the development of modern architecture and cites the 'Rationalist or structural approach to architecture' as English in origin but elaborated in France by Viollet-le-Duc and Choisy. This is the influence that continued in France both through Perret (backed by the technical studies of his own teacher Guadet) and to a certain extent through Le Corbusier into this century. The Dutch Master H. P. Berlage stood in this line too although his views stemmed as much from Semper as they did from Viollet-le-Duc. It is interesting, but incorrect in so far as Dutch developments are concerned, that Banham should imply that Semper's ideas were without issue. In so far as Dutch Rationalism runs through Berlage's working lifetime up to 1936 when the magazine *De Acht en Opbouw* were still debating the Rationalist–Functionalist basis of architecture shows the continuing validity of the Semper views. Berlage therefore offers one important key to the discussion on architectural Rationalism. His ideas on Rationalism (derived from the French and German/Swiss sources mentioned, as well as from Hegel and Schopenhauer) were linked with the 'New

Socialism' that was growing up rapidly in Holland at the turn of the century. Berlage was committed to the notion of the Idea. However his valuation of the Idea was somewhat different from Hegel's, as Dr Singelenberg in his masterful study of Berlage, *H. P. Berlage: Idea and Style* shows: 'The difference is that the philosopher practised aesthetics on a definite complex of phenomena, and that the artist wanted to escape from this motionless past by applying anew the strongest realization of the—Hegelian—idea in order to arrive once again . . . at the purpose of architecture. Berlage's whole written work is imbued with this way of thinking, which is often coloured leftist-Hegelian . . .'. Berlage held an optimistic belief that the twentieth century offered something very special for art, architecture and society. As far as his definitions of architecture were concerned he sought for its essence in the simple enclosure of space and its logical (rational?) expression through structure.

So what do rational and rationalist mean in their modern usage? Etymologically the word 'rational' is straightforward; it implies having the faculty to reason or endowed with reason. Its usage, passed down from the fifteenth and sixteenth centuries, is almost exactly the same today as it was then: based on or derived from reason or reasoning, reasonable, sensible and not foolish, absurd or extravagant (1601). Interestingly enough some of the derivatives are worth considering: to have a 'rational nature' was seen as a 'gift of God' (1788); 'rational dress', a term coined in 1889, brings in a utilitarian notion of a form of dress for women proposed as more sensible than that in general use (eg the wearing of knickerbockers instead of skirts for cycling). This latter definition comes close to our subject as it was the pioneer architect and brilliantly vitriolic journalist Adolf Loos who—at the turn of the century—saw in dress an aspect of modernity that was to prove of analogous importance to architecture. Loos was a man who took immense pleasure in practical and simple things, particularly if they were English or American. He saw the American plumber's boiler suit as the ideal type of rational dress for modern man; a point that did not escape Winston Churchill many years later when he was visiting the Allied fronts. Such dress was, of course, undecorated and utilitarian and as proletarian as the original Levis. Such various definitions make it very difficult to say exactly what the word means because of the sheer confusion that abounds in its adoption. Sometimes it appears to imply the old Platonic idea of order and harmony in geometric arrangements, sometimes it was used to justify what seems to have been a progressive radical development in the arts (Fernand Léger with his non-figurative Cubist experiments, Ozenfant and Jeanneret's Purism and Mondrian and the Stijl Group's desire for abstract geometries); at other times architects and designers looked upon machines as 'rational' objects and at 'machine forms' as the logical outcome of involvement with the mechanical process.

Many artists and architects felt that the new technology of the twentieth century, which brought with it the power and potential of the machine, would also bring with it a period of Utopia. That it did not do so is a matter of history. Not since Pericles, the Purists argued, had thought been so lucid; they believed that the modern age would realize the true aims and ambitions of the Greeks. How did the Purists aim to carry out this ambitious programme? In two or three different articles Ozenfant and Jeanneret indicated that they thought it would come through 'mechanical order'. 'Man', they wrote, 'is a geometric animal, animated by the geometrical spirit'. This emphasis was to be found at the root of the numerous arguments in *Vers une Architecture*, published soon after Jeanneret the painter became Le Corbusier the prophet of the new architecture.

The grandeur, order and harmony referred to by Le Corbusier in his writings are elements equated with the rational attitude, but it is not a cold view as 'emotional relationships' are linked to his view of architecture as its 'spiritual components'. We have therefore a dichotomy in Le Corbusier's definition: architecture is a product of a synthesis of reason and emotions. When Le Corbusier wrote his *L'Esprit Nouveau* articles he was still thinking largely in terms of the individual designer, as one isolated from a collective responsibility in the modern technological world. After the foundation of CIAM in 1928 and the strengthening of the bases of the 'New Building', architecture emerged as a collective struggle. If there was to be a wide acceptance of the principles of new building then this was to be a shared responsibility among the architects and designers involved. Much of this responsibility was seen in terms of working class housing. They demanded that architecture for the masses must be objectively expressed in technical, social and economic terms. This process of rationalization is one of the least understood aspects of the development of modern architecture. Ernst May, the leading figure in the second CIAM congress at Frankfurt in 1929 and Architect to the city, stated that the individual should have a *'ration'* dwelling specifically designed for his calculated needs. 'What does a man need?' was the question posed both by Giedion's pamphlet *Befreites Wohnen* published in 1929 as a popular summary of the aims of the Congress and the Congress publication called *Die Wohnung für das Existenzminimum* (housing for minimum existence). The answer was simple: 'light, air and space'. If anything, it was too easy a rationalization. But, as Martin Steinmann has pointed in the *AA Quarterly*:

'The description of the "Rational Dwelling" in biologically and socially comprehensible terms (absolute terms as Gropius called them) appears to debunk the human being to serviceable needs, which can be satisfied by constructional measures, without recognizing or acknowledging, that these needs are moulded by society. Without wishing to underestimate the tendency of Functionalism to regard itself as an end in itself, there were other reasons for the standpoints described. They consisted of the suitability of the demands to the conditions of the means of production most appropriate to the provision of the "consumer house", the house as a commodity, in large quantities; industrialized production. "The majority of people have similar needs. It is, therefore . . . in the way of an economic advance, to satisfy these similar mass needs in a single and similar way." This standardization however also took for granted that the satisfaction of such mass needs was as much a political and social claim as those of the work struggle.'

Through the desire to make this new attitude relevant, the opening salvos of the 'Architecture or Revolution' (Le Corbusier's phrase, once again) debate can be seen to have been concentrated on the technical, economic and scientific foundation of the new architecture. It was an intense investigation which leant heavily on the simple geometrical ideas and their relation to the machine and to the creation of a form vocabulary. 'Due to the machine', Le Corbusier stated, 'our environment is undergoing a comprehensive transformation in its outer aspect as well as its utilization. We have acquired a new vision and a new social life, but to that transformation we have not yet adapted building'. The work and convictions of the CIAM pioneers offered at the turn of the 30s the means for this adaptation. However Le Corbusier himself was ambivalent over the use of the term Rationalism, attributing it admiringly to the work of structural engineers on the one hand and advising Sartoris not to use it as part of a title for his book on 'Functional' architecture on the other. Le Corbusier was aware that the terms Rational and Reason were the province of the Academicians. That he failed to understand the Italian usage is not surprising; neither did the Italians. Nevertheless it was a group of Italian architects who organized the *Rationalist Architecture Exhibition* and founded the MIAR (Movimento Italiano per l'Architettura Razionale) in 1928, the year which also saw the formation of CIAM at La Sarraz, who perpetuated a nineteenth-century architectural term into the new century. Professor Bruno Zevi indicates his own distrust in the Italian use of the term in his contribution to this volume.

But how, it might well be asked, did other pioneers envisage a rational approach to the modern world, particularly as far as the practice and art of architecture was concerned? Some, of course, like Perret and Berlage, felt that the way forward was to continue to develop the nineteenth-century Rationalist views of Viollet-le-Duc and Gottfried Semper, as I suggested earlier, while others were more radical in outlook. Adolf Loos, acting as an irritant on the skin of bourgeois Viennese society and admonishing its love of decorative newness, cried out for simplicity, allied to practicality and utility. Ultimately he demanded no ornamentation in architecture.

Van de Velde looked upon Rationalism rather differently. In his *Vom Neuen Stil*, he entitled one chapter 'The Search for a Style Based on a Rational, Logical Conception' and set out, in the form of a 'credo' the 'honest' principles he felt were important for a new architecture. But his attitude took in the possibility of ornamentation, 'and if thou art animated by the wish to beautify ... forms and structures, give thyself to the longing for refinement to which thy aesthetic sensibility or taste for ornament—of whatever kind it is—shall inspire thee, only so far as thou canst respect and retain *the rights and the essential appearance of these forms and structures'* (my italics).

The German Werkbund, and Muthesius in particular, had a special view about the rationalization of machine production for the benefit of art. However, as Banham quite correctly indicates, the actual issue of *Rationalism* becomes somewhat obscured in their concern for Form. Muthesius also sought to establish national standards of good taste, his arguments for which were highly dubious. He, like many others in the period before the First World War, became understandably confused about the potential of the machine, standardization, types as well as the artistic leanings of individual artists and architects. Gropius, who benefited a great deal from his knowledge of the Werkbund's aims, was probably the first Modern Movement architect (after Behrens) to take the idea of the *Zweckbau* (the functioning building) seriously. During the years 1910–14 he indicated a practical desire for an approach to design based on the analysis of a buildings' functions. Due to the course of world events and the Utopian frame of mind that developed in the postwar years in Germany, this analysis was only continued after the brief interlude of Expressionism. During this period almost every architect searching for new architectural forms and ideas was caught up—momentarily—in what I am sure Richards and Pevsner would call an 'anti-rational' atmosphere. Mies was seduced by the free plan in his famous skyscraper project of 1922 (admittedly justified in terms of angles of light) and by Dutch brickwork; Arthur Korn, whose work in the mid-20s had an edge to it as precise and hard as his surname, was swept away in a post-Scheerbartian eulogy on glass.

Hannes Meyer, who took over from Gropius for a short time as Director of the Bauhaus at the end of the 20s, is often cited as the arch-Rationalist of the Modern Movement. Although he avidly debunked architecture as 'an emotional act of the artist' and as part of an historical line of which he did not approve, his contribution to architectural ideas was more concerned with the architect becoming 'a specialist in organization' than with the rationalization of the design process: geometry, form giving and structural honesty were less important to Meyer. 'Building', he wrote in 1928, 'is nothing but organization: social, technical, economic and psychological organization'.

In order to summarize the numerous ways architects and artists looked at rational approaches to design they could be grouped into four categories:
1   The search for simplicity and clarity.
2   The appropriation of relevant aspects of nineteenth-century architectural ideals, particularly in relation to integrity of construction and style and the refinement of constructional principles. A view that would be described as 'Structuralist'.
3   An objective (*Sachlich*) approach to the problems in the modern world, which often take into account social programmes: the 'Functionalism' of the 20s.
4   The 'mechanical' approach which although related to Functionalism was also very much a province of the individual artist seeking to justify a reason for his work.

In some cases these views overlapped; none were mutually exclusive. Behrens,

Perret and Berlage were all structuralists whereas Loos was not. Loos and Mies were interested in simplicity whereas Behrens and Berlage did not share this interest to the same degree.

I have tried wherever possible in this book to select from the material available that which best lends itself to a critical comparison of Rationalist views. I am aware I may have overstated my claim. However the confusion that reigns over definition of terms also affects the interpretation of ideas. This is reinforced by looking at the contributions in this volume by today's historians and commentators and comparing their views with the contemporary material. One can sense immediately their uncertainty about Rationalism and its interpretation. The present generation looks at the writing on the walls of the Modern Movement and finds it wanting. They see that Functional architecture is not so Rational as it was claimed to be. Indeed they seem to share a somewhat cynical belief that architects are not very Rational in their approach to ideas but are very good at justifying what they do for purposes of fashion and style.

PETER BEHRENS

by P. Morton Shand

P. Morton Shand's writings in The Architectural Review *in the 20s and 30s brought to the English reading public the latest developments in Continental architectural ideas. He introduced the pioneers of the Modern Movement to this audience and subsequently was instrumental in influencing the creation of the English MARS Group through his friendship with Fry and Coates.*

This article, one of a series under the title 'Scenario for a Human Drama', concentrates on Behrens as the dominant personality of the early period of modernism. It was published in 1934.

'Art ought no longer to be considered as one's own private affair, a mistress to be served as the individual artist's whim or fancy takes him. We do not want an aesthetic that derives its canons from romantic day-dreams, but one which bases its authority on the realities of life. But neither do we want a technology cultivated as an end in itself which goes its own sweet way, but one manifesting its solidarity with the artistic impulses of our age . . .
'I believe in type-art, which for me represents the highest goal in every branch of artistic activity. Type-art is the ripest and most intelligent solution of the problem presented by the design of a given object, since it is that which frees it from everything not strictly germane to its purpose. An artist's best designs will always constitute types. We see the proof of this in the standardized ground-plans and elevations which the domestic architecture of so many cities evinces.'

Peter Behrens

One of the disadvantages of a retrospective survey is that to render the from-to aspect of a phase of development comprehensible in terms of what was only gradually, haltingly, incompletely, or half-unwittingly achieved in it, it is often necessary to march and countermarch over the same ground: a rather disorganized retreat preceding a more orderly advance. Thus it is hardly possible to avoid an outline of Behrens's career in normal chronological sequence. For this alone will enable us to understand how, by 1909, he had come to evince the eminently unacademic attitude to a still eminently academic profession that his 'engineering' use of concrete, steel, and glass proclaimed; and the way in which his own progressive evolution from then onwards heralded so many of the characteristics subsequently manifested by modern architecture.

Peter Behrens was born in 1868 in the then free Hansa town of Hamburg, where people have always been independent enough to prefer thinking and shifting for themselves to obedience to military discipline. Like Corbusier, he started as a painter; but unlike that ascetic-visaged Swiss this towering, full-blooded North German neither passed through a school of architecture nor served an apprenticeship to a master builder. That is the first important thing about him. But if he never had what would now be called a 'recognized' architectural training, he duly studied art in Karlsruhe, Düsseldorf, and Munich, the three traditional German *Kunststädte*. In 1891 he settled in Munich, where he worked and exhibited as a painter and craftsman until 1899: a period to which he probably owes much of his universality as a designer. Even since the war he has been kept busy designing things as diverse as tea-services for the Prussian State Porcelain Manufactory, letter-boxes for the German Post Office, ecclesiastical vestments, a large monastery, churches, factories, slip-ways, bridges, stations, warehouses, huge administrative buildings for large industrial concerns, town halls, buildings for exhibitions, the tomb of the first German President, the replanning of one of Berlin's most important traffic centres, villas, a number of *Siedlungen*, blocks of tenements for the municipality of Vienna, new types of communal dwellings, and Mr Bassett-Lowke's house at Northampton. In 1919 the National Constituent Assembly of Weimar invited him to collaborate in framing certain sections of the Republican Constitution of the Reich; and in 1922 he was chosen to succeed Otto Wagner as head of the Vienna Academy of Fine Arts.

This list would be quite out of place here were it not that from 1907 onwards Behrens's primary significance was as a protagonist and exemplifier of standardized design in a steadily widening field. Yet another of his activities must be mentioned—and emphasized—in this connection, because handwriting and printing are necessarily based on standard models that have to be simple enough to be easily assimilable and generally acceptable. In 1902 he took up the reform of the spidery German calligraphy, which culminated in the latinized *Behrens Kursivschrift* (1907). This stimulated his interest in typefaces, and led to the cutting of the elegant *Behrens Antiqua* fount (1908).

In 1899 the Grand-Duke Ernst Ludwig of Hesse, the Maecenas of modern German art, invited Behrens to Darmstadt, where the Austrian architect Josef Maria Olbrich (1867–1908), the most gifted and versatile leader of the *Jugendstil*, was beginning to lay out the once famous *Künstlerkolonie* on the Mathildenhöhe, a height dominating the grand-ducal capital. Here Behrens built himself a house in 1901. Though this was his first building, it revealed him as a master of that all but untranslatable thing the Germans call *Raumgestaltung* (the spatial design of rooms as opposed to the solid surfaces circumscribing them). Behrens linked his rooms together as an organic, unstylistic unity in a far more forthright and uncompromising manner than Van de Velde had yet dared to. In some, generous and unorthodox fenestration was consciously used to produce an impression of extension into space beyond wall limits: a development he carried still further three years later in the corner living-room of a house at Wetter in the Ruhr. Though too tentative externally to rank as a landmark in domestic design, the Darmstadt house at least marks a break away from historical forms. It is more important as an attempt to use a synthesis of shapes directly dictated by comfort, convenience and function as an anticipation of a new, and more reasonable, kind of home life, at once simpler and more complex than any then existing. This design encouraged other architects to take increasing liberties with the respectable solidity of walls. Three other pre-war country houses of Behrens must be mentioned: the very English-looking Haus Obenauer at Saarbrücken (1905), with its plain whitewashed walls and almost entire elimination of detail; and two adjacent houses at Hagen (1908 and 1910) that have more hesitant, if definitely more transitional elevations.

From 1903 till 1907 Behrens was director of the Düsseldorf School of Art. To this period belong the pavilions for the Oldenburg Exhibition of 1905, and the Delstern Crematorium at Hagen (1907); both of which were based on geometric schemes of proportion. In spite of Tuscan mannerisms, these severely cubic stucco designs are of considerable importance because they accelerated the process of relieving the saving verities of structure of the furuncular rash of 'appropriate' ornamentation. None of his contemporaries felt the necessity for a drastic purge nearly so strongly as Behrens, and none applied it more resolutely to his own work. In so far as Behrens was influenced at this time by any other architect it was by Carl Friedrich Schinkel, Soane's contemporary and peer, the most austere of all the early nineteenth-century classicists.

Behrens realized very early that the machine was a powerful revolutionary idea as well as an inexorable physical fact. He saw in it a new intellectual principle which had already made an irreparable breach in the military tradition of manual execution, and would inevitably soon begin to transform the atavistic formalism of his age. If Behrens has been called a Modernist Romantic—and his brief

1 The corner living room at a house at Wetter in the Ruhr (1904)

2 The Obenauer house at Saarbrücken (1905)

Expressionist phase (Höchst, 1920, and the Dombauhütte Chapel at the Munich Exhibition of 1922) lends some colour to this charge—it is because he refuses to admit that the romantic element in architecture has suffered a final eclipse. This element he defines as the expression born of a conscious struggle of the coming with the existent: or in other words an incessant readjustment of the equipoise between form and function. To him we owe the *Deutscher Werkbund's* slogan of 'fitness for purpose' (*Zweckmässigkeit*). But he contemptuously rejects the dogma of *Sachlichkeit* (of which the rough and unprecise, though nearest possible, English equivalent is 'functionalism as be-all and end-all') as the abasement of design from the sovereignty of a full-fledged vehicle of expression to the bare bones of the primitive grammar on which that expression is based. His ultimate philosophy is that just as nature is nothing without culture, or culture without nature, so architecture remains a negation unless it achieves a fusion of culture and construction. 'Only problems interest me. I leave obvious solutions to others', is the quietly confident utterance of a man of singular personal modesty, which shows how much Behrens was inspired by the achievements of nineteenth-century engineers.

Though Friedrich Naumann was the intellectual pioneer of the Industrialization of Building, Behrens was its first practical sponsor. Naumann pointed out that the chief reason why building remained the only important decentralized industry was that it did not rely on a centralized power supply: a reason that has lost its force since dependence on the fixity of local steam-power units has been superseded by high-tension cable networks for the transmission of electric current. It was in 1910 that Behrens first publicly advocated the Industrialization of Building, after he had previously tried to make the directors of the AEG realize the significance of rationalizing construction as a first step towards a planned economy of industry. Such an idea, like Willett's contemporary campaign for daylight saving, was too much in advance of the spirit of his age. Naturally it was derided as impracticable. But if Behrens was unable to open the eyes of such a remarkable man as Rathenau to its implications, Naumann before him had encountered the same incomprehension in leading German industrialists like Siemens, Krupp and Ballin.

Baffled in the major field, Behrens soon succeeded triumphantly in a minor. The administrative headquarters of the Mannesmann Tube Works in Düsseldorf (1911) was far more than the European prototype of the standardized office block. It was the first practical exemplar of its kind, a model which has been followed with very slight modifications ever since. In planning it as a square steel-framed structure, Behrens used girders of standardized lengths and sections throughout, so that two or more of the normed cells into which the floors were subdivided could be easily thrown into one. The dimensions of the standard office unit were dictated by the

3 The first modern office building: the administrative headquarters of the Mannesmann Tube Company, Düsseldorf (1911)

space necessary for a team of six clerks to work in comfort at a writing-table, a typewriter stand, and a filing-cabinet. Its corners were defined by four 40 cm deep stanchions, spaced so as to provide a 90·5 cm breadth of window, the height of which was adjusted to light a floor area of 8 m². Externally this (then) huge building represents a rationalization of the slender verticality of alternating piers and windows first adopted by Messel in the Wertheim Store in Berlin, shorn of its Gothic reminiscences.

Behrens next turned his attention to household equipment. In 1912 he exhibited the standardized furniture he had designed for minimum working-class dwellings at the Berlin *Gewerkschaftshaus*. This was a sufficiently remarkable event in itself. It proves that his work with the AEG had had the effect of turning him into what we should call a 'social' architect even before he began to embark on housing schemes. The excerpt from the manifesto read at the Session of the *Deutscher Werkbund* during the Cologne Exhibition of 1914* which heads this chapter shows how rapidly his views on the scope of standardization crystallized in the interval. They were hotly attacked by Van de Velde, whose extreme individualism scornfully rejected the conception of the norm-type as degrading the artist to an artisan.

Even today Behrens's first housing scheme at Lichtenberg (1915), of which only a small part was realized, is still regarded as a model layout. In the Henningsdorf *Siedlung* (1917), built for the AEG's workmen during the war, he carried the standardization of the three-room dwelling still further in long uniform rows of three-storied tenements of a single type. Owing to the shortage of bricks, Behrens used large normed blocks of pressed refuse-destructor clinker as an *ersatz* material. Both Lichtenberg and Henningsdorf evince the same rational type of axial planning with rectilinear streets which he had originally adopted in the Eppenhaus Garden Suburb at Hagen in 1908. In this he was in diametric opposition to the most advanced contemporary school of town-planning, which based its picturesque contours on Camillo Sitte's axiom (typified by the whole of Art Nouveau) that only curved lines are beautiful.

In 1918, when a chastened and impoverished world was ready to listen to any

* This exhibition was organized by the *Deutscher Werkbund*, formed in 1907.

4 The prototype of the normed minimum dwelling: part of the Henningsdorf Siedlung, Berlin, built for the AEG's employees (1917)

5 Watertower in Frankfurt (1912)

6

6 The interior courtyard of a
block of tenements in the
Henningsdorf Siedlung, Berlin
(1917)

7 Block of flats at the Weissenhof
Siedlung, Werkbund Exhibition,
Stuttgart (1927)

8 The house in the Taunus
Mountains from the garden
terrace (1931)

method for saving cost and time in housing construction, even if, like the
'Industrialization of Building', it had only a theoretical basis, Behrens grimly
returned to the charge. His essay 'On Economical Building' (*Von Sparsamen
Bauen*) postulated that speed and economy could be obtained in three separate
ways: by rationalization of layout, by modernization of the technique of
construction, and by the maximum substitution of communal for individual
domestic services; and more concretely through:

(a) A harmonious combination of *Flachbau* (rows of small houses, each with its
own allotment garden) and *Hochbau* (multi-storied tenement blocks)—a combination which Gropius has never ceased to advocate—that would enable urban
Siedlungen to become self-supporting on good, and therefore relatively dear, sites;
and

(b) The cheapening of building materials, structural parts, and fittings by far-
reaching standardization and mechanical mass-production; together with the
cheapening of construction by the most extensive possible use of machinery in
assembly and erection.

At Praunheim, the first *Siedlung* built at Frankfurt-on-Main after the war, Ernst
May used precast concrete slab sections and semi-factory methods of assembly.
But in the next, at Niederrad, he was obliged to revert to traditional manual brick-
laying. The problem of the pre-fabricated house has preoccupied all the leaders of
the new architecture, more particularly Gropius and Corbusier; and though not
yet more than half mastered it is clearly only a question of time before it will be as
completely and satisfactorily solved as the mass-production of motor-cars.
Meanwhile it continues to exercise a growing, almost a paramount, influence on
modern architects. In America a mass-produced insulated steel house is already
being advertised—though if it comes to that the Japanese standardized timber-
framed, paper-walled house (unfortunately only habitable by the Japanese
themselves) has anticipated it by several centuries.

The next stage in Behrens's development as a social architect was the upshot of a
project for housing industrial workers at Forst in the Lausitz. Here the problem
which he set himself was to re-identify a mining population's *dopolavoro* with the
husbandry it had till very recently practised. He planned this *Siedlung* as a farm
suburb with communal market-gardens, tillage, pasturage, and agricultural
machinery; and its own co-operative organization for selling produce. A rather
similar scheme for a co-operative housing society in an industrial area of Silesia
led to Behrens's 'double gardens housing plan' (1920): a structural telescoping of
back-to-back houses into rows of two-storied dwellings, subdivided into four flats,

9

10

each of which overlooks and is entered from its own garden. This plan-form was the result of interrogating the wives of prospective tenants; and discovering that they demanded an absence of stairs within their dwellings, a minimum number to climb to them; and gardens that could be seen from their windows and reached directly from their front doors.

The same year saw the design for an urban housing solution known as the *Terrassenhaus*. In plan this is a pyramidal combination of structurally united one-, two- and three-storied buildings arranged on either side of a central four-storied block; the roof of each of the two sections of intermediate height providing a roof garden for that one step above it. The ground floor has an ordinary garden, and the top floors share a roof garden with an area of 144 m². Though never carried out, this revolutionary design exercised a radical influence on subsequent housing developments. Nor must Behrens's block of flats in the *Weissenhofsiedlung*, at Stuttgart, be forgotten: the solitary example of the work of the older generation at that 1927 exhibition of 'cultural Bolshevism'. Finally, in the house on the Taunus Mountains (1931), Behrens showed—as no one else except Mies van der Rohe has been able to, and then (Haus Tugendhat) on a far smaller scale—that the normed cubic idiom he had himself been predominantly responsible for evolving could be planned on the grand scale, and informed with that austere luxury which evokes a timelessly elegant modernity. Someone has described it as the first and last large country house to be built in the new architecture. Anyhow, it already stands empty, for the opulent Jewish family it was designed for has judged it best to flee from Germany.

9 The garden front of 'New Ways' in Northampton (1926) built for Mr Bassett-Lowke, who specified that the house should express his idea of the spirit of the age, with the height limited to two storeys and with every room being included within the four surrounding walls, omitting the customary collection of odd outbuildings

10 The lounge at 'New Ways', Northampton

AUGUSTE PERRET

by Peter Collins

1 Flats, rue Franklin, Paris (1903)

2 Garages, rue Ponthieu, Paris (1906)

3 Théâtre des Champs-Elysées, avenue Montaigne, Paris (1912)

The two outstanding features of the doctrine of Auguste Perret are the insistence on modenature—the profiling and management of projecting features—and the philosophy of the concrete frame. The former, exemplified by the house in the rue Reynouard, has inevitably remained a personal preoccupation in an epoch largely devoted to the suppression of such features, though many practitioners of the Modern Movement have benefited from the close attention to detail of this kind which was instilled into them when they were Perret's pupils. The concrete frame, however, exemplified by the skeleton of the Théâtre des Champs-Elysées, is a concept which has become an integral part of the philosophy of modern architecture, and remains the greatest of the many valuable contributions discussed by Professor Collins which Auguste Perret has made to architecture.

When Auguste Perret started his career as an architect, modern reinforced concrete theory had already been in existence, in a very elementary form, for about thirty years, and a few advanced architects were aware of the structural potentialities of the material in the construction of tall buildings. Nevertheless, the architectural problem in France had not changed so much as in, for example, America. Tall blocks of flats had been built in Paris for over two hundred years, and there was no great incentive to exceed the maximum height laid down in Napoleon I's legislation, which permitted about seven floors above ground level. This height was obtained quite satisfactorily and not uneconomically with the excellent stone of the region; a stone which allowed full scope for the rather florid architectural and sculptural decoration in vogue round about 1900. If reinforced concrete was used at all, it was introduced merely as an economical substitute for ashlar, and not as the answer to a new architectural problem.

Perhaps the most remarkable example of Perret's perspicacity was his early awareness that reinforced concrete has a structural dignity of its own; and it is significant that the first expression of his ideas should have been in domestic architecture, the small block of flats in the rue Franklin, Paris. These ideas had been fostered by three men; Guadet, who was his teacher at the Ecole des Beaux-Arts, his father, a building contractor with a strong and uncompromising temperament, and Choisy, whose history of architecture, which is essentially a history of construction, was his constant guide.

The general influence of Guadet is well known, especially in France, where his book on the theory of architecture is still a classic. Briefly, one may sum up his teaching by saying that he synthesized the traditional aesthetic values of French classical architecture and the structural Functionalism of Viollet-le-Duc and Labrouste. Perret found in him a master admirably suited to his temperament, and during a brilliant academic career became fully imbued with the idea that architectural forms are essentially structural forms, though capable of infinite and subtle modifications in the interests of proportion.

Perret first had to ask himself what was the true structural form for concrete, and arrived at the conclusion that it was a *frame*. The use of the expression 'reinforced-concrete frame' is now so common that it is almost impossible to appreciate how revolutionary the idea was at the very beginning of the century. Yet at that time, and for long afterwards, the general conception of concrete was as a substitute for masonry. The doctrine that reinforced-concrete construction was not similar to building in stone but to building in timber produced architectural

4

5

6

4 Parish church,
Le Raincy (1923)

5 Concert hall, Ecole
Normale de Musique,
rue Cardinet, Paris
(1929)

6 Flats, rue Raynouard,
Paris (1929)

7 Admiralty buildings,
boulevard Victor, Paris
(1931)

8 Private house,
Garches (1932)

9 Museum of the Office
of Public Works, place
Iéna, Paris (1938)

10 Place de l'Hôtel de
Ville (1952)

7

8

9

10

11

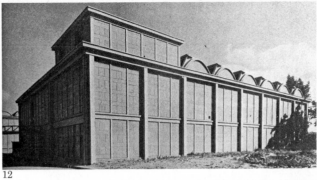

12

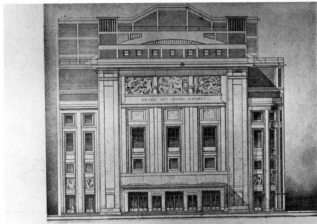

13a

13b

11 A primary influence on Perret was that of Guadet, his teacher, whose insistence on structure as a generator of form is exemplified by his house on the boulevard Murat

12 From Guadet's influence grew Perret's assertion that structure gives character to a building, even a utilitarian one like the warehouse of the Marine Nationale

13a and b Perret's theories were first exercised in a large public commission in the Théâtre des Champs-Elysées where they show clearly, in spite of elaborate surface treatment

forms of a new type, seen for the first time in the building in the rue Franklin. One must insist on the word *seen*. Other architects who later adopted the concrete frame covered the structural element with a screen wall which hid if it did not disguise the structural system. Perret, following Guadet, has always insisted that it is only structure which gives true character, proportion and scale to a building.

In order to arrive at a full technical understanding of the material, Perret, with the co-operation of the family firm of building contractors, constructed a series of utilitarian buildings of the utmost severity. These buildings, such as the garage in the rue Ponthieu, Paris, are barren of all refinements, exhibiting, like Romanesque churches, all the clumsiness of a healthy new architecture in the making.

In 1911, however, Perret had his first opportunity of realizing his aesthetic theories in a building of the first importance, the Théâtre des Champs-Elysées in Paris. Resistance to his ideas was strong, so that he had to use a good deal of tact. Until almost the official opening day, the directors were under the impression that the building was designed throughout in the style of Louis XVI. At the inauguration, critics were frankly hostile; they considered the staircases hardly suitable even for a factory, and were shocked by the unadorned simplicity of the columns. Yet even so Perret had made considerable concessions to popular taste; his façade, though indicating the structural system, was faced with marble, and the internal columns were finished with plaster.

It was in domestic architecture that important developments were next made. Always guided by the principles of half-timber construction, designs were

14

15

14 Service Technique des Constructions Navales, showing how Perret's conception of structural logic exacts a high degree of precision from the parts, which must fit together in a manner which is not only mechanically exact but also visually comprehensible

15 The concert hall of the Museum of the Office of Public Works showing his characteristic use of the column which tapers downwards like a table-leg

16 Building in rue Raynouard, Paris showing Perret's insistence on modenature, the profiling and disposition of projecting parts

17 a and b Perret's regard for the material itself in his manipulation and juxtaposition of textures is shown in his early works like the building in the rue Franklin (a) and late ones like the rebuilding of Le Havre (b)

perfected for precast window frames and precast concrete panels to fill the interstices of the monolithic structural frame. It was not sufficient that the general principle should be established. All the parts had to fit together like a delicate and complex mechanism, satisfying not merely practical but aesthetic requirements. In this way, the architectural forms were created, all capable of the infinite proportional variations which particular needs would dictate, yet all standardized and unified by common obedience to the rational structural system of which they formed part.

One of the most interesting and most misunderstood results of his systematic modification of the elements of architecture was the creation of the column which tapers downwards. Following the principles of timber construction, it became apparent to Perret that the stability of a concrete column was not due to gravity, as in a masonry column, but to the strength of the joint, as in a table leg. Just as he would have revolted against a table designed with each leg wider at the bottom than at the top, so he revolted against a similar structural error in concrete frames.

One of the most fascinating things about these new elements was that several of them, although created by a logical process of deduction, turned out to have the same form as purely decorative features of the architecture of the seventeenth and eighteenth centuries. The medieval timber floor beam, for example, had survived in French eighteenth-century masonry as a broad decorative string course; windows were framed round with mouldings merely carved in the surrounding stone; the wall surfaces were carved to give the impression of panelling.* The reintroduction

* The architects of the eighteenth century were not unaware that they were thus imitating timber forms. J.-F. Blondel (1705–74), who was rather a purist in these matters, criticized the main elevation of the Hôtel de Béthune as follows: '. . . l'avant-corps du milieu de cet attique paroît trop fréquemment subdivisé par des tables; ce genre de décoration paroît imiter la Menuiserie; c'est pourquoi il faut en user avec plus de prudence dans les murs de face, dont la matière exige une richesse qui soit relative à sa solidité naturelle' (*Architecture Française*, vol. i, page 252).

a

b

of these features, and the similarity between the structural concrete columns and decorative pilasters, gives a deceptively archaic quality to Perret's later work. Paradoxically, the element of imitation had occurred in reverse, since the eighteenth-century forms may be said more truthfully to prefigure those evolved by him. For several hundred years, the Roman architects and then the Renaissance architects had applied a decoration of trabeated architecture to their arch constructions, because they were convinced of its intrinsic beauty. Yet even in the late eighteenth century, when a determined effort was made to suppress all arches, the fact that architraves had to be composed of voussoirs brought about complications of thrust which continued to prevent architects from creating pure trabeated compositions. Perret discovered in reinforced concrete the material for a trabeated architecture suitable for modern needs, and in mastering its potentialities subdued it more and more to the discipline of ordered proportions.

The influence of Guadet's clear division between composition and proportioning is shown in Perret's later developments. Once having determined the general system of his architecture, he was not content to leave the elements in the crudeness of their initial form, but applied himself energetically and conscientiously to their refinement. In successive buildings, therefore, he carried out extensive improvements in surface treatment and *modenature*. The nearest equivalent to the word *modenature* is perhaps 'profiling'; the three-dimensional study of surfaces as determined principally by the depth of shadows. The French have always set great store by it; the early eighteenth-century architectural textbooks started off with an analysis of mouldings because, as Daviler puts it, 'mouldings are to architecture what letters are to handwriting'.

Perret's study of surface treatment involved experiments with different aggregates and different types of bush-hammering. Aggregates could be different in colour, texture and size, to give an infinite number of subtle gradations in tone, luminosity and scale. It was a long and anxious process, as there was a limit to the number of trial slabs which could be made, and in general the real effect could not be judged until the building was completed. It is a tribute to Perret's genius that these effects have been so successful, as anyone may see who cares to examine the relationships between various aggregates in the Musée des Travaux Publics.

As his fame grew and his commissions became more and more important, Perret became increasingly enamoured of this beautiful material, and exploited its potentialities with greater boldness. More and more surfaces were designed in bare concrete, with delicate modulations requiring the most skilful carpentry work in the preparation of the shuttering. Internal walls were made of precast panels, internal columns were left bare, ceilings displayed their ribs or coffers, everything was abolished which was a covering or a plaster veneer. 'Architecture', he was fond of saying, 'is what makes beautiful ruins', and he boasted that there was not a square centimetre of plaster in the whole of the Musée des Travaux Publics. Everything was done to take full advantage of the aesthetic possibilities of structural forms. Large concrete surfaces were used in the most unlikely places, such as the interior of auditoria. The concert hall of the Ecole Normale de Musique is a good example of such defiance, in the spirit of Guadet, of acoustic dogma. After the first concert there, Cortot is reported to have said: 'Perret promised me a hall which would resonate like a violin, but he did not tell me it would be a Stradivarius'.

This variety of work all showed one common feature: the tremendous care and study lavished on the smallest details. Working in Guadet's methodical manner, Perret ensured that the architect's ordering mind touched every inch of his building to refine and beautify. The elements were studied more and more. The classic problems, such as the transition from a round column to a square abacus, were studied in relationship to structural concrete and methods of shuttering. Greek optical corrections were applied to the silhouettes of cornices and the verticality of columns. Columns were 'fluted' with facets regulated by the number of laths composing the shuttering, and were diminished with a careful studied

18a

18b

18a and b Concert hall of the Ecole Normale de Musique where Perret used large, unmodulated areas of bare concrete which, contrary to acoustic theory, proved highly successful

entasis specified in large-scale drawings. And in all this one should remember the difficulties which had continually to be overcome. Apart from the initial expense of such refinements, which in the case of the church of Le Raincy were largely paid for by Perret himself, the workmen had to be taught and constantly supervised, for, since the essence of the system was the beauty of the structure, the forms once moulded were unchangeable. Any errors in shuttering or in pouring the concrete were thus almost catastrophic, since they could not be covered up, and could only be corrected by partial demolition and subsequent reconstruction. The expense was also a great obstacle in the beginning, although, now that the French contractors have become familiar with the method, prices compare favourably with those of other systems.

It is apparent from even a superficial study of his work that Perret has never sought originality in composition for its own sake. The Modern Movement, inheriting a tradition which goes back to Ledoux, became obsessed with new plan forms and volumes as the only way to create a contemporary architecture, although once having found exciting new compositions, the designers showed little concern with the surfaces of the geometric solids evolved. Perret learnt from Guadet that good composition, which is largely a matter of luck, is based primarily on a rational appreciation of plan requirements. He refused to be diverted by a search for novel plan shapes, or by extravagant new structural forms, from the pursuit of what he considered the true art of architecture. He ignored the new aesthetic values introduced by the modern schools of painters, showing that traditional French mistrust of painters and sculptors who turn their hands to designing buildings.

Nevertheless, there is no doubt that as he has grown older Perret's compositions have tended to conform more and more strictly to traditional types. The porticos at Le Havre, with shops and entresol, are openly modelled on the rue de Rivoli in Paris. The basic grid of the town shows a rigidity reminiscent of the early nineteenth-century doctrine of Durand. Are we to see in all this the retrograde steps of a man who, growing old, has lost his taste for adventure, and seeks merely to prove his skill at imitating the past? Perret's whole life history must surely

20

19 Le Havre, where Perret explored the problem of a column rising into a square abacus

20 Much of Perret's work at Le Havre, with its balconies and mezzanines over shops, exhibits close affinities with the types of urban development evolved for Haussmann's rebuilding of Paris

refute such a judgement. It would perhaps be nearer the truth to suggest that the classical theories on trabeated architecture have to some extent the objective validity which their creators claimed for them, and that Perret has demonstrated the fact in pushing his basic principles to their logical conclusion.

Auguste Perret has always fought against the conception of architecture as a deliberate expression of the artist's personality or originality, and one might suppose therefore that his purely objective doctrine, based on traditional principles, would appeal to many of his contemporaries. Those who like his work would expect such a logical use of a new structural material to have had an immediate, stimulating and lasting attraction for the younger generation. Those who dislike it for its traditional qualities would expect older and more conservative architects to have welcomed the new forms as a compromise between masonry and *modernismus*.

Perret's prestige in France has long been prodigious. In the first quarter of the century he was the natural rallying point for all the young architects eager to learn about reinforced-concrete design from the only man then capable of teaching it to them. Now, as Grand Officer of the Légion d'Honneur, Membre de l'Institut, President of the Ordre des Architectes, corresponding member of numerous societies and recipient of numerous gold medals, Honorary Inspector General of Buildings, Architect for the reconstruction of Le Havre, Amiens and Marseilles, *chef d'atelier* at both the Ecole des Beaux-Arts and the Ecole Spéciale d'Architecture, his opportunities for influencing both his own and younger generations are and always have been tremendous.

Yet when one looks at the achievements of his followers and imitators before 1945, their work is disappointing in both quality and quantity. Several of Perret's early students, such as Le Corbusier, had of course repudiated his doctrine in favour of an entirely different set of aesthetic values. But others who at heart remained faithful to Perret's principles were prevented by their clients' purses or tastes from putting them into practice. In this respect it may be observed that great as was Perret's genius and force of character, he himself could never have achieved so much without the tremendous financial backing of Perret Frères, the family

21 The influence of Perret is widespread and easily recognizable. Denis Honegger developed a personal note of technological aggressiveness in his Fribourg University, Switzerland

firm of building contractors and specialists in reinforced-concrete construction.

Perhaps only one disciple of Perret has shown himself equal to his master in fidelity to classical principles, sensitivity of design and tenacity of purpose: Denis Honegger. His is the only work which achieves a poetry of expression in reinforced concrete comparable to Perret's finest achievements; work which shows that a real individuality of design is possible within the strict framework and discipline of Perret's doctrine. The University of Fribourg was admittedly an ideal programme, but it was built in spite of great difficulties: wartime restrictions, local prejudices and severe financial limitations. Only a man with the utmost artistic integrity could have resisted so long and so stubbornly the temptation to compromise with his architectural principles.

Much of the work produced by other architects in the Perret idiom is nothing more than the adoption of certain forms he created, often applied in a way which has all the futility and irrelevance of the Italianate ornament introduced into French buildings in the early Renaissance. Some of this work, however, has been by architects who had never worked under Perret, and were ignorant of the doctrine from which such forms derived their significance.

Perret's work has attracted little attention in England, but this is understandable. The English have never had the same rational, analytical approach to classical design as the French, and have in the past worried more about the accuracy than the appropriateness of their Palladian details. It is no accident that the only Englishman who has thought it worth while to write at length on the principles of architectural composition should have been trained at the Ecole des Beaux-Arts. The fact also that London is so largely built of brick is not without influence, for it is not easy for those used to designing in brick to be sensitive to the subtleties of profiling and contrasts; nor can generations brought up to regard Nash's buildings as the high-water mark of English achievement be expected to despise cement rendering as something sham and unworthy.

The tragic devastation of France by allied bombing has brought to many of those who believe in Perret's doctrine a magnificent opportunity to show their capacities. Under the enlightened patronage of the municipal authorities of Le Havre, and with the moral authority of Perret as Architect-in-Chief, a team of architects has rebuilt the demolished city with a classical regularity and scale worthy of the best French tradition in civic design. Based on a general plan kept in harmony by a rigidly imposed 20 foot grid, the rhythm of columns, the gradations of surface tones and textures, the subtleties of profiling, and the contrasts of void and solid form a variety of elements in a unity of design which make Le Havre a monument to reinforced-concrete craftsmanship on a large scale, and one of the most significant creations of European architecture in this century.

22 The Witwatersrand Dental Hospital, South Africa, one of the largest and most Perret-influenced buildings outside Europe, designed by John Fassler

ADOLF LOOS:
Ornament and crime

by Reyner Banham

Everyone knows that Modern Architecture is undecorated. This concept is the layman's recognition check: flat roof, big windows, no decoration. It is also one of the great seminal half-truths that have now become rules of design morality. But how did this state of affairs come about? Did the spirit of the times command? Did the Zeitgeist, *like a baroque angel, swoop down to stay a thousand pencils as they held poised above the beginning of an Ionic volute or an Art Nouveau lily?*

In Reyner Banham's original introduction to this article (1957) he wrote: 'To us, now, the idea of an undecorated architecture has so nearly the status of a Mosaic commandment, to be flouted in practice but never queried in theory, that it is difficult to conceive of it as the thought of one man, and much easier to refer it back to the collective unconscious of the pioneers of modern design. But the surviving literary evidence from the first twenty years of this century does not reveal any widely diffused hostility to decoration. There were ideas like Significant Form that were later to reinforce such a hostility when it had taken hold; there was a certain suspicion of past styles of decoration; there was even a certain indifference to ornament, articulated by Geoffrey Scott and earlier by Auguste Choisy, as the feeling that ornament was something that one might do without if one's command of formal composition was sufficiently sure. But only in the writings of one man, the Viennese architect Adolf Loos, will one find a positive anathema on ornament.'

Did Adolf Loos beat ornament single-handed? He certainly thought so himself, for he wrote in the introduction to his book *Trotzdem*, published in 1930, 'I have emerged victorious from my thirty years of struggle. I have freed mankind from superfluous ornament'. This is an uncommonly big claim even for a big-talking movement like Modern Architecture, and it needs scrutiny. But scrutiny will be facilitated if we look first at the weapons with which he fought. The example of his buildings was not decisive—their exteriors are sometimes, but not always, plain; the interiors, though devoid of decorative objects for the most part, exhibit almost a milliner's sense of the decorative qualities of wood and marble, fairface brick, turkey carpets, glass and metal. His doughtiest blows at ornament were struck in print, and the doughtiest of all in one single essay, published in 1908.

Its title is an eye-blacker for a start, *Ornament und Verbrechen:* Ornament and Crime. It brings the reader up with a jerk and sets his stock responses jangling. It is probably the first appearance of that pugnacious moral tone that was to characterize the writings of the 20s and 30s, and the opening paragraphs fully sustain this bourgeois-blasting, damn-your-delicate-feelings attitude:

'The human embryo goes through the whole history of animal evolution in its mother's womb, and when a child is born his sensory impressions are those of a puppy. His childhood takes him through the stages of human progress; at the age of two he is a Papuan savage, at four he has caught up with the Teutonic tribesmen. At six he is level with Socrates, and at eight with Voltaire. At this age he learns to distinguish violet, the colour that the eighteenth century discovered—before then violets were blue and tyrian was red. Physicists can already point out colours that they have named, but that only later generations will be able to distinguish.

Children are amoral, and so, for us, are Papuans. If a Papuan slaughters his enemies and eats them, that doesn't make him a criminal. But if a modern man kills someone and eats him, he must be either a criminal or a degenerate. Papuans tattoo their skins, decorate their boats, their oars—everything they can get their hands on. But a modern man who tattoos himself is either a criminal or a degenerate. Why, there are prisons where eighty per cent of the convicts are tattooed, and tattooed men who are not in prison are either latent criminals or degenerate aristocrats. When a tattooed man dies at liberty, it simply means that he hasn't had time to commit his crime.

The urge to ornament oneself, and everything else within reach, is the father of pictorial art. It is the baby-talk of painting. All art is erotic.

The first ornament born, the cross, is of erotic origin. The earliest art-work, the first creative act of the earliest artist, was smudged on the cave wall to let off emotional steam. A horizontal stroke, the reclining woman; a vertical stroke, the man who transfixes her. The man who did this felt the same impulse as Beethoven, was in the same heaven of delight as Beethoven composing the Ninth.

But the man of our own times who smudges erotic symbols on walls is either a criminal or a degenerate. It is clear that this violent impulse might seize degenerate individuals in even the most advanced cultures, but in general one can grade the cultures of different peoples by the extent to which lavatory walls are drawn upon. With children this is a natural condition, their first artistic expressions are erotic scribblings on the nursery wall. But what is natural to children and Papuan savages is a symptom of degeneracy in modern man. I have evolved the following maxim, and present it to the world: The evolution of culture marches with the elimination of ornament from useful objects.'

This is still a tremendous performance nearly a half-century after its composition. ... But it won't stand re-reading. This is *Schlagobers-Philosophie*, that whisks up into an exciting dish on the café table, and then collapses as you look at it, like a cooling soufflé. It is not a reasoned argument but a succession of fast-spieling double-takes and non-sequiturs holding together a precarious rally of clouds of witness—café-Freudianism, café-anthropology, café-criminology. The testimonies of these various witnesses don't really support one another, but they must have appeared convincing at the time, partly because they were all new and hot, but more especially for an overriding reason that will be discussed later. But Loos has no intention of giving the reader time to pick the argument to pieces, he wants to detail the poor response that the world made when presented with his 'maxim'.

'I had thought with this rule to bring a new joy into the world, but no one has thanked me for it. Rather, people have pulled a long face and hung their heads. What oppressed them in my discovery was the proposition that no new ornament could be invented. Were we, men of the nineteenth century, to be incapable of doing what the simplest negro, the men of every previous age or nation, had been able to do?'

'Men of the nineteenth century'—this must mean that the maxim had been enunciated in the 90s originally, and at that time, with Viennese Art Nouveau flourishing like a rain-forest, it must have sounded more mad than sad. Loos, however, followed it up with Old Testament rhetoric.

'Then I said: Weep not. Behold the true greatness of our age, that it can no longer bring forth ornament. We have vanquished decoration and broken through into an ornamentless world.

Behold. The time is at hand and fulfilment awaits us. Soon the pavements of our cities shall glisten like marble; like Zion, the holy city, the Capital of Heaven.'*

But no one thanked him. What had gone wrong? Almost inevitably, he alleges an Imperialist plot: Certain reactionaries rejected his prophecies, the Austrian state continued to support and subsidize a reign of ornamental terror, retarding

* Depressingly enough, Loos's views on clothing were entirely consistent with his views on architecture. His ideal was *der Mann im Overall*, so his Holy City would have looked rather like a set for *1984*.

progress, making people wear felt boots instead of rational footwear, because it had found that a backward people was easier to govern. Some citizens of the Austro-Hungarian Empire were so backward that they had not yet been converted to Christianity, would have been looked down on by the Goths and Visigoths. Happy the country that has no such stragglers! Happy America!

America for Loos, as for so many of the pioneers, was the promised land of technology. Not a word about the Indian reservations or the hookworm belt, nor the coloured slums of the northern cities, which he must have seen on his visit to the US. Americans were his ideal twentieth-century men and

'When two men live side by side, all things else being equal, the twentieth-century man gets richer, the eighteenth-century man gets poorer, assuming that each lives according to his inclinations, for the man of the twentieth century can cover his needs with smaller outlay, and thus make savings.

The vegetable that tastes good to him when simply boiled in water and glazed with butter, is only palatable to the other when served with honey and nuts, after the cook has slaved over it for hours. Decorated plates are expensive, whereas the plain white crocks that modern man prefers are cheap. One saves, the other overspends, and it is the same with nations. Woe to a people that hangs back from cultural progress. The English get richer, and we get poorer.'

What would he have made of a Cadillac economy, where undecorated goods are apt to be in an inaccessible luxury price-bracket, while ornamental products are within the reach of all but the most depressed strata of society? One can guess, for a few paragraphs later he sketches in a satirical draft of a high-obsolescence economy, where everything is highly decorated and thrown away almost as soon as it is made, and everyone swims in wealth and well-being. But it is only a satirical view of a vulgar 'land of cockayne'. He is not envisaging it as a way of life that need be taken seriously, nor one that he wants any part in. He exhibits here that peasant streak so common in reformist aesthetes, and can see objects of use only as possessions whose market value must be maintained, not as equipment to be discarded when technically obsolete. Not for him the scrapping economy implicit in Futurism's 'every generation its own house', or Le Corbusier's 'on jette, on remplace'. In fairness one should note that he could accept expendability in trashy materials: 'I can accept papier mâché in an artists' club, run up in a couple of days, torn down when the exhibition is over. But to play ducks and drakes with golden sovereigns, to use banknotes to light cigars, to crush pearls and drink them—*das wirkt unästhetisch*'.

But in skipping on thus far we have overpassed the vital paragraph that holds the historical key to 'Ornament and Crime', and explains the instance of its writing and the immediate power of conviction that it undoubtedly possessed.

'Now that ornament is no longer organically integrated into our culture, it has ceased to be a valid expression of that culture. The ornament that is designed today has no relevance to ourselves, to mankind at large, nor to the ordering of the cosmos. It is unprogressive and uncreative.

What has happened to the ornamental work of Otto Eckmann? What has happened to Van de Velde? The artist used to stand for health and strength, at the pinnacle of humanity, but the modern ornamentalist is either a cultural laggard or a pathological case. He himself is forced to disown his own work after three years. His products are already unbearable to cultured persons now, and will become so to others in a little time. Where are now the works of Eckmann, and where will those of Olbrich be ten years from now? Modern ornament has neither forbears nor descendants, no past and no future. It may be received with joy by uncultured folk, to whom the true greatness of our time is a book with seven seals, but even by them in a short time forgot.'

That fixes him in time. Where other men of his day may have had an uneasy feeling that Art Nouveau was losing its impetus, he had a personal quarrel with

Hoffmann and the *Wiener Sezession*, and any stick would serve to beat the *Wiener Werkstätte*. For all that, it took courage—truculence even—to launch these personal attacks at a time when the world reputation of both *Sezession* and *Werkstätte* were at their height, and had made Vienna a centre of artistic pilgrimage. On the other hand, the crack-up was already signalled. Long-witted operators like Peter Behrens were quietly sloughing off Art Nouveau, and that symptomatic young person Charles Edouard Jeanneret was, in the very year of 'Ornament and Crime', telling Josef Hoffmann he could keep his *Werkstätte*, recognizing that it was no longer creative. In articulating his quarrel with the *Sezession*, Loos was polarizing the attitude of a generation to decoration, as surely as Marinetti in the next few months was to polarize its attitude to machinery. In a time of decision his was a decisive gesture.

The decision taken, his position was clear: all forms of cultural regression are crime and waste; ornament is cultural regression and must therefore be a waste and a crime; worse than that, sex-crime. With his position so clearly given, and in such forthright terms, it comes as a further shock to find him hedging the issue with soft options.

'I address myself particularly to those natural aristocrats who stand at the summit of human progress, and yet have the deepest understanding of the needs and impulses of lesser men—the Kaffir who weaves an ornament into his cloth after a receipt so subtle that it is only seen when the whole is unpicked; the Persian knotting his rugs; the Slovak peasant working her lace; the grannie who works wonders with crochet-hook, beads and silk—he understands them and lets them alone, for these are consecrated hours in which they work. A vulgar revolutionary might burst in on them and say "that's a lot of rubbish", just as he might shout to old ladies performing their Stations of the Cross "There is no God". But under an aristocracy even an atheist takes off his hat when passing a church.'

Then he goes on to relate a touching parable of the dismay of his shoemaker on being asked to make a pair of utterly plain shoes, even at a third over the price of the normally ornamented model. Ornament, he says, is the culture of the poor, and we—aristocrats who have Beethoven and Wagner—have no right to deprive them of it. But a cultured man who goes to hear the Ninth Symphony and sits down to design a sampler is either a show-off or a degenerate.

'The death of ornament has brought the other arts to unbelievable heights. The symphonies of Beethoven could never have been written by a man who had to wear velvet, silk and lace. Anyone who goes around today in a velvet coat is no artist, but a clown or a housepainter. Wandering tribesmen wore bright colours to distinguish themselves from one another, but we have grown subtler and more refined—we moderns wear our clothes as a mask.

So unbelievably powerful is a modern personality that it can no longer be expressed through clothing. Freedom from ornament is a sign of mental strength, and modern man may use the ornament of historic and exotic cultures at his discretion, but his own inventive talents are reserved and concentrated on other things.'

In spite of the slight crescendo for the coda this is still a stingless tail, all passion spent. Nevertheless, 'Ornament and Crime' is still good fighting talk. In its author's own eyes it ranks with *Architektur*, written a year later, as one of his two prime writings, but not necessarily as his unique blow against ornament. To revert to the introduction to *Trotzdem*, we find that it continues 'Ornament was once synonymous with beautiful, but thanks to my life's work it now means inferior'. Life's work, he says, and on the narrow stage of Austria this might be true, but on the wider screen of the Modern Movement at large much of his writing after 1900 went by default for lack of republication on foreign presses. It is on the reprinting history of 'Ornament and Crime' that his claim to have liberated mankind must rest.

But it rests securely. Already in the nineteen-teens it had attracted enough

1 Kärtner Bar, Kärtner Durchgang, Vienna (1907). At a time of opulence in interior decoration, Loos's design appeared simple and restrained

1

notice outside Vienna to earn republication, first in Herwarth Walden's expressionist magazine, *der Sturm*, in 1912, and then in Georges Besson's sprightly translation in *Les Cahiers d' Aujourd'hui* in 1913.

These reprints brought Loos—and the essay—to the notice of an interested if restricted international readership. They also presumably brought Loos's ideas to the notice of the Futurist Sant'Elia, the first writer outside Vienna to be visibly influenced by them—Marinetti, the leader of the Futurists, had contacts with *der Sturm* as well as Parisian circles.

The French version was once more reprinted, unaltered, in No. 2 of *L'Esprit Nouveau*. One should remember that at this early date (March 1920) *L'Esprit Nouveau* still had a third director beside Ozenfant and Le Corbusier, and while its appeal to those two for its relevance to architecture and design is obvious enough, its appeal to the third director, Paul Dermée, would be equally strong. For though he was a poet, he was also close in with the Dadaists, and one can imagine how gratefully any attempt to equate Beethoven with a cave artist, and a comfort-station muralist, would fall upon the ears of those who were trying to get the Morgue accepted as an object of sentimental interest and had already moustached the Mona Lisa. The reappearance of 'Ornament and Crime' while Dada was still going full blast was uncommonly timely, and guaranteed it a favourable hearing at another moment of decision.

For this reprint appeared after Le Corbusier had finished with his flower-box-smothered house-projects of the war years, but before the Villa at Vaucresson that ushered in his new style. It was read, and of this we can be certain, by Erich Mendelsohn, between his first and second Dutch visits; after the decorated Luckenwald factory, and before the undecorated Sternfeld house. It appeared after Gropius's decorated Sommerfeld House had been designed, but before the 'reformed' projects and the undecorated Jena theatre, and again we can safely posit communication between Paris and Germany. Riding hard behind this timely reappearance came the publication of Loos's first book of collected essays, *Ins Leere Gesprochen*, which covers the years 1897–1900 only, but shows him in his plumbing-before-art-work mood, and remains to this day better known and more widely read than *Trotzdem*.

For, by the time *Trotzdem* appeared, Loos had ceased to be timely. He caught no mood of disgust with Art Nouveau, nor any Dadaist mood of disgust with art in general. Not only had the mood changed, but the ideas he had pushed had now been so thoroughly absorbed and understood that they looked more like Laws of Nature than the Works of Man.

All his best ideas had been pirated by younger men. His advocacy of Thonet chairs and *fauteuils grand-confort 'Maple'* had been so thoroughly taken over by Le Corbusier that Loos began to deride Thonet as *eine falsches Modell* in order to maintain some show of independence. But even the anti-ornament campaign had been plagiarized without acknowledgement, and in the introduction to *Troztdem* he says, following what has been quoted already,

'But even the echo as it answers believes the note to be its own, and that perfidious book *Die Form ohne Ornament*, published in Stuttgart in 1924, conceals my efforts even while it falsifies them.'

He might well complain. *Form without Ornament* was the catalogue *de luxe* of a Werkbund exhibition that toured Germany in 1924–25. Its illustrations make a brisk start with Jena glass and Stuttgart soap, but then trail off through such objects as Breuer's early Bauhaus furniture until they wind up with products so arty that they can only be described as *Sezession ohne Ornament*. The impossible, as Loos had seen it, had taken place, and the fine art designers had climbed on the anti-ornamental bandwaggon. Wolfgang Pfliederer says, in his introduction to this 'perfidious' book, 'If we survey the field of artistic handicraft today we find that it is not unified, but draws ... from two sources ... Technical form and Primitive form.'

Technical Form and Primitive Form. Engineers and peasants had been identified by Loos in that other prime essay, *Architektur*, as the two good, clean formgivers who did not commit the crimes of architects and artists, and to suggest that they might be tributary to the artistic handicrafts was to turn his arguments upside down and inside out. Within three years he was dead anyhow, and rapidly passing into that special limbo of oblivion that is reserved for those who have ideas that are too good to belong to one man alone. He had settled the problem of ornament as Alexander settled the Gordian knot, shockingly but effectively, and his ideas had gained an empire wider than the Macedonian's wildest dream. It is impossible now to imagine how the Modern Movement might have looked as a decorated style, but it might have been just that, had not its creators had ringing in their ears Adolf Loos's challenging equation: Ornament equals Crime.

Loos's essays still remain substantially unpublished in the English language with the exception of 'Ornament and Crime' which has appeared in the following publications: L. Munz and G. Künstler, Adolf Loos: Pioneer of Modern Architecture, *London 1966 (this volume also includes translations of 'The Plumbers' and the wonderful anti-Hoffmann essay 'The Story of a Poor Rich Man'); U. Conrads,* Programmes and Manifestoes on Twentieth-Century Architecture, *London 1970. Three further Loos essays, 'Potemkin's Town' (1897–8), 'Cultural Degeneracy' (1908) and 'Architecture' (1910) appear in T. and C. Benton and D. Sharp,* Form and Function, *London 1975.*
The essays have been re-issued in German, edited by Franz Glück and published by Verlag Herold, Vienna. (Editor)

FRANK LLOYD WRIGHT'S
peaceful penetration
of Europe

Nikolaus Pevsner's article on Frank Lloyd Wright is something of a classic. It was published originally in The Architects' Journal *in May 1939 on the day that Wright spoke at the Royal Institute of British Architects. It is included in this anthology of writings on Rationalism because it examines Wright's influence on Europe, principally through the Dutch and German architects associated with Modern Movement developments.*

There lived near London an architect known to many for his adventurous early buildings and designs, his brilliant writings on the social movement of the arts and crafts, his Campden experiment in craftsmanship, husbandry and community life, and his charming personality, Mr C. R. Ashbee. He was about seventy-five,* and could claim amongst his other titles to fame that of having discovered Frank Lloyd Wright for Europe. They got to know each other when Mr Ashbee was staying in Chicago in 1900. Correspondence ensued, and when Wright came over to Europe in 1910 he visited Mr Ashbee at Campden. Some time before this journey, Professor Kuno Francke, a German professor in aesthetics at Harvard, had visited Wright and strongly suggested to him to go to Germany, where his work would be hailed by the progressive architects. Soon after this visit, a proposal came from E. Wasmuth, the best-known German architectural publishers, to bring out a complete monograph of Wright's work. While in Florence, Wright signed the introduction to this first portfolio, a copy of which is now at the Architectural Association. Immediately afterwards he suggested to Mr Ashbee to write the text to a second smaller and more popular volume also to be brought out by Wasmuth's. This appeared in 1911, and can now be studied in the library of the Victoria and Albert Museum.

The two books, including all that was most important of Wright's early style from Winslow to the Robie and Martin Houses, must have had an almost instantaneous effect on young German architects. This is most clearly reflected in certain details of Gropius's model factory at the Cologne Exhibition of 1914. The brick technique, above all, in the odd long slots of the upper floor windows, the heavy entrance with the two bands of windows on the left and the right, the projecting string courses above and the flat slab roofs, all these motifs prove beyond doubt the impression of Wright's (besides Peter Behrens's) work on Gropius. In the meantime, however, Berlage, the great old man of Dutch architecture, had gone to the United States in 1911, unacquainted in all probability with the Wasmuth volumes. Travelling in America he discovered Wright again independently. In articles published in the *Schweizerische Bauzeitung* of September 14, 21 and 28, 1912, and in a Dutch book of 1913 dealing with his American impressions, Berlage praised Wright as 'a master without an equal in Europe'. In discussing the Martin House, he stressed its bare ground floor walls, the long bands of windows on the upper floor, the living-rooms leading into each other without separating doors, the lovely vistas across caused by this spatial arrangement, the intimate connection between house and garden, and the widely projecting roofs. It can be assumed that those young Dutch architects who learned their craft or set up in practice just before the war became familiar with a man so sincerely admired by their great example, Berlage, and with the two German

Frank Lloyd Wright in the Bride of Denmark, the private bar in the offices of the Architectural Press, decorated in the style of a Victorian pub

* C. R. Ashbee died in 1942.

3

1 Frank Lloyd Wright: Robie House, Chicago (1908–9)

2 Walter Gropius: model factory at the Werkbund Exhibition, Cologne (1914)

3 R. van't Hoff: Huis ter Heide, near Utrecht, built of concrete (1915)

publications of 1910 and 1911. One of the first palpable proofs of Wright's influence on building in Holland is a house designed by Van't Hoff in 1915. Similar features can easily be detected in the early work of Jan Wils and H. Th. Wijdeveld (who, incidentally, saw illustrations of some houses by Wright in an American book as early as 1900, when he was only fifteen years old. He says: 'I could not sleep the first night I possessed the book; I was so thrilled'). During the first postwar decade Wright's idiom became one of the chief ingredients of Dutch architectural expression. There was, eg, the Kijkduin Estate near the Hague, by Bijvoet and Duiker, there were private houses by Wouda, La Croix (ill. *Nieuw Nederl. Bouwkunst*, 1924, Figs. 21–23), and even by Berlage himself. The centre of Wright enthusiasm, however, was Wijdeveld, not by imitating Wright's style, but by spreading knowledge of it. In 1921 and again in 1925 he published in a magazine, *Wendingen*, then edited by him, illustrated articles on Wright, and collected these in 1925 into a lavishly produced book with English text and contributions by Oud, Mendelsohn, Mallet-Stevens, and others. This book, it seems, opened at last the eyes of young English architects to Wright's genius, although nothing comparable to the Dutch vogue followed. When Wijdeveld splendidly finished his propaganda for Wright by staging an exhibition of his work at the Municipal Museum in Amsterdam, which was then sent round to Berlin, Cologne, Munich, and Antwerp, no arrangements could be made for the exhibition to be shown in London. Paris does not appear to have been interested either, and this came probably from the strangely isolated development of the Modern Movement in France until after the war. To those eager for innovation and a true contemporaneity, Garnier's Cité Industrielle of 1904, and Perret's achievements in ferro-concrete had played the part assumed in Germany to a certain extent by Wright's forms and experiments. However, despite this, it seems unlikely that Mallet-Stevens or Le Corbusier can have been in complete ignorance of Wright when they formed and evolved their styles. Mallet-Stevens, in fact, paid a debt of gratitude to Wright in his article for

Heer Wijdeveld's volume. But Le Corbusier, although he had lived in Berlin for about six months just in 1910–11, answered, when asked to contribute to the Wijdeveld book: 'I do not know this architect'.

Here is a first instance of the difficulties which one meets in trying to follow the course of one man's style in the intricate tissue of European postwar architecture. Wright's influence on early Gropius—a transitory one—or on Dutch buildings of about 1920–24, is comparatively easy to grasp, but the historian of style finds himself in a much more precarious position directly he tries to analyse certain deeper and wider effects of Wright on Europe. A few examples may illustrate this.

There are, eg, the so-called Phantasts in Holland, the school of architects recognizable by their odd, deliberately crude, chaotic details, originally, one may surmise, instigated by Indian native temple art. De Klerk is perhaps the best known of them (Eigen Haard 1914 and 1917, Spaarndamerplantoen 1913 and 1917, Amstellaan 1920); Kromhout and, for a time, Piet Kramer were other representatives of this mood which leads back to Van der Mey's mad Scheepvaarthuis of 1912–13, and even to certain details in Berlage interiors. When the large estates of tenement houses around Amsterdam were erected immediately after the war and began to impress German town planners and architects, it was in this fantastic attire that they became known. And as at exactly the same time riotous post-war feelings prevailed in Germany, sometimes of a constructive revolutionary, sometimes of a post-defeat desperado, and sometimes of a jazzy *Après-nous-le-Déluge* character, the Dutch Phantasts found response in more than one school in Germany. Poelzig's and Bruno Taut's most soaring architectural dreams belong to these years, but Mendelsohn also succumbed to such feelings for a short time, and even Gropius's now destroyed War Memorial of 1920 at Weimar re-echoed the strident outbreaks of Expressionism.

Now, Expressionism was originally a pictorial movement, and the effects on architects of new forms in painting should not be underestimated. Cubism, the French counterpart of German Expressionism, has certainly deeply impressed architects, and helped them to develop compositions of bare cubes and façades without any mouldings mediating between different planes. But Cubism again could be interpreted decoratively and functionally, and both interpretations can be found in buildings of the first ten years after the war. The Rue Mallet-Stevens of 1927 can serve to illustrate the decorative, J. J. P. Oud's splendid Rotterdam estates the functional exegesis of Cubist tenets. Dudok, one may say, stands between the two.

Functionalism, however, is in itself a complex phenomenon. Even without Cubist pictures—and pre-war Cubism of Picasso and Braque or pre-war abstract art of Kandinsky were far from precise and geometrically rigid—Functional architecture would probably have found its own immediate expression, simply by evolving Loos's and Peter Behrens's forms of about 1910. This is what Gropius did. He certainly understood Cubist painters or else he would not have appointed them to professorships in the Bauhaus, but while teaching there they probably adopted more from his direct and courageous architectural style than he from their configurations in the flat.

The Dutch and German Phantasts, Expressionism, Cubism, Functionalism—an intricate pattern of tendencies in European art between 1920 and 1925, and yet, in fact, not intricate enough, for once more Frank Lloyd Wright's influence must be introduced into it. There was not one of these conflicting schools of thought which has not at one time or other experienced some stimulus from Wright. And as if this were not enough of confusion yet, one has to add that by then—as is known— Wright had changed his own style considerably. Midway Gardens, Chicago (1913), and the Imperial Hotel, Tokio (1916–20), represent a new Wright, gone all romantic, fantastic, Eastern—far more personal and inimitable now than he had been when Europe first got to hear of him. To copy this new style or even to accept influence from it was bound to be fatal to any but the strongest decorative genius. How far now did the Dutch Phantasts find themselves confirmed in Wright's

4 Frank Lloyd Wright: Midway Gardens, Chicago (1913)

5 H. Wouda: country house, 'De Luifel' at Wassenaar, near the Hague (1924)

6 W. M. Dudok: School at Hilversum (1921)

seconda maniera? Van der Mey comes before Midway Gardens, but Berlage may have felt the first symptoms of a change, the result of which was naturally just as palatable to him as Wright's earlier style. Wijdeveld's volume of 1925 is certainly an instance of Wrightian Phantasm interpreted by a Dutch architect who had gone through a phase of native Dutch Phantasm.

It is the same with Cubism. An architect grown up in admiration of Wright's genius would find access to Cubist painting easy; an architect ready to translate Cubist revelations into building would see his theories corroborated in Wright's practice. Who would be prepared to define what comes from Wright in Dudok's work at Hilversum, and what from Cubism, or what in Mendelsohn's uncouth brick houses of 1922 and 1923 is the outcome of Wright's idiom and what of Dudok's?

However, these questions seem simple when held against any arising from a consideration of Wright's most profoundly architectural qualities. So far, only forms have been discussed. But what effects of Wright's research into modern building materials can be traced, what effects of his brilliant spacial flexibility, or his revolutionary theories on the social future of art and architecture? It will, in all probability, never be possible to assess correctly the share, in the use of composite walling materials in German post-war experiments (Gropius, Luck-hardt, etc), which belonged to Wright's Unity Temple of 1908, a monolith with walls all of concrete slabs. And how far would Gropius himself be able to remember whether the lovely unity of house and garden in his Bauhaus staff dwellings at Dessau owed something to early impressions gathered from the perusal of the

Wasmuth volumes? Or take Mies van der Rohe's ravishing ballets of space, his Barcelona Exhibition Pavilion of 1929 and the famous Tugendhat House at Brünn with rooms rhythmically flowing into each other and no inner divisions. Had Le Corbusier spurred him, or at a much earlier stage Wright, who was the first so boldly to unite room with room? And—to mention one last instance—what of Wright's ideas on art education? Taliesin, his Wisconsin community, is only a few years old.* But it was preceded by his plan for what was to be called the Hillside Home School of the Allied Arts. The prospectus of this went out about the end of 1931, and Heer Wijdeveld was mentioned as future principal, Heer Wijdeveld who only a few months before had published his own plan for an international guild of architectural and general artistic training and community life to be built in Holland. Did Wijdeveld know about the Bauhaus? Is the name of guild derived in some roundabout way from Mr Ashbee's Guild and School of Handicraft at Chipping Campden, which Wright on his part knew? If there is a connection here, it would be a welcome proof of an ultimate derivation of Taliesin as well as Heer Wijdeveld's Elckerlic school from the Arts and Crafts Movement and William Morris. But these relations are, of course, not meant to be in any way direct or conscious. They are subtler, more concealed, and therefore perhaps all the more important. For the deeper the impression an architect of original genius receives from another of equal calibre, the less apparent will the links be . . .

* At the time of writing. (Editor)

WALTER GROPIUS

by Hermann George Scheffauer

Hermann George Scheffauer was one of the first continental commentators to write in The Architectural Review *on the new architecture movement in Germany. In a series of four articles in 1922–3, he discussed the work of Bruno Taut, Erich Mendelsohn, Hans Poelzig and, lastly, Walter Gropius. Although something of a historical curiosity his article remains a useful critique of Gropius's ideas for an architecture of synthesis—'architecture', Scheffauer argues on behalf of Gropius, 'is of an orchestral nature—the precipitate of the whole (of art)'.*

This article is followed by a Memorandum on Gropius's early housing programme. It was written when Gropius was 26 years old in 1910 and originally presented to the AEG, the giant German electrical combine which employed Peter Behrens as its chief designer and architect.

Walter Gropius is the leader of the most revolutionary arts and handicrafts school in the world, the Staatliche Bauhaus at Weimar. This well-organized, fruitful, and heretical institution has been established upon ancient and venerable foundations—those of the former Royal Saxon Academy of Arts and Crafts—and upon many new and dynamic theories in the arts and the teaching of them. The Staatliche Bauhaus is the enemy and antithesis of the academic. It is a great institution with a well-selected staff of 'form-masters', and many 'apprentices' and 'journeymen'. It has workshops and garden-colonies, and is, in effect, a modern abbey in which the acolytes of the arts are trained to priesthood according to a curriculum which seeks to amalgamate all the virtues of the old guild system with modern means, methods, and necessities. Thus, mass-fabrication is calmly faced as an inevitable phase of modern economic conditions, and efforts are made to refine and ennoble it to the service of art. Among the teachers of the Staatliche Bauhaus are some of the most distinguished European creators and exponents of the new—such as Vassily Kandinsky, Lyonel Feininger, Johannes Itten, Adolf Meyer, and Walter Gropius himself. The motto of the Bauhaus reads, prosaically enough:

'To train artistically-gifted man so that he may become creatively-productive, as an artisan, a sculptor, a painter, or an architect'.

Walter Gropius belongs to that group of younger German architects to whom the war and its accompanying cultural, social, and political phenomena meant a deep, never-to-be-closed cleavage with the past. The seeds and spores of the impending change that came finally in the shape of a cataclysm instead of a gradual evolution were already active in him before the war. As a creative artist of quick and responsive sensibilities the discord and the separatism, the fatal dualism of the modern age, were palpable to him long before the whole structure was shaken and riven to its centre. He *knew*, as every true architect must indeed instinctively *feel*, that the world-spirit of an epoch crystallizes itself most clearly in its edifices, that its spiritual and material capacities find in them a simultaneous and visible expression. We thus have an infallible mirror for discerning the features, the harmony or cacophony of an epoch. A vital architectural spirit, rooted in and fed by the entire life of a people, must embrace all domains of human endeavour, all arts and all technics. Gropius felt the great, painful discrepancy, and became vividly aware of the fatal fact that the architecture of today had degenerated from the great art, inclusive of arts, to a mere study and routine. The lamentable confusion to be seen everywhere was but a reflection of an old, dismembered world and of the lack of cohesion and co-operation between creators.

The art of great building or of architecture in the grand style is conditioned not only by material considerations of immense scope, but also by the ability of large groups to possess themselves of, or be possessed by, a new inspiration—a new artistic dispensation arising from sublimated knowledge, insight, and experience—and the capacity to act in unison. The art of great architecture is, therefore, a multiple, a communal art. True architecture, in contradistinction to other individualized manifestations of art, is of an orchestral nature—the precipitate of a whole.

Walter Gropius began his revolt against the anaemia of the academic with the example of Morris, Ruskin, Van de Velde, Olbrich, and Behrens, and later, the splendid work of the 'Deutscher Werkbund' before his eyes. His artistic nature is of an earnest and brooding cast, and the dualism between the world of art and the world of reality affected him deeply. He saw architecture, bound with the swaddling-cloths of mummified traditions, delivered up to the cold conceptions, the scant imaginations of engineers and merchants. His recoil from the conventional and from outworn forms first threw him into the arena of the scientific, into a struggle with the new materials, such as steel and concrete, and into a compromise with the utilitarian. The stripping process became one with the creative or formative. He began a passionate search for the naked form, the primal form that would also serve as the ultimate. Instinctively he felt that a *tabula rasa* was necessary. Upon this clean slate or cleared ground, new life, expressed by chastened bulk and transfigured line, was to arise. Every architect had the duty of becoming an ascetic, of preparing himself and his work for the message his age was to write, the symbols, forms, and ornament it was to create.

This period of combat with technical demands, this debate and compromise with new materials, this search for fresh solutions is visible in such structures of Walter Gropius as the office building at the Werkbund Exhibition at Cologne in 1914. Here we have the spectral, translucent encroachment upon and envelopment of brick,

1

1 Side view of the office building at the Werkbund Exhibition, Cologne (1914)

2 The front of the office building at the Werkbund Exhibition, Cologne (1914), showing the glass enclosed staircases and brickwork front

2

3 Front view of the machinery
hall, Werkbund Exhibition,
Cologne (1914)

4 The machinery hall and tower,
Werkbund Exhibition, Cologne
(1914)

stone, and wood. We become conscious of a new audacity. The walls vanish. Staircases, skeletonized as by an architectonic X-ray, sweep their suspended helices through the air. The corner towers become transparent and seem to mock at all traditions of permanence. The corbelled-out pilasters on the front throng one another so closely as to leave mere slits, and echo the massiveness of Assyrian façades. We have the wide, insolent rake of tin roof cornices floating on clerestorys of glass. The supporting pilasters of a longitudinal wall are masked by a free wall of glass. Brick enters into a new law of marriage with other brick and with sculpture—as in the entrance portal of this horizontally-attuned edifice that glistened and smouldered with a new message upon the raw grounds of this exposition—like a bubble before the cannon-blast of the impending war.

The same influence, but expressed in less restless and more monumental terms, is visible in the machinery exhibition hall of the Deutz Motor Company, and the remarkable octagonal tower that adjoined it. Here the round and the triangular are also invoked, as well as colour, striking and living colour that gave the whole complex an additional rhythm and vibration. The effect of the whole was grandiose—a lay temple of symphonic symmetry, a hall in which the machine and the building, the one wholly, the other in part, of metal, celebrated a new reconciliation. Here utilitarian architecture, aided by the element of spectacular display, takes on a dignity and beauty through its own high and fearless honesty, the frank, graceful avowal of its purpose.

It is a pity that this element was not preserved in the shoe factory, at Alfeld an der Leine. Here we have an expression of naked use and an unabashed confession of the purely expedient. One of the oldest optical-material principles of architecture is defied and even repudiated by the glass ends of this factory, enclosing the staircase hall, and supporting the heavy, super-incumbent angle of the brick fascia on fragile glass and spidery muntins. Here the hunger or itch for

5 The shoe factory for Karl Benscheidt, Alfeld an der Leine (1911): the entrance and offices

6

8

7

9

6 The staircase hall in the house
of A. Sommerfeld, Dahlem-Berlin

7 A house at Zehlendorf-Berlin

8 The main façade of the
Municipal Theatre at Jena

9 The auditorium of the
Municipal Theatre, Jena

independence may have resulted in an unnecessary, even disturbing *tour de force*, yet one which undeniably demanded courage. A fine balance and harmony of walls and fenestration is also visible in his factory of agricultural machinery, clear-cut masses, without cornices, save in the central tract, and traversed by the long, white-mullioned parallelograms of the windows.

The sheer, uncompromising barrenness, the stern, absolute negation of all extraneous decorative elements which mark Gropius's industrial buildings are not retained in his domestic designs. An example is the remarkable solid timber-frame house which Gropius, in association with Adolf Meyer, built for Herr Adolf Sommerfeld at Dahlem-Berlin. The framework is of solid beams or dressed logs, cross-mortised into one another—round-faced on the ground-floor wall and peak-faced on the upper story. This house is built with a set will and tenacity that convert it into something original and organic, within and without. Externally it is devoid of all ornament, save that of the expressionistically carved door, and the beam dentils, and the oiled and varnished grain and pattern of the logs themselves. Within, apart from the patterns of the boarding and the symbolical carvings of the staircase buttresses, we encounter the same nudity which goes so far as to banish such impedimenta as pictures. But the material itself once more comes into its own. The old love for a beautiful, warm, and friendly material—wood—which has been lost to us so long, and which survives only in parts of Scandinavia, Russia, and Bavaria, has been recovered and accentuated here.

Another dwelling, recently completed at Zehlendorf-Berlin, and built massively of concrete, confronts us with a front that is practically windowless, except for the deeply recessed opening on the second floor. Here we have heavy and naked severity, redeemed by a certain shadowplay, bizarreness of line and balance of parts. The abrupt bifurcation of the front is remarkable; the elevation, however, is held together by the cornice and roof over the entrance.

Gropius is one of those German architects who have been influenced by the cold, sober objectivity of American commercial architecture as expressed in the work of Frank Lloyd Wright. Applying this alien American element to their own problems, they have, to a certain extent, rarefied and even ennobled it, as may be seen in countless designs for projected *turmhäuser*, as the Germans have categorically christened the skyscraper. But in the application of this American element to American problems, they have over-americanized it under the false assumption that the American was purely utilitarian. This accounts for the lifeless desolation, the schematic abstraction of most of the German designs submitted in the competition for the 'Chicago Tribune' office building—among them one by Walter Gropius, a sheer, bleak problem of acrobatic engineering and geometric planes.

In the Municipal Theatre at Jena (Jena Stadt-theater), Gropius, again in association with Adolf Meyer, has tried to give us the absolute theatre, the theatre stripped, as it were, for action. He has created a blank, polished, chromatic shell for the medium of the drama. Here his aversion to even the simplest survivals of 'byzantinism', has forced him to fight for the achievement of the pure, unadorned, essential playhouse—the bones and soul of the theatre. This fabric, built up of cubistic masses within and without, and held together in a strange harmony by blocks and expanses of pure and direct colour, is something which first offends, then overwhelms, then fascinates by its very starkness, and by its rude, almost brutal repudiation of all attempts to conciliate by means of concessions to the conventional. Photographs, unfortunately, give only the dead bulk, the light and shadow, without the vibration and movement that result from the relationship between the static and the dynamic masses.

The front of the theatre is a snow-white wall with parallel wings and bevelled corners, the whole elevated upon a long plinth. The treatment of the central and side entrances, the hoods and illuminating bodies, in form and colour—different greys, viridian green and brass—as well as in delicate symmetry, is full of subtle refinements, such as the flat, entasis-like curve of the line of the front fire-wall. The door and window openings have the appearance of being cut directly out of the smooth, external skin of the building. The entrance lobby is steeped in a sunny vibrant yellow. Two thick square columns are capped with light-boxes of matt glass and surrounded with seats of silver-grey plush. The floor is set with large Roman tiles of brilliant red.

The auditorium at once seizes and submerges us by its walls of vivid salmon-red. The 'friezes', balcony fronts, and proscenium walls are a dull grey, the wooden wainscot and doors a greyish-yellow, the doors themselves armoured with great discs of copper. The heavy, optically even top-heavy projections which step off the angle between wall and ceiling oppress one at first sight, as well as the ponderous light-boxes. The square, blunt forehead of the gallery front is supported on huge lintels, reminiscent of Stonehenge or of Aztec motifs. The stage itself opens, without any preliminary transition, abruptly from the wall, and is closed by a curtain of brilliant ultramarine. The stage settings themselves are so built as to continue and extend the architecture of the auditorium into the realm of the footlights and to bring about a new harmony with the scenery. Once adjusted to the play and interplay of these cubicular and geometric forms, and to the static and active forces dwelling in these masses, one succumbs to their power and to the spell exercised by the huge facets of courageous colour.

There can be no doubt that there is a new music or at least a new rhythm in this architecture of Spartan simplicity. It may be the architecture or at least the step towards an architecture of a new transition, the cleared field for the growth of wonders to be, or the adumbration on a small scale and in terms of concrete, steel, and stucco, of the cyclopean architecture of the future. The clear, stark, masculine note of this architectural challenge, must, despite its asperities, be recognized and honoured. It may or may not be a plinth for a new renaissance, but it is at least a wall built against reaction, possibly a forest clearing for the planting of something sublime.

The work of Walter Gropius may also be summed up, like the simple, yet in the best sense of the word sensational, monument he designed at Weimar for the dead in the March revolution—an immense stone lightning-bolt darting from an irregular plinth into the heavens—as a challenge of earth to the obtuse, blundering gods. The gesture is the gesture of Ajax, and it is the attitude of Ajax that impresses us in the architecture of Walter Gropius—however much this attitude, contrary to that of the Greek warrior, is the result, not of a tempestuous temperament, but of a deliberate programme, growing out of a philosophy.

Programme for the establishment of a company for the provision of housing on aesthetically consistent principles

by Walter Gropius

Underlying idea

The company which is to be established regards the industrialization of housing as its aim, in order to provide for the building of houses the incontestable advantages of industrial production, ie best materials and workmanship and a cheap price.

It is the fault of speculative builders and entrepreneurs that housing has deteriorated so much in the last decade both as regards taste and durability. The public consciously or unconsciously is affected by this state of affairs. Everybody with an inborn or acquired sense of quality must find the bragging, purely superficial, sham comfort unbearable which entrepreneurs, in the houses they build, try to produce for the sake of advertising, but at the expense of good material, solid workmanship, distinction and simplicity. It can be said that pomposity and a false romanticism instead of good proportions and serviceable simplicity have become the trend of our time.

10 Farm labourers' cottages in Pomerania, designed by Walter Gropius (1906)

The reason for this malaise is the fact that the public is always at a disadvantage, whether it builds with an entrepreneur or with an architect. The entrepreneur is justly avoided by many, because he unscrupulously hurries projects through in order to save costs, and because he does damage to his client by saving materials and wages in order to increase his own profit. The architect on the other hand who provides designs only is interested in raising the cost of a job, since final cost determines his fee. In both cases the client is the sufferer. His ideal is the artist architect who sacrifices all to aesthetic aims and thereby does economic damage to himself.

These points demonstrate patently the unhealthy situation in today's building trades. Enterprises based on craftsmanship still exist in the building trade, but can no longer resist the competition of industry. For in the case of quantity production overheads spent on creation and design while developing a type which could in the end be established as an ideal, are negligible in proportion to turnover, whereas they cannot be afforded in production by ones.

The fundamental principle of industry is subdivision of labour. The creator concentrates all his energies on making his idea, his creation come to life, the manufacturer concentrates his on durable and cheap production, the merchant on well organized distribution of the product. This use of specialists is the only way by which essential, ie spiritual, creation can be made to work economically and the public can be supplied with products of aesthetically and technically good quality.

It is true also of the building of houses. To a certain extent industrial production has already entered this field, but the types introduced by entrepreneurs for the sake of making profits are immature and technically as well as aesthetically bad and therefore inferior in quality to houses whose parts are still produced by hand. However, the craftsman's work is probably too costly, and entrepreneurs have for the sake of cheapness tried from the start to eliminate it as far as possible.

The new Company is to draw the consequences from this situation and combine by means of industrialization the aesthetic activity of the architect and the economic activity of the entrepreneur. This would result in healthier conditions and patent aesthetic advantages. For whereas up to now the busy architect had to rely more or less on trained assistants and was unable to attend personally to all the details of his designs, money can be spent profitably by the Company on the slow and most careful working through of all details by the architect himself, before they go into production. Thus a happy union would be established between art and technics and a large public enabled to possess mature works of architecture and reliable and durable products.

The reason why careful detailing in all respects can, even where a simple house is concerned, be of such high cultural significance lies much deeper. It lies in the concept of a *Zeitstil*.

The way private houses are built today, the tendency deliberately to stress uniqueness, ie the opposite of the principles of modern industry, cannot possibly create a type of housing characteristic of our age. Methods based on craftsmanship are antiquated and must be replaced by the acceptance of a modern concept of industry. The search for the odd, the wish to be different from one's neighbour makes unity of style impossible. It is a search for what is novel, not for the perfect type. The example of all styles of the past shows that they all worked to established formal principles with variations only to fit special cases.

Conventions in the good sense of the word cannot be hoped for by emphasizing individuality. They depend on the contrary on unification, the rhythm of repetition, ie the consistency of forms, recurrent because recognized as good. Our age, after a sad *interregnum*, is approaching a *Zeitstil* which will honour traditions but fight false romanticism. Objectivity and reliability are once more gaining ground.

The necessity of conventions can also be demonstrated from their practical advantages. The more an individual groundplan differs from what is based on the needs of an age and has been worked out by generations, the more will its own qualities suffer. What is true of the plan, is true of the whole house. Past periods respected traditions. The Dutch brick house, the French block of flats of the eighteenth century, the *Biedermeier* house of about 1800 were all repeated in series. In England this desire for conventional identity, based on a firm power to organize, led to terrace housing of exact identity continued without any break through whole districts. The result was great economies and at the same time, and admittedly unintentional, aesthetic consistency. However, because the English builders did not intend to produce works of art, their single-minded pursuit of economic advantages produced in the elevations a drab uniformity.

The new Company intends to offer its clients not only inexpensive, well-built and practical houses and in addition a guarantee of good taste, but also take into consideration individual wishes without sacrificing to them the principle of industrial consistency.

The realization of the idea

I. Use of the same parts and materials for all houses
The idea of industrialization in housing can be translated into reality by repeating individual parts in all the designs promoted by the Company. This makes mass production possible and promotes low costs and high rentability. Only by mass-producing can really good products be provided. With the present methods of building houses it is a matter of luck whether one finds efficient and reliable craftsmen. Mass-production in a factory guarantees identity of products.

Nearly all parts of a house can be produced in factories, such as

Building	*Decorating and furnishing*
Staircases	Furniture
Railings	Panelling
Windows	Ceiling panels
Doors	Floors
Cornices	Wallpapers
Doorways	Door furniture, handles,
Balconies	key-holes, etc.
Bay windows	Linoleum
Verandas	Lincrusta
Dormer windows	Light fittings
Grilles*	Textiles
	Ceramics
	Cutlery

Given the trend of our age to eliminate the craftsman more and more, yet greater savings by means of industrialization can be foretold, though in our country they may for the time being still appear utopian. In America, Edison pours in variable iron forms whole houses with walls, ceilings, staircases, plumbing, etc., and can thereby dispense even with the bricklayer and joiner.†

For all parts the best dimensions have to be decided first of all. These standard dimensions form the basis for the designs and are to be kept in future designs. Only by this means can mass sales be guaranteed and special making in the case of replacements and repairs be avoided.

Of each item there are available a number of designs of different execution and price, but the same size.

All questions of form, colour, material and internal equipment are put down and catalogued as variants. All parts fit exactly, as they are made by machine to the same standard dimensions. For the same reasons they are all interchangeable.

Internal features such as ceiling panels, stone floors or wooden floors, panelling, wall coverings in pressed materials are designed for all parts of the home so that they can be supplied at once.

Furnishings promise to be an important field. Experience shows that turnover is quick and sales easy. Furniture, light fittings, rugs, textiles of all kinds, linen, ceramics, cutlery, etc, are to be made to a variety of tested designs and can be supplied quickly and inexpensively.

In the same way all technical and sanitary installation, ie hot and cold water, bathroom equipment, electrically operated ventilation, electric lighting and cooking apparatus will be ready-made and offered according to what arrangement and price are suitable.

* For example, one may assume that one house has twenty doors of the same dimensions. Even if the turnover were only 80 houses a year, 600 doors of the same dimensions would be used, without considering possible sales to outside builders. (Author)
† This was reported in *Building News* XCI, 1906, p. 249. *See* P. Collins: *Concrete*, 1959, p. 90. The whole question is taken up again by Gropius in the chapter 'Rationalization' in his *The New Architecture and the Bauhaus*, 1935. (Editor)

Colours and combinations of materials are set down in tables.

The client can compose his house from all these materials and forms according to his personal taste. He first chooses from among available types of house. However, even the type is variable as will be demonstrated later. The same plan can be had with a proper upper storey or an attic storey, with larger or smaller kitchen, and with a wide variety of details. The choice of materials also is the client's. He can specify rendering, brick, or stone, a slate or a tile roof.

It is by the provision of interchangeable parts that the Company can meet the public's desire for individuality and offer the client the pleasure of personal choice and initiative without jettisoning aesthetic unity. Each house is in the end its own self by means of form, material and colour.

Contracts with suitable specialist manufacturers secure that all objects and parts satisfy the standards laid down by the Company and are, if possible, permanently in stock. As soon as an order comes in, all parts, catalogued in some numerical arrangement, can be obtained at once and need only be assembled on the site according to plans which are equally readily obtainable.

The individual parts and especially those belonging to the furnishing of houses can also be sold to outside clients and entrepreneurs. Royalties from their sales go to the Company, because it is the Company that provided the designs. It is quite possible that such sales will raise the turnover considerably. As soon as it has been proved that there is demand and that the Company is developing, contracts with firms can be drawn up increasingly profitably.

II. Multiple use of designs

From the rich material of years of experience and the study of traditional building methods of all civilized countries of the world, the best has been used for inspiration and tested for suitability in the historical and climatic conditions of today. After this study of tested traditions, old as well as current, the work of designing started. Its result after many attempts is a series of designs for houses of different categories which contain the sum total of all practical, technical and aesthetic experience. They now seem suitable to establish exemplary standards for quality production in varied forms.

The designs must be ready in every detail to be used on the site, when the Company starts operations. As in every other type of industrial standardization, large turnover will be the means of profiting from the long period of preparation of the designs and the intellectual effort contained in them and their practical and technical ideas. Moreover, they will be of value to many, not just to a few. Large sales allow for low prices of the individual products in spite of high accuracy of execution.

The guiding idea of the Company is to be that comfort is not obtained by overdone bogus-splendours, but by clear spatial arrangements, and by the conjunction and selection of tested materials and reliable techniques. It is in this field that higher excellency will be offered and confirmed by guarantees granted over several years. For it is exactly here that the Company believes to be able to establish and maintain its reputation.

All types of houses, variable in size and arrangement, and variable also, as has been described, according to the wishes of the client, are ready with all drawings, estimates and detailed specification of necessary parts. The houses as designed are independent, coherent organisms not tied to any site, devised to fit the needs of modern civilized man in any country, not even only Germany. Interchanges between civilized nations are growing with the growing facilities of traffic. The result of this is the establishment of new international needs and a unified direction in all vital questions. National costumes tend to disappear and fashion is becoming a common factor in all civilized countries. In the same way there is bound to be a common convention in housing transcending national frontiers.

All designs for houses and their parts must be registered. Even if imitations were to appear, however, they could not do damage, because of a cheapness, reliability and reputation which could not easily be emulated.

To satisfy the changing needs of the public, the Company has prepared detached houses of different types and sizes from the working-class house to the upper-class villa. They will be put into operation according to demand. The advantages of detached houses need not be reiterated. Everybody wishes to own property. The strength of this wish even among the poorer classes is demonstrated by the allotments round our cities.

Modern industry has for a long time recognized the importance of working-class housing. Indeed, by the initiative usually of private companies more and more working-class estates are appearing in Germany. Their number and development in the near future is, as far as one can foretell, going to grow enormously. Experience collected for decades in English, American and German working-class housing has been used by the Company in the preparation of its designs. With the help of the principle of industrial production it can thus offer the possibility of building working-class cottages of high aesthetic value and good workmanship at minimum cost and in the shortest time. The advantages of the principle of industrial production are particularly obvious in working-class housing; for clients who are manufacturers or owners of large agricultural estates will as a rule need not one house but larger numbers. It is evident that the largest number of houses built at the same time and with the same parts will result in the cheapest price. This even applies to the wages of foremen, etc, and other overheads, since they can be set against not one house but many erected at the same time. As cost is a primary factor in putting up working-class estates, the Company is, on that score alone, going to be superior to those erecting individual houses with the services of individual craftsmen and solely when opportunities offer themselves.

The second group of designs is larger detached houses.

For the wealthier urban population, manufacturers, professional men, merchants, etc, who want to have houses of their own and who can spend some 25,000 to 50,000 Marks on them,* there is no possibility except in England to get a house of good workmanship and with the space and comfort that can be obtained, if one is ready to live in a flat. They must put up with the hygienic and aesthetic defects of flats as speculative builders offer them, or with small, primitive detached houses which have much less space than the flats in the towns.

By means of the multiple use of the same designs and of the industrial production of parts the Company is in a position to satisfy these large groups of clients and offer them a good and aesthetically well-organized house of six to twelve or even more rooms with all the comforts of the modern metropolis for a capital corresponding to the rents they have at present to pay for flats.

There is also a public which wants houses in the suburbs, but has not as much capital as the previous groups, or can, for some reason, not settle down for a long duration. The Company caters for this public by offering designs for semi-detached houses or detached houses of several storeys for the use by two or more rent-paying families. The advantages of the detached house can be preserved, even if it is planned to consist of a small number of flats, and rent takes the place of ownership. Special care has been taken to separate tenants as completely as possible.

In these cases the Company's clients are not the tenants, but entrepreneurs who would regard such a house in a suburb close to the centre as a good investment. For, thanks to the principles of industrialized housing, these houses are so cheap that, thereby alone, they guarantee a good income from rents, quite apart from the advantages of good workmanship and comfortable fitments and furnishings.

For the largest types of the houses there would be, according to location and if a need can be established, the possibility of simplifying the economic running by centralization [of services†]. Since for town-dwellers with their nostalgia for

* This, in 1910, represented £1250 to £2500. Voysey's *Holly Mount* at Knotty Green near Beaconsfield cost £1429 in 1906. (Editor)

† Editor's addition.

nature the idea of a garden is always tempting, the Company proposes to undertake the provision of a garden for every one of its houses. Although each garden is an individual case, if only for reasons of the contours of the site, and, therefore, repetition in quantity from one and the same design is out of the question, the provision of gardens yet appears important as a publicity asset. Moreover, certain principles and certain formal details can be laid down, according to which in each case the garden architect employed by the Company can easily work out a plan suitable for each particular house and site.

III. Architectural unity for estates

It is likely that the Society will make sufficient profit from the sale of such detached houses. However, it will also be desirable, taking into consideration the appearance of a town as a whole and also higher profits, to lay out and build coherently larger estates inside and outside a town. This could be done under contracts with entrepreneurs.

For the estates outside the town, where transport conditions must be a determining factor, the multiple repetition of detached or semi-detached or terrace houses for one family or several families would be the programme, in the manner of similar English estates, but with all the advantages of good workmanship, taste and comfort which it is the programme of the Company to offer. The visual treatment, the beauty and intimacy of inner courtyards which our age has lost, though southern countries still possess it, will be emphasized especially and similarly the treatment of corners, of the middle axis of buildings and of the surrounding gardens.

The principle of creating coherent streets out of rows of identical houses can also be applied to blocks of flats in cities. Here in any case a type, though not a good one, has recently been developed, as regards the plan as well as the elevation with the never ending pairs of bay windows. Only, builders hide the identity of forms under an unjustifiable mess of stucco and bad ornament, instead of drawing the logical conclusion and aiming at complete repetition which would be of enormous economic advantage. The price of mass-produced terraces of flats must, of course, be considerably lower than that of detached houses, since to build on a large scale in one place and at one time with identical materials and parts being taken to the site must be a great saving.

In the case of the largest types of such blocks of flats one could again, where opportunity arises, think of simplifying the running by means of centralization [of services].

The building of large estates could be done on behalf of other companies and big financiers. According to available capital either a large number of houses could be built as a speculation and then sold to a bidder (which would result undeniably in the quickest service to the public and the lowest prices), or the site could be laid out and divided up into plots according to the plan of the Company and the plots then sold individually as the demand arises.

Whenever an adjoining block is tackled afresh, new building types will be used, both for aesthetic and practical reasons. However, quite apart from that, each plan type allows for innumerable combinations of the parts so that there is none of the danger of that uniformity which is so typical of English suburbs.

The sites are to be prepared even before the houses are built. Gardens also and walls and fences are to be provided in advance. By means of an early planting of trees and by their grouping each garden is to appear completely separate from its neighbours. Thus the public will be at once attracted by the beauty of the gardens and the unity of the whole estate and its rentability will increase accordingly.

The organization of sales

I. Commercial principles

So far the products have been explained. Selling them is proposed to be handled in the following way. To protect an enterprise against competition, it is important to establish sound commercial principles for the selling of the products, principles surpassing those of competitive enterprises. Several significant advantages result *per se* from the idea of the present enterprise.

By mass production in factories and mass consumption of its goods the Company is in the advantageous position to offer its goods, in spite of their best workmanship and excellent materials, so cheaply that the goods of competitors made singly and by hand cannot keep pace with them either in quality or in price.

Moreover, it has so far been the worst evil for the client that it was impossible to fix in advance exactly what a building will cost. It is well enough known that a client from the beginning calculates with costs exceeding the estimate by 20 per cent and that even this tacitly accepted figure is often exceeded. This alone prevents innumerable people from having houses built for themselves. The Company is capable of fixing in advance and with absolute certainty the total cost for each of their houses, since experience gained in previously executed projects is a guarantee of no detail being forgotten in the estimate, of all parts being purchasable from factory stock at fixed prices, and of all types of parts chosen by the client being entered with their prices at once in the printed estimate for each project. The varying costs of transport from the factories, of wages and materials are written into specially provided columns of the estimate according to current prices in the relevant part of the country. The Company gives a guarantee that the estimate will be kept.

Similarly, the Company will be immune against another evil in the building of houses, the loss of time and especially of interest on capital caused by the time taken over drawings, sub-contracts, etc. All designs are ready, all by-law permissions granted, all parts ready to be delivered. Thus the Company can execute orders with little manpower and at a speed inaccessible to competitors and thereby prevent losses of time and especially of interest on capital.

II. Organization

These are the commercial principles of the enterprise. Its internal organization is planned to be as follows:

The whole organization will be conducted by a board of directors responsible for artistic, commercial and technical departments.

The function of the art department is to design types and parts, site plans and layouts for gardens and to specify materials and methods of construction.

The techno-commercial department is responsible for the running of the business. It deals with advertising, with the client whose individual wishes must be matched against the variable items of plans and parts, with the sale of houses or perhaps sites and, when an order has been placed, with the ordering of materials and parts. Nearly the whole correspondence can be reduced to printed forms, and the filling in of numbers from catalogues and of quantities. Dealings with suppliers, the making out of contracts and necessary journeys also belong to the responsibilities of the commercial department.

The art department has at its disposal a design office which is entirely separate from the commercial offices. Here the products are developed according to basic ideas and types, ie new types of houses are created and parts improved in accordance with technical progress. Gardens are also designed in the design office and sites are planned. The art department in developing designs consults the commercial department and takes advantage of its experience gained in dealing with the public.

Once a design is ready it is handed on to the central commercial office which looks after sales. This central office undertakes all correspondence, all accounting work and all advertising.

As a help to the central office branch offices will be established, when the growth of the Company justifies them. The head of each of these branches is a man of commercial experience. He is to get orders and to represent in his own region the commercial directors, all the while keeping in close touch with them. If necessary he can have by his side a manager of the building enterprises in hand. The number of such branch offices will grow as the Company grows. As soon as possible there should also be foreign branches. Designs, however, are issued only from the centre.

In all offices, apart from ample catalogues and illustrations, there are to be samples of materials and parts.

The internal organization of the business is supported by equally well thought-out advertising. On this, especially at the beginning, depends the number of orders necessary for financial success. The aesthetic intentions of the Company must be expressed powerfully in its advertising.

Well-designed leaflets illustrating and describing the various types of houses and pointing out their advantages for the purchaser are to be printed in large editions.

In order to make the public aware of the idea of the Company, shorter leaflets or articles in important journals will be issued. They should be written by well-known economists or journalists.

Public lectures with lantern-slides should also be held. The achievements of the Company are to be shown by travelling exhibitions in museums or other premises suitable for exhibitions. The types of houses should appear in models and plans. In addition, samples of parts and furnishings are to be on view so that the practical advantages, the high quality of materials and workmanship and the consistency of the style throughout can be demonstrated.

Posters announcing exhibitions are also to be produced by the design office. They are to be of high artistic distinction in order to convey at once the character of the enterprise.

The best handling of publicity is, as has been said before, of the greatest importance to the enterprise. For in contrast to other building enterprises overheads hardly change when turnover increases, and so every order taken after overheads have been paid for can be regarded almost entirely as profit.

MIES VAN DER ROHE

by Peter Carter

In this specially commissioned article, the architect Peter Carter outlines Mies van der Rohe's career and his rationalistic outlook on architecture. Carter sees Mies as 'a Rationalist who worked with the creative interpretative grasp of the poet' who also never lost his respect for tradition.

In his *Discourses on Architecture*, the nineteenth-century architect and theoretician Viollet-le-Duc suggested that 'the more the artist reasons on his art, the more he tries to perfect the expression by which he would interpret his meaning, he is led to strengthen the original expression—to render it clearer'. This definition of the rational creative process accurately describes the philosophical outlook and the way of work followed by Ludwig Mies van der Rohe (1886–1969), a founding father of modern architecture, master builder in steel and glass, and initiator of a rationally based method of architectural education.

Through his early discovery of Saint Thomas Aquinas's proposition 'reason is the first principle of all human work', Mies van der Rohe came to reject open speculation and personal expression as bases for creative architecture and to work instead within a context guided by reason and founded upon fact—to focus upon the objective and general, rather than the subjective and particular. On this matter he was quite unequivocal: 'If you do not follow this course you may go astray', he cautioned, 'and that would slow down architectural development or even make it impossible'. His respect for reason and the rational brought an understanding of the traditional premises of architecture. Indeed, among the pioneers of the 1920s who strove to release architecture from the anachronisms of historical eclecticism (an aim only previously achieved for a decade during the 1880s by the architects of Chicago), Mies van der Rohe may be considered one of the most committedly traditional in outlook. Traditional in the sense that he thought of architecture as being primarily a building art (*Baukunst* is the word he used) wherein clear construction, guided by structural principle, creatively serve the needs of the time through the means at its disposal. As he would tell his students, 'architecture begins when two bricks are put carefully together'.

These convictions had their roots in the experiences of his early years. The son of a master stone mason, Mies van der Rohe was born on March 27, 1886 at Aachen (Aix-la-Chapelle), Germany's oldest settlement on its border with the Netherlands and the first capital of Charlemagne's Holy Roman Empire. The town had acquired many fine buildings from the early middle ages and the clear and honest construction of these structures stimulated Mies van der Rohe's interest in architecture and exerted a lasting influence upon his own creative work. These impressions, together with a respect for the nature of materials that he had learnt from his father, aided his understanding of building construction when he came to study at a local trades school and work as an apprentice on building sites. Employment as an architectural draftsman followed this practical training and brought him eventually to Berlin, where, wishing to improve his knowledge of construction in wood, he became apprenticed to the furniture designer Bruno Paul.

In 1907, at the age of twenty-one, Mies van der Rohe had sufficient confidence in his understanding of the practical aspects of building to accept his first independent commission: a house for the philosopher Professor Riehl, who sent him on a study tour of architecture in Italy as preparation for this work. The successful completion of the Riehl House brought him to the attention of Peter Behrens (1868–1938), then Germany's foremost architect and industrial designer. During the three years that he worked in Behrens's office (where he was entrusted with supervising construction of a new German embassy in St Petersburg), Mies van der Rohe became stimulated by Peter Behrens's great sense of form and also came to share his master's respect for the buildings of the nineteenth-century classicist Karl Friedrich Schinkel (1781–1840), noticing in particular their careful proportioning and the articulated separation of their various architectural components. Upon establishing his own practice in 1912, Mies van der Rohe's work showed the influence of Schinkel's sparse Neo-Classic manner, while endorsing the constructional integrity characteristic of the Dutch architect H. P. Berlage (1859–1934), whose Stock Exchange in Amsterdam he had greatly admired.

At the conclusion of the 1914–18 war the newly established Weimar Republic offered few opportunities for building in Germany, and this circumstance, coupled with the fact that many new developments in the arts were finding an hospitable centre in Berlin, encouraged radical investigations into architecture's direction also. Stimulated by this new intellectual climate, Mies van der Rohe participated fully in these activities. He directed the architectural programme of the Novembergruppe, financed and wrote for the magazine G (Gestaltung: creative force), and prepared a remarkable series of projects in which he explored the architectural possibilities of reinforced concrete, structural steel, and plate glass. By the mid 1920s these contributions brought him recognition as one of modern architecture's most vigorous leaders.

Foremost among Mies van der Rohe's projects of this period is undoubtedly the Glass Skyscraper: 1922, in which a multi-faceted, non-load-bearing glass skin encloses the open framework of a skeletal structure, producing great richness in reflection and transparency. In contrast to this glass sheathed tower, his project for a Concrete Office Building: 1923 reverses the relationship between skin and structure: the structural system now being the dominant exterior visual element, with the glass recessed in unbroken horizontal bands around each floor. A third project, the Brick Country House: 1923, develops the concept of decellularization of interior space which Frank Lloyd Wright had initiated at the turn of the century—Mies van der Rohe having become familiar with Wright's work through an exhibition held in Berlin in 1910. The brick walls of the Country House project are load-bearing, individually defined so as to appear free-standing, and through being placed in a semi-overlapping manner produce a series of interlinked spaces and a minimal definition between interior and exterior.

This decellularization of space is further developed to a most refined and poetic degree at the German Pavilion, International Exposition, Barcelona: 1929, a building which had no specific functional requirement other than to suggest the social and political openness that was an aim of the new German Republic. While the free-standing walls of the Brick Country House project fulfilled both load-bearing and space-defining functions, those of the Barcelona Pavilion are set free of structural obligations, being purely space-defining elements freely disposed within the regular framework of an open structural skeleton. During the course of preparing the plans for this building Mies van der Rohe suddenly became aware, as if after years of rumination, of the architectural potential inherent in the separation of structural from space-defining elements, a discovery that proved to be of great significance for his future work.

The Barcelona Pavilion, together with the Tugendhat House, Brno, Czechoslovakia: 1928–30—a work that interprets the architectural concepts of the Pavilion in terms of residential functions—and the furniture that he designed especially for them (which was an addition to concurrent studies for a full range of metal framed pieces) established Mies van der Rohe as an architect and furniture designer of international stature.

In 1930, at the recommendation of Walter Gropius, Mies van der Rohe was appointed Director of the Bauhaus; but, by 1933, when the political trend in

2

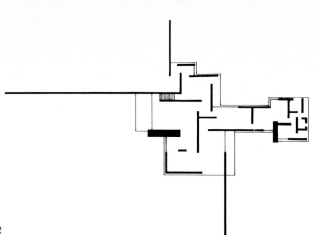

1 Glass skyscraper project (1922)

2 Brick country house, project (1923)

3a German Pavilion, International Exposition, Barcelona (1928–9); (b) Plan; (c) Interior

3a

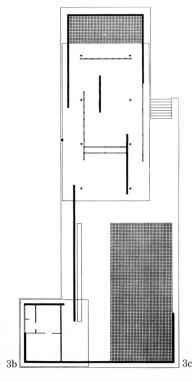

3b   3c

Germany became evident, he courageously closed the school as a gesture against the Nazis. After working for the next five years on buildings which were to remain in the project stage (these include studies for single storey court houses), he decided to leave Germany and accept an invitation to settle in the United States. Through the initiative of John Holabird, the architect, and Henry Heald, the president of Armour Institute (later to become Illinois Institute of Technology), Mies van der Rohe arrived in Chicago in 1938 and began a twenty-year tenure as Director of the School of Architecture at Illinois Institute of Technology; two of his former colleagues from the Bauhaus, Ludwig Hilberseimer, the city planner, and Walter Peterhans, the photographer, joining him so as to form a strong nucleus for the faculty.

While he was preparing the school's curriculum, Mies van der Rohe became convinced of the necessity for a method of architectural education that would radically oppose the excessive emphasis many schools of architecture place upon individualism and personal expression. He held that 'the function of education is to lead us from irresponsible opinion to truly responsible judgement; and since a building is a work and not a notion, a method of work, a way of doing should be the essence of architectural education'. Accordingly, the curriculum that he evolved for his school at Illinois Institute of Technology—and which continues there today—had its basis in reason: 'At our school we tried to develop a system of training and education in which everything leads to reason; I thought that if there were nothing in the course against reason, the student would attack everything with reason'. The curriculum comprises a three-year foundation course, followed by a two-year period for the creative application of this knowledge; its parallel components of (a) training for practical purpose, and (b) education for the comprehension of values, provide a framework for the study of principles and, therefore, encourage general rather than special solutions. Mies van der Rohe was convinced that if students are guided in this way, their individual creative abilities may develop secure in the knowledge that the basic vocational skills have been assimilated. Upon the successful launching of his school, Mies van der Rohe re-established his architectural practice in Chicago and from then on divided his time between his office's activities and his teaching duties. The North American technological environment facilitated the realization of his architectural ideas over a broad base and stimulated him to create a body of work which includes a number of the seminal buildings of our time. The philosophy of architecture expressed by this work—already well established in his mind before he left Europe—had its origins in the interaction of certain principles that he had become aware of while studying the great architectural epochs of the past, namely, that architecture is derived from and eventually becomes an expression of the ethos of a civilization; that its physical realization is accomplished through the use of clear construction; and that the universality of its language, as well as the sound foundation for this language's creative interpretation, arises from an organic structural ordering of its constituent parts.

Mies van der Rohe deduced from these principles that architecture is an integral part of the epoch. It is neither a fashion, nor is it something for eternity. This realization brought him to accept as the determining factors for his work the significant driving and sustaining forces of our epoch: those of science, technology, industrialization, and economy, together with the social patterns and needs they bring about. He strove to interpret these forces in terms of a creative architectural language through the use of contemporary building technology, disciplined by constructional clarity and guided by the principle of structure. Structure in this context does not imply columns, beams or trusses—these are components of construction. It refers, rather, to the emergence of a morphological and organic ordering of things, which permeates the whole building fabric and illuminates each part as necessary and inevitable: a condition where form becames a consequence of structure and not the reason for the construction.

Regardless of their individual functions or magnitudes, as a group Mies van der

Rohe's buildings clearly belong together and speak with a single language. This consanguinity is principally due to the following shared characteristics: (1) Constructional clarity and athletic repose have appeared through the removal of all unnecessary weight from a building. (2) The materials used are predominantly industrially produced and the manner in which they are used acknowledges the specific nature of each. (3) The structural systems employed are in accordance with the requirements of each building's functions, and the components of these systems are revealed both internally and externally. (4) To underline and complement the clarity of the structural system, the non-load-bearing enclosing skins and interior space-defining elements are separately articulated from the stressed members, leaving no doubt as to what is structural and what is not. (5) The employment of the module, a subdivision of the structural bay relative to function, provides a tool for planning. (6) The detailing is accomplished with great care and thoroughness and always exemplifies the practical refinement of what is necessary and no more. (7) Free-flowing as opposed to compartmentalized space characterizes both interior and exterior situations. The concept of form following function was an idea that held little credence for Mies van der Rohe, because he realized that functional requirements in our time may often change, while form, once rigidly established, cannot easily be modified. On the contrary, he thought that building solutions should allow for an optimum of flexibility in order to insure that people may arrange or modify their living and working spaces as they see fit. For this reason he selected a structural system with respect to the magnitude of a building's functional requirements as a whole, rather than to their individual and specific needs; and he fixed only the essentials of a plan. Furthermore, that there could exist a direct relationship between the groupings of functions relative to their overall space requirements, and the structural systems that are capable of appropriately and economically accommodating these requirements, was a conviction that led Mies van der Rohe to concentrate his creative energies upon the development of three distinct *building* types: the low-rise skeleton frame building; the high-rise skeleton frame building; and the single-storey clear span building.

The predominant characteristics of low-rise and high-rise building types—horizontal spread and vertical extention—ultimately determine their respective possibilities and limitations with regard to such matters as site, function, economy, structure, servicing, and vertical transportation. The effect, for example, of the last two considerations upon the planning of a low-rise building is negligible, while for a high-rise building they are of critical significance if a balanced plan and an economical structural bay is to be achieved. In Mies van der Rohe's low- and high-rise buildings the structural bay provides a regular framework within which the needs of similar and dissimilar functions may be accommodated. The steel frame or reinforced concrete flat (or waffle) slab structural systems employed take the form of repetitive bays of square or rectilinear configuration—the bays being subdivided into modules for lighting, air-conditioning and window wall components. The open structures thus formed provide a neutral overall space, within which only the vertical transportation and service shafts are permanent elements. The flexibility afforded by this arrangement permits the location of individual functions and activities for their optimum convenience and efficiency in operation, both at the time of the initial installation, as well as later when changes may prove necessary.

The low-rise building type is less restrictive than the high-rise type in determining the structural bay since limitations which could result from multiple vertical repetition and accumulative weight do not apply, and larger spans, if economically feasible, may be functionally desirable in view of the different type of occupancy. These factors permit a more varied spatial character and a more open type of plan than is usually possible in high-rise structures. In Mies van der Rohe's low-rise buildings, accommodation which requires natural light is planned at the periphery, while the interior zones—free of the high building's extensive lift and service cores—are opened up to provide circulation spaces around those functions for which natural light is not essential. The closed character of these interior circulation spaces is relieved by the introduction of a garden court, so providing visual and physical contact with the outside and bringing nature into the heart of the building.

Two examples of the low-rise building type are located on the campus of Illinois Institute of Technology in Chicago, the master plan for which Mies van der Rohe prepared in 1940. The Metallurgical and Chemical Engineering Building: 1945–6 accommodates classrooms, laboratories and workshops at its periphery, with a free-standing lecture auditorium, administrative offices and toilet block in the central areas surrounded by circulation spaces which open on to a garden court. This two-storey steel framed building is planned on a module of 12 ft and has a 24 ft square structural bay. Its enclosing skin is attached to the exterior of the structural frame and comprises black painted welded steel components, aluminium sash, clear plate glass, and panels of buff-coloured brick. The Commons: 1952–3 accommodates student and faculty dining and meeting facilities, a post office, and various shops. It is a single story building with a basement, having an un-fireproofed exposed steel structure set above a fireproofed sub-structure. The module is 4 ft and the structural bay 24 ft × 32 ft with a clear interior height of 16 ft on the main level. The enclosing skin is set between the structural frame and comprises steel framing members, clear plate glass and panels of buff-coloured brick; all exposed steel is painted black. Mies van der Rohe employed the high-rise skeleton frame building type to accommodate either apartments or offices. In order to release the valuable perimeter space of these buildings for subdivision as different apartment types or office requirements may dictate, the lifts, fire stairs and service shafts, together with kitchens and bathrooms in the case of apartment buildings, and tenants' toilet facilities in the case of office buildings, are gathered together in the central areas of the plan to form continuous vertical cores. These cores stand visually free at the ground floor, which is given over entirely to providing an inviting and appropriately sized entrance lobby for the building with access from all surrounding streets. The glass enclosure at this level is set well back from the building's periphery in order to afford protection during inclement weather, to ease the pavement crush on constricted sites, and to lighten visually the mass of the building above.

The apartment buildings at 860 Lake Shore Drive, Chicago: 1948–51 exemplify the validity of Mies van der Rohe's insistence upon a high degree of flexibility, in that over the years the planning of the apartments on individual floors has varied in response to the increase or decrease of space required by the residents. The two 26-storey steel framed buildings are planned on a module of 5 ft 3 in and have a structural bay of 21 ft square. The enclosing skin is placed contiguous with the outer face of the fire-proofed structure and comprises black painted steel components, aluminium glazing frames and clear plate glass. The introduction of projecting steel mullions at the module points, including where the columns occur, has caused the building's structural frame and its glass infill to become architecturally 'fused', each element losing a part of its particular identity in the process of establishing a single architectural statement. At ground level roman travertine is used to pave the entrance lobby and surrounding exterior terraces, and also as a facing to the building's lift cores.

The Seagram Building, New York: 1954–8 (designed in association with Philip Johnson as co-architect and Phyllis Lambert as director of planning) is a 39-storey air-conditioned multi-tenancy office tower. The building is set 100 ft back from Park Avenue and the open space thereby created provides an area for it to stand in commensurate with its magnitude, a landscaped plaza for use by the general public, as well as being incidentally beneficial to Seagram's neighbours. The building is planned on a module of 4 ft $7\frac{1}{2}$ in and has a 27 ft 9 in square structural bay. The enclosing skin, which is placed in front and free of the building's structural frame, comprises bronze mullions, spandrel panels, glazing members

4a

4b

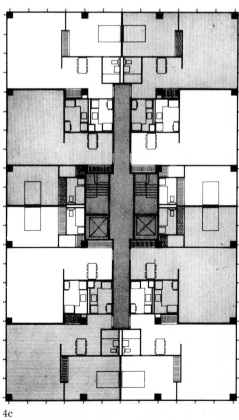

4c

4a 860 Lake Shore Drive
Apartments, Chicago (1945–6);
(b) Model; (c) Plan

and column covers, with bronze tinted plate glass. At the ground level, the cores are faced with roman travertine, the soffit is of pinkish-grey glass mosaic, and the lobby and plaza areas are paved with a pinkish-grey granite.

The third building type to be analysed is the single-storey clear span type. The column-free spaces of the past usually accommodated only one function and were spatially singular in character; in his clear span buildings Mies van der Rohe reinterprets this type of space for today's needs, giving it an entirely different meaning through his introduction of function defining elements of a non-structural nature, freely disposed within the peripherally supported structure. This arrangement (first stated as a conceptual idea in a 1941 project for a concert hall) permits one or more related activities to be brought together and unified within a single space; and provides complete flexibility for planning changes precisely because the structural enclosure is independent of the functional subdivisions. In these buildings, subsidiary functions for which enclosure is essential are accommodated either in free-standing cores, or on a level below the main floor; while rain-water pipes, air-conditioning and electrical services are brought to the roof through free-standing and non-structural duct shafts. Mies van der Rohe's clear span buildings range in magnitude and function from a weekend house, to an academic building, a headquarters bank, a drive-in restaurant, an art gallery, and a convention and exhibition hall.

Set in a low lying meadow adjacent to the Fox River, the Farnsworth House, Plano, Illinois: 1945–50 is first seen as a tranquil pavilion of steel and glass, poised above the ground and visually open to the landscape. The two 28 ft × 77 ft 3 in horizontal planes which form the house's floor and roof are held 9 ft 6 in apart— and well above the ground level as a precaution against the spring floods—by eight externally located wide flange columns, from which they cantilever in their longitudinal direction. A point to note is that the welded connections between the columns and the channel fascias at floor and roof are detailed so as to allow each component to retain its individual identity, while at the same time permitting the characteristics of the material and the method of its assembly to be clearly stated. The space that has been created between the floor and roof planes is divided into contiguous exterior and interior living areas: the exterior area being approached by a flight of steps broken at mid point by a floating terrace; the interior area being enclosed by large sheets of clear plate glass, and subdivided into living, sleeping and kitchen spaces by a free-standing service core. The materials and finishes of the house were chosen so as to avoid conflict with the seasonal changes of nature, and they are therefore kept within a neutral tonal range: roman travertine on the floor, terraces and steps; primavera panelling for the service core; natural colour shantung curtains; and all of the exposed steel surfaces are painted white.

A larger building of the clear span type is Crown Hall, Illinois Institute of Technology, Chicago: 1950–6, which houses the Institute's School of Architecture and City Planning, and the Department of Design. The building's 120 ft × 220 ft steel framed roof plane is carried by four externally exposed steel portal frames, cantilevering 20 ft beyond the extreme portals. The enclosing skin comprises welded steel components holding large sheets of clear and translucent plate glass; all exposed steel surfaces are painted black. The main hall is 18 ft high and is subdivided into student work areas, and exhibition and administrative spaces by low oak panelled walls and two non-structural service shafts. The floor of this hall is raised 6 ft above the ground in order to provide natural light for the workshops and lecture rooms which are located—together with toilets, storage and mechanical plant—at the lower level. The entrances to the main level are provided on the building's long sides, one taking the form of a flight of steps, interrupted at mid point—as at the Farnsworth House—by a floating platform; this structure is separately articulated from the building and the ground, and upon mounting it one is imperceptibly lifted from the one to the other.

The structural and spatial principles upon which Mies van der Rohe's individual buildings were developed also influenced the manner in which he brought

5 The Seagram Building, New York (1948–51)

6a and b Farnsworth House,
Plano, Illinois (1945–50); (c) Plan

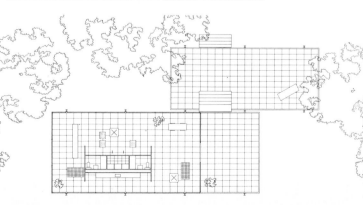

7 Crown Hall, Illinois Institute of
Technology, Chicago (1950–6) (see
also illustrations on p. 152)

buildings together in groups, enabling the buildings and the space between them to
create a spatially varied, yet conceptually unified environment. These groupings
share certain distinctive characteristics, one of the most evident being the manner
in which the buildings are invariably placed in a partially overlapping,
asymmetrical relationship. This spatial concept originated with the free-standing
treatment of the walls in the Brick Country House project of 1923, and which in
this different context gives identification to individual exterior spaces, while also
allowing the larger whole of the total project to be sensed. The resulting
interpenetration of space is reinforced and complemented by landscaping planted
in a natural free-flowing manner, which in its interaction with the pristine
qualities of the architecture introduces a poetic aspect to both interior and
exterior milieu.

The Master Plan for the campus of Illinois Institute of Technology: 1940–1
exemplifies these characteristics, as does also, for a totally different purpose, the
highly successful 'down-town' housing development of Lafayette Park, Detroit:
1955–6, which Mies van der Rohe planned in association with Ludwig Hilberseimer and the landscape architect Alfred Caldwell. In this 78 acre urban renewal
scheme, building groups, which combine low-rise terraces of houses for families
with 21-storey apartment buildings for the smaller dwelling units, are set amongst
well landscaped surroundings and are serviced from the site's perimeter by cul-de-
sac roads. These mini-neighbourhoods are distributed around a large public park
through which the residents may walk to schools and shops without crossing
roads.

Mies van der Rohe's centrally located urban schemes are, without exception,
treated as vehicle-free pedestrian precincts, with the building groups set among
landscaped plaza spaces that are noticeably free of architectural clutter and
fortuitous changes in level and so encourage activities in which the general public
is included. Many of these urban schemes incorporate single-storey buildings
accommodating special functions, and the human activity that is visible within
these pavilion-like structures brings additional life to the plaza areas throughout
day and night. These attributes apply to the Federal Center, Chicago: 1959–73,
Westmount Square, Montreal: 1965–8 and to the Toronto-Dominion Centre:
1963–9 (realized in association with John B. Parkin and Bregman and Hamann).

8 Toronto-Dominion Centre,
Toronto (1963–9)

This 5·5 acre project comprises two multi-tenancy office buildings of 56 and 46 storeys respectively and a 150 ft square clear span banking pavilion set in landscaped plaza spaces, and incorporates an extensive shopping concourse, restaurants and a cinema. The lunchtime plaza concerts and other activities which the Centre's management sponsor during the summer months have proved to be popular with the general public and are always well attended.

Mies van der Rohe's last major work, the New National Gallery, Berlin: 1962–8, stands in the city where he had begun his architectural career in 1907 with the Riehl House. During the intervening years he had completed over 160 designs for buildings and building groups, of which 82 were constructed and stand today in the United States, Canada, Mexico, Czechoslovakia and Germany. Throughout this creative life Mies van der Rohe held to the conviction that:

'Architecture is an historical process, it has little or nothing to do with the

9 New National Gallery, Berlin
(1962–8)

invention of interesting forms or with personal whims. I believe that architecture belongs to the epoch, not to the individual. That, at its best, it touches and expresses the very innermost structure of the civilization from which it springs.... Only a relation which touches the essence of the time can be real. This relation I like to call a truth relation. Truth in the sense of Thomas Aquinas, as the: Adequatio est rei intellectus; or as we would express it in the language of today: Truth is the significance of facts'.

He therefore realized that a practising architect should understand that there exists a relationship between the significant objective facts of the epoch and the ideas that are capable of guiding these in a direction beneficial to human society in general. In his own work he endeavoured to reach a practical synthesis between this ideal and the disciplines set by the principle of structure, with the objective of contributing towards the evolution of a truly contemporary language for architecture—one that comes from the past yet is open to the future.

Because Mies van der Rohe developed this concept of architecture in a logical manner from one building to another, his work as a whole is endowed with a unity of purpose and expression. A unity in which clarity of structure and construction is complemented by a neutrally open and somewhat ambiguous type of space, a gentle relationship to nature and an expressive response to changing conditions in light and weather, and above all by a respect for and celebration of human activity. Furthermore, in his hands, the critical interaction between function and construction, which lies at the heart of architecture, frequently touches that concomitant to all great architecture—poetic expression. A Rationalist, Mies van der Rohe could certainly be classified; but as the Barcelona Pavilion, 860 Lake Shore Drive, Farnsworth House, Crown Hall and Seagram Building clearly demonstrate, we are talking about a Rationalist who worked with the creative interpretive grasp of the poet.

SELECT BIBLIOGRAPHY
Peter Blake, *Mies van der Rohe: Architecture and structure*, New York 1960
Werner Blaser, *Mies van der Rohe: The art of structure*, London 1965
Peter Carter, *Mies van der Rohe at Work*, London 1974
Ludwig Glaeser, *Ludwig Mies van der Rohe: Drawings in the collection of the Museum of Modern Art*, New York 1969
Ludwig Hilberseimer, *Mies van der Rohe*, Chicago 1956
Ludwig Hilberseimer, *Contemporary Architecture, Its Roots and Trends*, Chicago 1964
Philip C. Johnson, *Mies van der Rohe*, New York 1947

Twentieth-century living and twentieth-century building

In these two articles by Le Corbusier a very personal view of architectural rationalism emerges. In the first, reprinted from The Studio Year Book on Decorative Art, 1930, *Le Corbusier examines how structural systems determine architectural systems and the way the thought processes of the modern world determine the 'new architecture'. The second piece is concerned with education. It is a long forgotten contribution Le Corbusier made to a British student journal which shows him in an optimistic light. It illumines the rational process of his design.*

Structural systems determine architectural systems. Technical processes are the very abode of lyricism. There is a modern spirit which is a process of thought and which determines a new architecture.

Let us try and formulate some basic truths.

The house is a shelter, an enclosed space, which affords protection against cold, heat and outside observation. It is formed of floors, walls and roof. It contains various compartments, in which are performed definite, daily and regular functions. Life within these compartments is carried on in accordance with a series of rational, definite, daily and regular actions.

The day consists of twenty-four hours only. This regulates the size of the house and the rôle it has to fulfil. For the twenty-four hour day is short, and our acts and thoughts are spurred on *by time*. If we were taught to regard the hand of the clock as a beneficent but implacable god, we should order our lives more rationally.

The house is a question of materials. Its walls, floors and roof are questions of suitability: which part supports, which is supported, which does neither one nor the other. The various compartments of the house raise the question of utility: what function is served by one or the other: what is its appropriate form, its size and its capacity for providing light. Why is furniture movable, and need it be so. What actually is furniture, for what is it used, where exactly ought it to be. Life within the compartments of the house raises the question of *moving about*: fatigue hampers us, efficiency is precious. The necessity for free movement inside the house suggests a number of architectural ideas, tending to an effect of orderliness. Are the moments we spend each day in the interior of the house enjoyable or wearisome? The house is a product of the spirit; as we ourselves are, so can our house be, if we bring our natural tastes and logical reasoning to bear on it. The question of our dwelling is a question of attainable well-being. Teach this to the children, you who are schoolmasters! *But first teach yourselves*, else your precepts might only be falsehoods. Alas, are not our present-day houses (now and then very charming I admit) often a monstrous lie? If the social relations between men were as false as the taste (or more exactly the ethics) which govern the construction of our houses, we should all be in prison!

Having thus briefly set forth the true meaning of the house, I have turned my back on the Schools, on the history of styles, on the pedantic composition of the Masters. I have washed my hands of the burdensome accumulations of vague, pedantic and dangerous teachings. I am *free*, but I am stripped bare. A problem arises: it is ahead of me, and must be faced. It is my task to fashion an entirely new kind of implement, that is to say, an implement which is pure, efficient, healthy, loyal, clear as crystal. Do I therefore turn my back resolutely on tradition? Do I break down bridges? Reject the past? Do I no longer believe in anything which has previously existed?

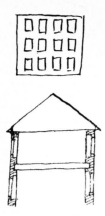

1 The supporting façade; surface gnawed away by windows and support walls thereby weakened; *below* section of supporting façade

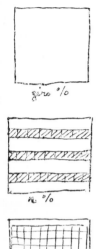

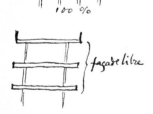

2 The free façade. The whole wall surface, which is free from the necessity to support, may be used for windows: *from top to bottom* no windows: 50 per cent window space; 100 per cent window space; section of free façade

No! *I deny academic teaching.* And inspired by the spirit of honesty, I search *in the past* and *in the present*, in my own country and in other countries, in my own race and in others, for *vernacular* houses, *human* houses for human-man and spirit-man, which are shining exhortations, marvellous examples of efficiency, economy, lyricism and intelligence. That is the one school in which I shall look for Masters on the day when my task is to construct the house of the machine age.

I shall find my clue in cold analysis. At each stage my duty will be to put the question: 'Why?' *Nothing has any right to exist which cannot give a precise answer.*

Modern science brings us a *new construction.*

The culmination of Western cultures came with *supporting walls* (supporting the floors and roofs). These walls were of necessity pierced by windows, of which the dimension and number was limited by the fact that they weaken the capacity of the walls. This system was *bastard, hybrid, confused* and even *expressed total contradiction.* The supporting mass was gnawed away by the apertures of the windows (diagram 1).

Ferro-concrete or metallic construction have abolished this bastard architectural system (which was responsible for the whole Renaissance and the Louis periods, culminating in Haussmann). They give us the *independent framework* and the *free façade. The façade no longer has to support either the floors or the roof*; it is itself supported by the floors. The façade fulfils its true destiny; *it is the provider of light.* It can provide light with *either 0 or 100 per cent of its surface.*

The façade is enabled to supply 100 per cent of light, because support is provided by the framework, of which the uprights are in the interior of the house and of which the crossbeams (borne by these uprights) terminate behind the surface of the façade and its windows (diagram 2).

From this emerges the true definition of the house: stages of floors, light interior partitions varying on each floor and in strict conformity with the functions of the interior (*the free plan*): all round them *walls of light.*

Walls of light! Henceforth the idea of the window will be modified. Till now, the function of the windows was to provide light and air and to be looked through. Of these classified functions I should retain one only, that of being looked through. Air is provided by scientific methods of ventilation, which include heating in winter and coolness in summer. Light? Glass in many different forms fulfils this function without having to reckon with windows (the most restricted organ of the house). We have submitted to the laboratories of St Gabain the basis of a new lighting substance which may have far-reaching consequences. *To see out of doors, to lean out,* that is henceforth all that the window need be used for. Is this necessary in every part of the house? No! And where the window is built into the luminous façade it will be as a definite organ, in the form of a complete mechanism. *Plate glass* replaces window panes. The sashes run horizontally, unhampered by the clumsy accessories of the sash window. They make possible the *lengthwise window,* the source of an architectural motive of great significance.

These illuminated walls date back a long way; for instance, the cathedrals of the middle ages (the Sainte-Chapelle in Paris). Then in particular the steel palaces of the Paris International Exhibitions which abjured 'classicism' (the Hall of Machinery, the Palace of Industry). In 1900, however, the Academy was responsible for a premature decline; the *Grand Palais* was in the clutches of the Institute. The façades were not of glass (that would have been neither Roman nor Greek nor Classical!); a facing of stone was superimposed on the metal framework and the *Grand Palais*, which had been destined for art exhibitions, was as dark as the inside of an oven!

In 1914, Walter Gropius reintroduced the glass façade at the Cologne Exhibition. My skyscraper (*Esprit Nouveau*, 1921) was built of clear glass from top to bottom.

The *free plan* (resulting from the interior framework) the *free façade* (resulting from the surface available for lighting being 0 to 100 per cent)—these are the great architectural reforms due to the new technical possibilities of ferro-concrete and

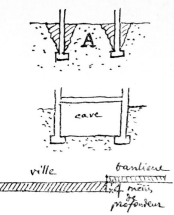

3 Sectional diagram of supporting walls: *above* the walls sunk in the ground, leaving 'core' A to be excavated for cellar; *centre* the cellar after earth is excavated; *below* the excavated earth removed from site and transported outside the town

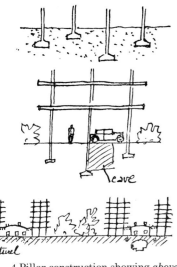

4 Pillar construction showing *above* spaced out pillars; *centre* space beneath available for shelter, garage, garden, etc; *below* the 'double street'

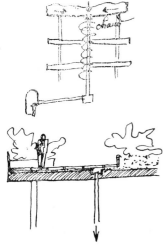

5 The roof garden showing *above* drainage of snow water inside the house, with heating system; *below* trees and plants established on the roof

metal construction. History teaches us that technical achievements have always overthrown the most ancient traditions. It is destiny. There is no escape!

The two magnificent corollaries of this solution are: *pillars* and the *roof garden*.

PILLARS. Formerly the building of support walls necessitated their being sunk deep in the earth. The excavation of the foundation trenches left a core (A) between them, which was also removed. *Cellars* were formed, compartments with a constant temperature, usually damp, deprived of light, unfit for habitation. And in this way there resulted this futile operation: the town soil for four metres deep was transported to the outskirts (3). What an expensive process! What a ridiculous state of affairs! The new static methods are based on the *supporting framework*. The weight of the house is exactly calculated, and distributed over the spaced-out pillars, whose function is reckoned out meticulously and in conformity with the resistance of the soil. Costs are considerably reduced. But instead of *fruitlessly* incurring the expense of flooring raised 60 centimetres above the ground (as is required by hygienic regulations in most countries), the pillars are erected three to four metres in height. The first floor will be *up in the air*, on *naked pillars, and the space beneath the house will be completely restored.* Children will play there, sheltered from rain or sun. The car may be conveniently housed there. The entrance to the house will be under cover. The garden will extend underneath the house. There will no longer be either a back or a front to the house.

And the soil of the town will no longer have to be transported to the outskirts. Extensive use of pillars will make possible the *double street* (heavy weight on the ground, light weight on the raised ground level). And lastly (a considerable advantage), the town pipes (a modern organ of vital importance), will no longer be *buried in the ground*, a system which is evil, barbarous, ruinous and lamentably idiotic (diagram 4).

THE ROOF GARDEN. Ferro-concrete normally provides a roof surface which is flat, water-tight and homogeneous. Severe climates, such as snow in high mountain districts, demonstrate that the drainage of snow water, melted *under the influence* of central heating (a present-day problem which is very disturbing) should take place in the interior of the house, *in the warm*, protected from frost. Expansion is the great enemy of ferro-concrete and metal construction. *The establishment of gardens on the roof* successfully combats expansion. Plants, flowers and trees grow better in roof gardens than in the open ground; they are practically under the conditions of a greenhouse. Gardens planted on roofs do splendidly. A client of mine said to me this spring: 'Come and see the lilac on my roof; it has over a hundred clusters of blossom!' (The house was completed in 1924) (diagram 5).

Let us sift the advantages of pillars and roof gardens. The plan of the modern house *can be reversed*. The reception rooms will be at the top, in direct communication with the roof garden, in the fresh air, away from the street with its noise and dust, and in full sunshine. The roof becomes a *solarium*, and the demands of modern hygiene are satisfied. Generalization: the whole ground surface of the town is free, available for walking on. The ground is in a sense doubled; transported to gardens up aloft, right in the sun (diagram 6).

At Moscow this year, the President of the Labour Soviet, after the explanations I had given about the plans of our *Centrosojus Palace*, made this resolve: 'We will build the Centrosojus Palace on pillars, for if we did not do so we should be renouncing the fundamental idea which will solve for us the problem of the urbanization of Moscow'. And Mr Krassin reminded a recalcitrant member of the Soviet that the Russian 'isbas' had always been built on pillars. I finished my explanations by pointing out that man, desirous of health and security, had since the beginning of the human race, and right up to our own times, constructed buildings on pillars, in Europe, in Africa, in America and Asia.

The new construction upsets the conventional. I shall be accused of being fanatical! But I say this: if the inhabitants of the great towns die of suffocation, or are a prey to diseases, it is owing to this prevailing 'sentiment'. *Prevailing*

6 Roof garden and pillar construction. Sectional diagram showing garden on flat roof, living rooms below with direct access to the garden. Ground floor 'in the air' and space beneath free for car, etc

sentiment bars the way to proved solutions, to indispensable solutions, to urgent and to honest solutions. A sentiment which is false puts us in danger of dishonesty, of slackness. This sentiment is artificial. *It is not human, it is academic.* It leads to laziness. Academicism does not look ahead, its gaze is fixed steadfastly backwards. Academicism in setting out to honour the past *denies the past*, for all the great epochs from which it pretends to draw inspiration have been revolutionary manifestations, *acts of creation. Creation*, that is to say: faith, courage, initiative, enthusiasm, curiosity, the joy of discovery. Academicism, that is to say: *imitation, servility, senility, laziness, lassitude, fear of responsibility.* Academicism is an army which turns tail. It is paralysis for a society, for a country. It is a public danger. I define academicism thus: *it does not reply to the question 'Why?'* Academicism is cultivated by the Institutes but (we must not delude ourselves) it is rife also in modern architecture! A man is academic once he no longer possesses a *clear* judgement. Academicism is supreme in religion, as in diplomacy or the higher command, even in machinery! and in morality!

But why has the case of academicism such dramatic relation to the present epoch? It is because our 'today' is the result of a hundred years of Science. This century of gigantic achievement, in which inventions have been our 'great adventure', has given us the *machine age.* Is this word empty of all meaning! Has nothing changed—is it just a figure of speech? Pitiable creatures are they who affirm such monstrous notions!

The world is turned upside down. The ideas of village, district, and country are abolished. The framework of society is broken, and the tension is at the point of cracking social laws. Capital, a new and modern power, a sudden evil, as though it were not understood and not under control, is not administered according to its natural constitution. Capital is the dust raised by labour, which spreads throughout the inactive state, and by means of a simple mechanism is suddenly converted into a power for active work on a gigantic scale. Anything can be undertaken if reason balances action. This equilibrium is the *eternal phenomenon of cause and effect*, which is the law of the universe, which acts, develops or assimilates in nature and which *selects. Artificial equilibriums*, arbitrarily maintained, are a danger; they contain in themselves the reactions which one day will be the overthrow of everything. Violence exists (we are well aware of it!), but also claim, steadfast and certain progress. To balance, that is, to *harmonize*, is the human task in this world of movement. *To harmonize is to reply with a new solution to the eternal 'why' which each nation propounds.*

Architecture is the outcome of the spirit of an epoch. This conclusion, proclaimed by every great period of history, sets us face to face with the task of the present day.

What then is the spirit of the present day? Are we in a period of *regionalism*, that is to say, in a period when each district and each village affirms and develops its own peculiar spirit (costume, customs, trades, materials, construction)? Are we in a period when contact is difficult or almost non-existent between districts, countries, nations or continents? Are we in an age when empiricism rules in our achievements, when formulas patiently established by time are handed down from father to son? Is ours an age of handicrafts, of products lovingly and painfully fashioned by skilled fingers poorly aided by precious tools? Is ours an age of ornamentation, when the laboriously finished task attracts to itself the ingenuous lyricism of him who so patiently executed it? The unique piece, the rare piece, the exceptional piece, do they occupy in our empty dwellings the chosen place of a household god? We are in an age in which the steam engine has destroyed frontiers, abolished districts, is disturbing local folklore, killing local customs. The steamboat has thrown bridges from continent to continent. The aeroplane has abolished our ideas of distances; telegraphy and the wireless have made possible universal interpenetration. Printing (a stupendous thing) in eight days distributes throughout the world discoveries great and small, in vivid pictures. The exodus of races is a *fait accompli*. State schools (a new departure) have demolished local individuality. The universal fact is revealed to all, is within the reach of all. The

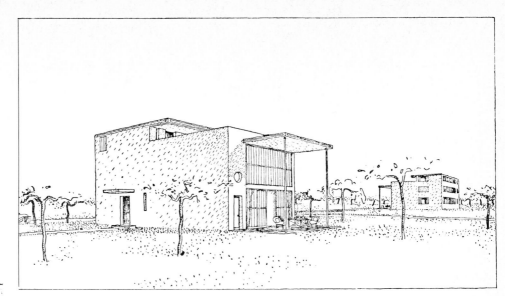

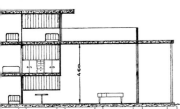

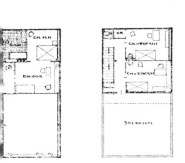

7 Theory put into practice: 'Maison Citrohan' designed by Le Corbusier and Pierre Jeanneret, Paris. *Above right* elevation showing pillar construction and flat roofs. The front of the house is composed almost entirely of windows; *above left* section showing arrangement of the various floors; *centre and below left to right* plans with basement, ground floor, first floor and roof with the solarium

laboratory, scientific analysis, expert, accurate, precise calculations reveal the object to the mind more quickly than the hand can execute it. The hand (conscious but inexact) is replaced by the machine (unconscious but exact). The idea of exactness has become omnipotent. Our eyes behold a new spectacle. The son thinks differently from his father, and the grandson will leave the son, with his conceptions of 'another age', far behind. Thirty years are a sufficient space of time for three generations to overlap each other: three conceptions, in reality three separate stages, which are uninterrupted but startling in their regular course. The machine has destroyed the lyricism of local habit and local poetry. Indeed, throughout the world there exist countless works, new in spirit, constant, universal. The dwelling is filled (and will be filled) with useful implements. Useful, but also harmonious (for the aesthetic function is at the base of human work: the conception is an aesthetic phenomenon; the attempt at harmony is simply a need for equilibrium, completeness, security, ease). Efficacious, efficient, exact and so much the more sensitive, mathematical and so much the nobler, the modern product bears witness to a tremendous revolution. A new age is born. We are in it, and we do not see it because we are in it. *Cause, effect.* The cause is outside us, it is destined. The effect is all round us, unavoidable, daily apparent.

A new construction, resulting from the most scrupulous research by experts, has established a new system of architecture.

New technical and scientific processes with rich possibilities of application, not to be compared with those of previous epochs, have placed new products in our hands, have placed gigantic resources ready to our hand, resources which will enable those of intrepid spirit, animated by civic enthusiasm and sincere love of humanity, to conceive new cities, to transform cities, *to evolve the city of today*, magnificent, more stately than before, efficient, practical: the city which will save men from the diseases which are at present tearing at the rotten heart of ancient towns, and which will instil into the inhabitants the spirit of pride which brings content. Technical processes are the very abode of lyricism. A modern lyricism exists. The phenomenon of the day, the machine age, is a state of affairs of great poetic significance. Day by day there emerge its marvellous manifestations. Happy are they who can discern the profound poetry of modern times.

There is a modern spirit which is a process of thought. To think clearly, to see ahead, to act, to create! The highest joys of creation, joys of the spirit, wealth within the reach of all! A new architecture is born as a result of the technical labour of a hundred years of science. Breaking down the regional and national boundaries, prevailing from continent to continent, it is formed of inspiring associations which bind its elemental constituents. A single man can set them in motion, can make them apprehensible and clear. Architecture, an exalted art, is a function of the nobility of the individual.

If I had to teach you architecture

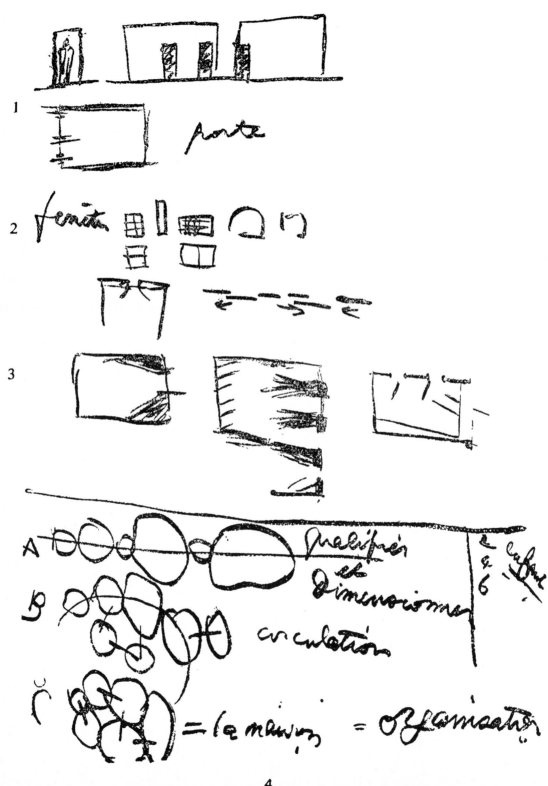

by Le Corbusier

The architecture of the new age has triumphed the world over. But it is still subject to violent and insidious opposition. It upsets too many prejudices, too many vested interests. The whole country is controlled by commercial obstructiveness, and by architects who employ old-fashioned technique, and so find it impossible to meet the demands of a new clientèle. They invoke sacred traditions, good taste, beauty—Pericles or Louis XIV, whichever you like.

The teachers in the schools are extremely worried by the curiosity of their pupils, by their indiscreet questions, and their almost irrepressible enthusiasm. Life is no longer a joke for the majority of the teaching staff in most schools.

The immense future of modern architecture, which is, after all, the equipment of a new civilization, should not have to be mixed up with vested interests. Life is just beginning for a new architecture, and it has a long life ahead of it. Why deny it the possibility of achieving beauty and greatness? That sort of objection is futile and groundless.

All the same, it is important to recognize that a great many mistakes have been made in the field of modern architecture, especially by young people who imagine that the modern man's house is like a soap box. But the greatest harm of all has been done by plagiarists, who take the superficialities of modern architecture and merely apply them to the same old carcases. If the task is not yet finished (and it most certainly isn't), it is the duty of authorities to realize that the world is continually evolving and that consequently architecture as the expression of an age must go ahead. Architecture must be afforded the necessary opportunity for practical experiment.

One of the crucial aspects of the whole question lies in the teaching of architecture in schools. In this respect, certain countries are asleep and cling to tradition: the students are all right, but the instructors. . . . They still don't hesitate, two thousand years afterwards, to become more Roman than the Romans, more German than the Germans, etc. Nationalism only serves to encumber architecture with all sorts of trappings which have nothing to do with the actual problem. All over the world I have noticed that the teaching of architecture, however envisaged, is always scrappy and superficial—sometimes apparently on the old Beaux-Arts model, sometimes lacking in any aesthetic significance (as in some Oriental countries), sometimes gently ticking over (as in the most technically progressive countries, like America).

What is even more ludicrous to see is the fierce opposition of our fathers and grandfathers (magistrates, town councillors, etc.) to any manifestation of the modern spirit. Who are the towns of the future designed for? For those who will soon be dead, with their habits anchored to the pit of their stomach, or for those who are yet unborn? Their defensive attitude is comic.

Architecture provides the framework for a civilization (housing, work, leisure, circulation); so architecture is also town planning. It is no longer possible to separate architecture and town planning—they are one and the same thing.

But what signs are there of modern town planning? It has only just been born— it's a new science with few professors. And they're all young. Surely they deserve universal recognition.

If I had to teach you architecture? Rather an awkward question. . . .

I would begin by forbidding the 'orders', by putting a stop to this dry rot of the orders, this incredible defiance of the intelligence. I would insist on a *real* respect for architecture.

On the other hand, I would tell my pupils how moving are the things on the Acropolis at Athens, whose pre-eminent greatness they would understand later. I would promise an explanation of the magnificence of the Farnese Palace and of the wide spiritual gulf between the apses of St Peter's and its façade, both constructed rigorously in the same 'order', but one by Michael Angelo and the other by Alberti. And many others of the simplest and truest facts about architecture, whose comprehension demands a certain mastery. I would emphasize the fact that nobility, purity, intellectual perception, plastic beauty, and the eternal quality of proportion are the fundamental joys of architecture, which can be understood by everyone.

I would strive to inculcate in my pupils a keen sense of control, of unbiased judgement, and of the 'how' and 'why'.... I would encourage them to cultivate this sense till their dying day. But I would want them to base it on an objective series of facts. Facts are fluid and changeable, especially nowadays, so I would teach them to distrust formulae and would impress on them that everything is relative.

I ask a young student How do you make a door? How big? Where do you put it (1)? How do you make a window? But, incidentally, what is a window for? Do you really know why they make windows? If so, you will be able to explain to me why a window is arched, square, or rectangular (2). I want reasons for that, and would add: Think hard: do we need any windows at all today?

In what part of a room do you make a door? ... Perhaps you have several solutions. You are right, there are several solutions, and each one gives a separate architectural sensation. You see—these differences of solution are the very basis of architecture. According to the way you enter a room and according to the position of the door in the wall, you get a particular impression, and the wall which you pression, and the wall which you pierce takes on particular characteristics. You feel you have discovered architecture. By the way, I forbid you to draw an axis on your plans—axes are merely formulae to dazzle the unwary.

Another point, just as important: Where do you make the window-openings? You realize that according to where the light comes from you get a particular feeling, so draw all the possible ways of arranging window-openings and then tell me which are the best (3).

As a matter of fact, why have you made your room that shape? Think out other workable shapes, and put in openings for doors and windows. You had better buy a big notebook for this job—you'll need pages and pages (5).

Now draw out all the possible shapes of dining rooms, kitchens, bedrooms, each with its special requirements. Having done this, try to cut down the dimensions to a minimum. A kitchen. This is a question of town planning—circulation and working space. Don't forget that the kitchen is a holy of holies.

The next thing is to draw a business man's office and that of his secretary, his typists, and his workmen. Remember that a house is a machine for living in and that an office or factory is a machine for working in.

You don't know anything about 'orders', nor the '1925 style'; and if I catch you designing in the 1925 style, I'll box your ears. *You must not be a stylist.* You articulate, you plan—nothing more.

Now try solving one of the most intricate of all contemporary problems: the minimum house.

First of all for a single man or woman, then for a married couple—don't bother about children. Next you move house—two children have arrived.

Then you have to accommodate four children.

As all this is very difficult, you will begin by drawing a straight line, round which you will build up the necessary units in their proper order, each with the minimum area (4).

Then on a sort of genealogical tree you work out their circulation, putting the appropriate units next to each other.

5

une chambre à coucher

?

?

Quelle forme?

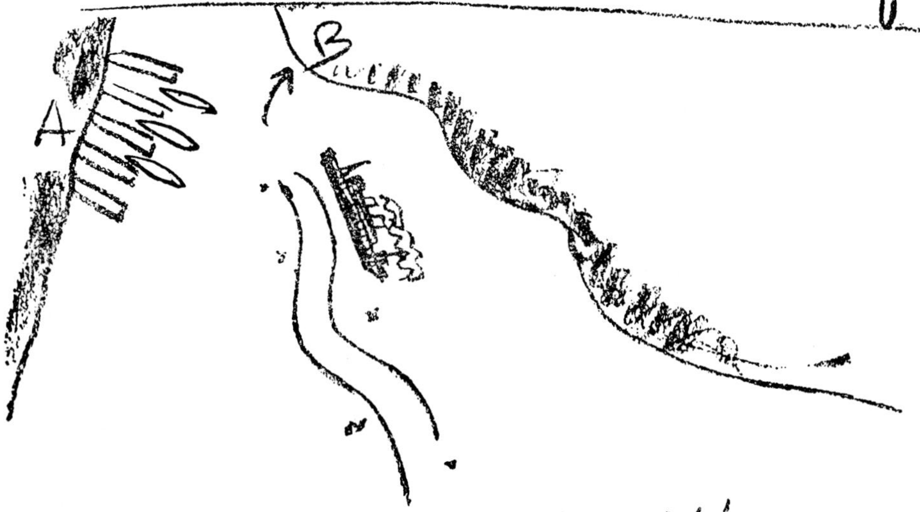

A

B

6

?

étudier
les
refuges

7

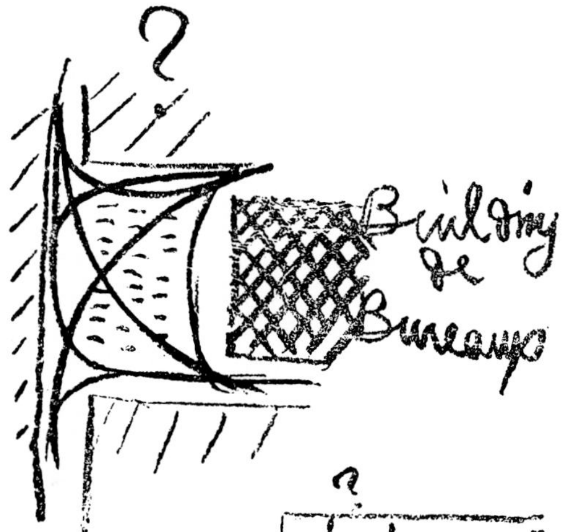

Building
de
Bureaux

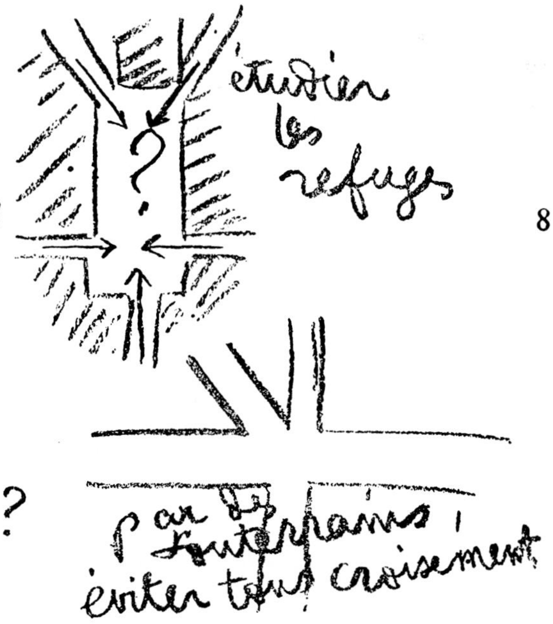

8

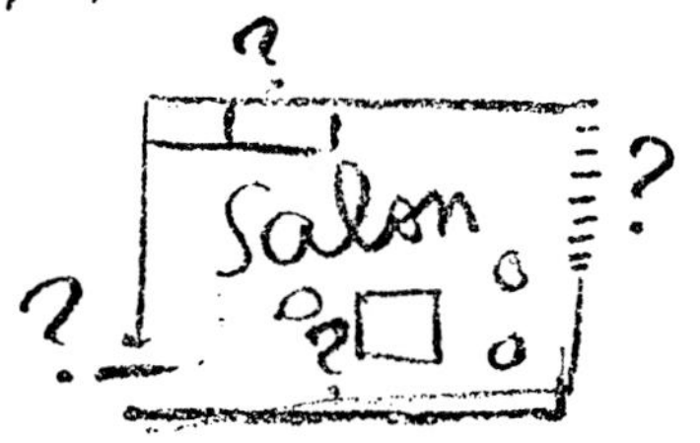

?

Salon

?

?

?

par les souterrains,
éviter tout croisement.

9

To finish up, you will try to assemble the component units to make a house—don't worry about the construction: that is another matter. If by any chance you like playing chess, it'll come in useful here, and you won't have to go to a café to find an opponent!

You will go on to buildings in course of construction and see how they make reinforced concrete, flat roofs, or floors, and how windows are put in. Make sketches, and if you see anything idiotic, make a note of it, and when you get back ask questions. Don't imagine that you learn construction by doing mathematics. That's a deceit practised by the Academies to get the better of you.

Nevertheless, you will have to study a certain amount of statics. This is easy. Don't think you need to know exactly how the formulae of resistance are arrived at by mathematicians. With a little practice, you will understand the mechanics of calculation, but above all remember how the various parts of a building work. Make sure that you understand moments of inertia. Once you understand them, you will be free to do anything. All this is quite straightforward: leave higher mathematics to the mathematicians.

Your studies are not yet finished. You will have to research into questions of sound, temperature, and expansion. Of heating and refrigeration. The more direct experience you can pick up at this stage, the more thankful you will be later on.

Try drawing a harbour with buoys marking the channel, and show how a liner comes alongside the dock and gets under way again (6). It will do to cut the rough shape of the ship out of coloured paper and show its successive positions on the drawing. This may give you some ideas about designing docks.

Now draw a block of two hundred offices with a square in front for parking cars: find out how many cars to allow for, and, as with the steamer, show clearly all their manoeuvres (7). Perhaps you will get some idea of what size and shape to make islands and parking spaces, and of their relation to the street.

Here is a golden rule: use coloured pencils. With colour, you accentuate, you classify, you clarify, you disentangle. With black pencil you get stuck in the mud and you're lost. Always say to yourself: Drawings must be easy to read. Colour will come to the rescue.

Here is a square in a town, where several roads meet (8). Work out how traffic crosses it. Try to think of every kind of square, and figure out which are the best for circulation.

Set yourself the problem of a drawing room with its doors and windows. Arrange the necessary furniture conveniently. This is another problem of circulation, and is common sense and lots of other things as well! Ask yourself if your room serves any particular purpose like that (9).

Now I set a written problem: Get out a comparative and analytical report on the reasons for the existence of towns like London, Birmingham, Liverpool, Hull, Glasgow. Rather a hard task for a student, but you realize that before putting anything down, you must always know exactly what you are considering and why it exists. Splendid exercise for developing your power of discrimination.

One day, go to the station, ruler in hand, and make an exact measured drawing of a restaurant car with its kitchen and service. Do the same for a sleeping car. Then go down to the docks and go over a liner. Draw coloured plans and sections, showing how it works. As a matter of fact, have you any clear idea of what does go on inside a liner? Are you aware that it is a palace accommodating 2000 people, of whom a third live in luxury? Do you realize that here is an hotel system with three separate and entirely independent classes, a gigantic system of mechanical propulsion, with its staff of engineers and mechanics, and besides this a system of officers and sailors to operate the ship? When you can express clearly by means of coloured sections and plans the organization of a liner, you will be able to go in for the next competition for a League of Nations Palace.

And now, my friend, I beg you to keep your eyes open.

Do you keep your eyes open? Have you been trained to keep your eyes open? Do you know how to keep your eyes open? Do you keep them open continually and usefully? What do you look at when you go out for a walk?

Look at the backs of buildings if you want to learn anything. Shut your eyes to the street front. Then go and measure some of those buildings which are decent behind their façades. Study this vernacular with a view to later execution on a larger scale, perhaps in steel (a prefabricated house), or in reinforced concrete (assembled from standard units).

Now that I have appealed to your sense of honesty, I should like to inculcate in you, and in all students of architecture, a hatred of 'drawing-board stylism', which is merely covering a sheet of paper with alluring pictures, 'styles', or 'orders'— these are fashions. But architecture is space, breadth, depth, and height, volume and circulation. Architecture is a conception of the mind. It must be conceived in your head, with your eyes shut. Only in this way can you really visualize your design. Paper is only the means for setting down the idea, and transmitting it to the client or contractor. Everything is in the plan and section. When you have achieved through plans and sections a working entity, the elevations will follow, and if you have any power of design, your elevations will be beautiful. Say, by all means, that houses are for living in, but you will be a good architect only when your elevations succeed. Proportion is enough, but you need plenty of imagination as well, and the more modest the problem, the more imagination you need.

Architecture is organization. *You are an organizer, not a drawing-board stylist.*

Where do we stand?

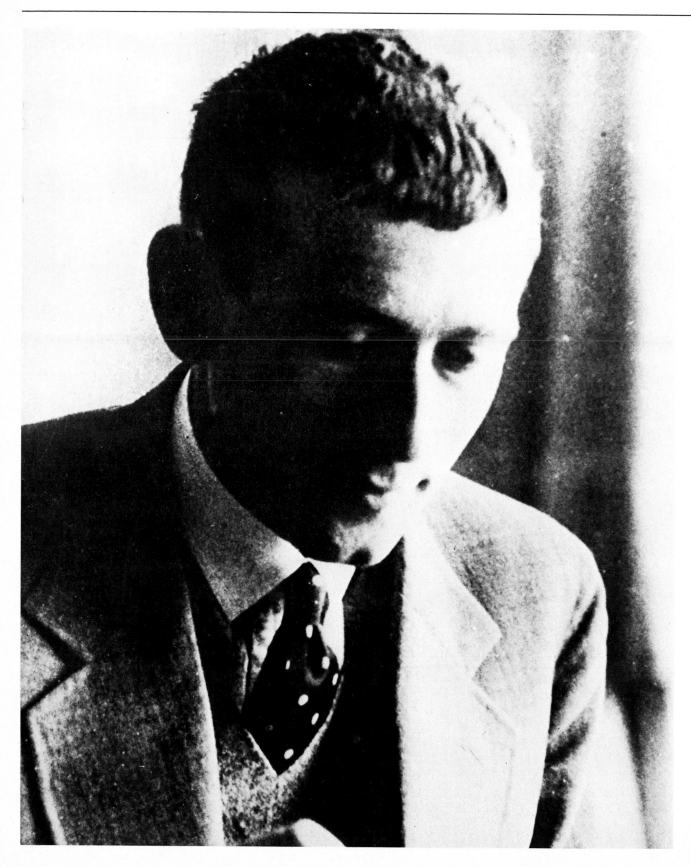

by Marcel Breuer

Marcel Breuer, former Bauhaus student and teacher, came to Britain in the mid-30s after completing the Dolderthal flats, near Zurich for Sigfried Giedion. He was in partnership for two years with F. R. S. Yorke. This article, which examines the ideology of the Modern Movement, was published in The Architectural Review *in April 1935.*

I would ask my readers to be resigned to a purely theoretical handling of this question, since I shall assume that they are already familiar with the tenets of the New Architecture and what it looks like. They will know, for instance, that these buildings are conceived of in severe terms—a maximum simplicity, wide openings for light, air and sunshine; balconies, flat roofs, minutely studied practical floor-plans, a scientific basis, strong emphasis on mechanization; industrial methods of production with a tendency towards standardization; light colours, new materials used for their own sake and a reconception of housing and town-planning in the light of social and economic research. Therefore I want to confine myself to a statement of what is really fundamental in our thought and work.

In the past I have been opposed to over much of this theorizing about the New Architecture, believing that our job was to build, and that our buildings sufficed, since they speak plainly enough for themselves. I was, moreover, not a little alienated to observe that there was often a considerable discrepancy between these theories and the personalities who advanced them. The danger of all theorizing is that, by carrying one's arguments too far, one is apt to leave the world of realities behind one.

Parts of the principles of the Modern Movement have been extensively adopted, but they have been compromised by being used separately without any co-ordinating relation to the aims of that Movement as a whole. A closer examination of the ideology of the New Architecture has therefore become a pressing necessity.

The protagonists of the Modern Movement have been occupied with the classification and development of their intellectual principles and the carrying out of their individual designs. This meant that further propaganda was left to chance, industrial advertisements and the technical press. Much has been distorted, much overlooked, as a result. Modern terminology has been put under tribute for snappy slogans; and each of these serves only some isolated detail. A correlation of these heterogeneous parts to their unifying whole is still lacking. Whereas the pioneers of the Modern Movement have now succeeded in establishing a very broad intellectual basis, which is in harmony with their own work, the younger generation still confines itself to rigid formalization.

I should like, therefore, to give a more general survey that will cover a wider field than these catch-phrases. To do so, however, is not such a simple matter. Architecture is an alarmingly many-sided complex, and as soon as one leaves the technical sphere all conceptions tend to become vague and overlapping.

I intentionally renounce historical comparisons,and leave to others the task of contrasting our age with epochs of the past, and showing us from history what leads to progress or decay, what to art or architecture.

What, then, are the basic impulses of the New Architecture? In the first place an absence of prejudice. Secondly, an ability to place oneself in immediate objective contact with a given task, problem or form. Thirdly, being unfettered by tradition and the usual stock-in-trade of the intellectual departmental store. Let those who prefer respectful transition from the principles of one school or style to those of another, adopt them if they will. What we believe is what we have perceived, experienced, thought, proved and calculated for ourselves.

At this point I should like to consider traditionalism for a moment. And by tradition I do not mean the unconscious continuance and growth of a nation's culture generation by generation, but a conscious dependence on the immediate past. That the type of men who are described as modern architects have the sincerest admiration and love for genuine national art, for old peasant houses as for the masterpieces of the great epochs in art, is a point which needs to be stressed. On journeys what interests us most is to find districts where the daily activity of the population has remained untouched. Nothing is such a relief as to discover a creative craftsmanship which has been developed immemorially from father to son, and is free of the pretentious pomp and empty vanity of the architecture of the last century. Here is something from which we can learn, though not with a view to imitation. For us the attempt to build in a national tradition or an old-world style would be inadequate and insincere. To pride oneself on such things is a bad symptom. For the modern world has no tradition for its eight-hour day, its electric light, its central heating, its water supply, its motor roads and filling stations, its bridges and its steel motor-liners, or for any of its technical methods. One can roundly damn the whole of our age; one can commiserate with, or dissociate oneself from, or hope to transform the men and women who have lost their mental equilibrium in the vortex of modern life—but I do not believe that to decorate their homes with traditional gables and dormers helps them in the least. On the contrary, this only widens the gulf between appearance and reality, and removes them still further from that ideal equilibrium which is, or should be, the ultimate object of all thought and action.

It may, perhaps, seem paradoxical to establish a parallel between certain aspects of vernacular architecture, or national art, and the Modern Movement. All the same, it is interesting to see that these two diametrically opposed tendencies have two characteristics in common: the impersonal character of their forms; and a tendency to develop along typical, rational lines that are unaffected by passing fashions.

It is probably these traits that make genuine peasant art so sympathetic to us— though the sympathy it arouses is a purely platonic one. If we ask ourselves what is the source of the solid unselfconscious beauty, the convincing quality and reasonableness of peasant work, we find that the explanation lies in its unconsciously, and therefore genuinely, traditional nature. A given region only has a few traditional crafts and uses a few definite colours. Roughly speaking, the same things, or variants of the same things, have always been made there. And even these variations are obedient to a regular and recurrent rhythm. It is their uninterrupted transmission through local and family associations which conditions their development and ultimately standardizes them as typeforms.

In one direction at least our modern efforts offer a parallel—we seek what is typical, the norm; not the accidental but the definite *ad hoc* form. These norms are designed to meet the needs, not of a former age, but of our own age; therefore we naturally realize them, not with craftsmen's tools, but with modern industrial machinery.

If one examines a *bona fide* example of industrial standardization, one cannot fail to perceive that it is representative of an 'art', and that that art has only reached this point of perfection by a sort of traditional development which is the result of exploring the same problem over and over again. What has changed is our method: instead of family traditions and force of habit we employ scientific principles and logical analysis.

Please do not misunderstand me. I do not for a moment mean that peasant art and the Modern Movement have any connection in fact with one another. All I wanted to do was to bring out the similarity between certain tendencies which have led, or can lead, to relative perfection in each. In any case, we can all admit that there are numbers of old peasant farmsteads that we find far more stimulating than many so-called 'modern' houses.

To sum up: it is quite untrue to say that the Modern Movement is contemptuous of traditional or national art. It is simply that the sympathy we feel for each does not take the form of making us want to use either as a medium for the utterly different purposes of the present day.

I should like to divorce the 'unbiased' aspect of the New Architecture from association with terms like 'new', 'original', individual', 'imaginative', and 'revolutionary'. We are all susceptible to the persuasion of that word 'new'. Society pays its meed of respect to anything new by granting it a patent. It is common knowledge that international patent law is based on two principles: 'technical improvement' and 'newness'. Thus novelty becomes a powerful commercial weapon. But what is the Modern Movement's real attitude to this business of 'newness'? Are we for what is new, unexpected and a change at any price, in the same way that we are for an unbiased view at any price? I think we can answer this question with an emphatic negative. We are not out to create something new, but something suitable, intrinsically right and as relatively perfect as may be. The 'new' in the Modern Movement must be considered simply a means to an end, not an end in itself as in women's fashions. What we aim at and believe to be possible is that the solutions embodied in the forms of the New Architecture should endure for 10, 20, or 100 years as circumstances may demand — a thing unthinkable in the world of fashion as long as modes are modes. It follows that, though we have no fear of what is new, novelty is not our aim. We seek what is definite and real, whether old or new.

This perhaps invites the retort, 'Be sincere. Look into your motives without trying to make your introspection too moral or positive. Don't all of us get sick of everything after a time? Doesn't everything, even architecture, become tiresome in the end? Isn't our thirst for change greater than we care to admit?'

Here we reach a point where logic ceases to be logical, where consistency loses sense, and anticipation is impossible, because history provides examples for and against. It were easy, but futile, to indulge in prophesy. I would rather interrogate that unwritten law of our own convictions, the spirit of our age. It answers that we have tired of everything in architecture which is a matter of fashion; that we find all intentionally new forms wearisome, and all those based on personal predilections or tendencies equally pointless. To which can be added the simple consideration that we cannot hope to change our buildings or furniture as often as we change, for example, our ties.

If by 'original', 'individual', or 'imaginative' artistic caprice, a happy thought or an isolated flash of genius is meant, then I must answer that the New Architecture aims at being neither original, individual, nor imaginative. Here, too, there has been a transformation in the meaning of terms. According to our ideas, modern architecture is 'original' when it provides a complete solution of the difficulty concerned. By 'individual' we understand the degree of intensity or application with which the most various or directly interconnected problems are disposed of. 'Imagination' is no longer expressed in remote intellectual adventures, but in the tenacity with which formal order is imposed upon the world of realities. The ability to face a problem objectively brings us to the so-called 'revolutionary' side of the Modern Movement. I have considerable hesitation in using the word at all, since it has recently been annexed by various political parties, and in some countries it is actually inculcated into school-children as an elementary civic virtue. In fact, revolution is now in a fair way towards becoming a permanent institution. I believe that what was originally revolutionary in the Movement was simply the principle of putting its own objective views into practice. It should also be said that our revolutionary attitude was neither self-complacency nor propagandist *bravura*, but the inward, and as far as possible outward, echo of the independence of our work. Although, as I have just pointed out, to be revolutionary has since received the sanction of respectability, this causes us considerable heart-searchings: the word inevitably has a political flavour. In this connection it is necessary to state that our investigations into housing and town-planning problems are based primarily on sociological, rather than on formal or representational, principles. In short, that our ideas of what developments were possible were based on the general needs of the community.

All this has led some people to believe that the Modern Movement either was, or was bound to become, a political one. Our opponents resuscitated this old accusation so as to be able to assail us with political propaganda. Other bodies of opinion tried to force us to define our position by such arguments as: 'You make radical proposals for improvement which can only be realized in a radically different form of society. Architecture is the expression of its age, and so, of the circumstances, social structure and political conformation of that age. If your work has no political bias and it is not your main object to realize a political programme, you are simply Utopians who, as things are today, will sooner or later be dragged into impossible compromises'.

To which I would reply:

'It is an error to imagine that architecture in its broadest sense is determined by political considerations. Politics, of course, play an immensely important part in architecture, but it is a mistake to identify that part with any one of its different functions. To come down from the general to the particular:

'The technical and economic potentiality of architecture is independent of the political views of its exponents.

'It follows that the aesthetic potentiality of architecture is also independent of their political views; and likewise the intensity with which particular architects may apply themselves to the solution of particular functional problems.'

Politics and architecture overlap, first, in the nature of the problems presented to the latter; and, secondly, in the means that are available for solving them. But even this connection is by no means a definite one. For instance, how does it help us to know that Stalin and the promoters of the Palace of the Soviets competition are Communists; or the reasons why they became Communists? Their arguments are very much the same as those of any primitively minded capitalistic, or democratic, or Fascist, or merely conservative motor-car manufacturer with a hankering for the cruder forms of symbolism. In spite of the undeniable influence of politics in every sphere of life and thought, no one can deny that each of these spheres has a highly important unpolitical side to it, and that that side determines its nature. As an architect, I am content to confine myself to analysing and solving the various questions of architecture and town-planning which arise from their several psycho-physical, co-ordinating and technical-economic aspects. And I believe that work of this kind leads to material advances which have nothing to do with politics.

The second dominant impulse of the Modern Movement is a striving after clarity, or, if you prefer it, sincerity. No romantic tendencies are implied in either of these terms. They do not mean that we wear our hearts on our sleeves, or invite all and sundry to pry into our homes and private lives through our long horizontal windows.

This particular exemplification of 'clarity' has caused a great deal of harm—in the same way that the desire to show construction openly arrived at has often led to the violation of structural principles or their naïvely childish over-emphasis. Clarity interpreted in this spirit has been responsible for a decidedly uncomfortable world full of screw-heads and intellectual exhibitionism. With a little goodwill and a pinch of crass stupidity, the famous principle of inside-out 'exteriorization' can be relied upon to conjure up a perfect wilderness.

The principle of clarity, as we understand it, expresses itself in the technical and economic fields of architecture, through emphasis on structural laws and practical functions; and in the aesthetic field by simplicity and a renunciation of all irrational forms. The New Architecture might be compared to a crystalline structure in process of formation. Its forms correspond to human laws and functions, which are other than those of nature or organic bodies. In its more immediate conception this New Architecture of ours is the 'container' of men's domiciles, the orbit of their lives.

Are our buildings identifiable with descriptions such as 'cold', 'hard', 'empty-looking', 'ultra-logical', 'unimaginative and mechanistic in every detail'? Is it our aim to trump the mechanization of offices and factories with the mechanization of home life? Whoever thinks so has either only seen the worst examples of modern architecture, or else has had no opportunity to live in or make a closer inspection of the best. Or possibly there is some confusion in his ideas. Does he perhaps mean pompous when he says 'human'; dark-brown wallpapers when he invokes cosiness, empty pretence when he demands 'peacefulness', and a brothel when he refers to love? Anyhow, he attributes intentions to us which we have never had and can hardly be accused of embodying in our work.

The origin of the Modern Movement was not technological, for technology had been developed long before it was thought of. What the New Architecture did was to civilize technology. Its real genesis was a growing consciousness of the spirit of our age. However, it proved far harder to formulate the intellectual basis and the aesthetic of the New Architecture intelligibly than to establish its logic in practical use. I have often found that something like a functional kitchen equipment has made hypercritical people far more accessible to our ideas; and that they have not infrequently ended by becoming reconciled to our aesthetic as a result. The ease of this method of approach led certain modern architects to outbid each other in broadcasting technical progress, and to rely on theoretical deductions supported by columns of figures. A deliberately statistical attitude to architecture ensued, which degenerated into a competition as to who could go furthest in denying it any sort of aesthetic moment. The engineer was proclaimed the true designer, and everything was declared beautiful that was technically efficient.

I think we can take it that this tendency has nearly seen its day. Engineering structures are by no means necessarily beautiful *qua* engineering structures, though they may often be beautiful either because their builders had a marked talent for formal design, or as a result of that scientific tradition which in process of time evolves a satisfactory industrial form for everything—the norm type, the standard. There is, of course, a great deal to be said for the practical objectivity of engineering methods in facing technical problems. The engineer has been responsible for several things which, in contrast to many architectural designs of the last century, were at least useful.

But we must call things by their proper names, and not bamboozle ourselves into believing that the achievements of engineering are *ipso facto* beautiful.

To sum up again: clarity to us means the definite expression of the purpose of a building and a sincere expression of its structure. One can regard this sincerity as a sort of moral duty, but I feel that above and beyond this it is a trial of strength for the designer, which sets the seal of success on his achievement. Nor do I see any puritanism in our cult of simplicity, but rather a zest for obtaining greater effect with less expenditure; and the satisfaction of fashioning something out of nothing with intelligence and arrangement as one's only resources. By which I mean winning colour, plasticity, and animation from a flat white wall. Simplicity in this sense connotes both attainment and quality.

Where does rationalism end and art begin in the New Architecture? Where is the dividing line between them, and how is it fixed? I could not trace that frontier if I tried. Architecture seems worthy of notice to me, only in proportion as it produces an effect on our senses, and our senses are strangers to rationalizing processes. It is the same to me whether this effect, which we can, if you like, call 'beauty', has been created by an engineer or an artist; whether it is the result of what is called speculative research, or what is called intuition. I care nothing for any differentiation as between these methods, but I care a great deal whether I feel at ease in the finished building. Besides, I do not wish to invalidate the super-rational basis of the Modern Movement which is its unwritten law, by any passionate assertion of principles. All the same, a few of them can be indicated here.

We have no use for beauty in the form of a foreign body, of ornament, or of titivating of undesigned structural elements; nor even as an arbitrary magnification of certain dimensions, a purely transient vogue. We have no use for architecture that is labelled Symbolist, Cubist, Neoplastic or 'Constructivist'. We know that the essential and determining elements of a building can be wholly rational without this rationalism in any way affecting the question of whether it is beautiful or ugly.

Everyone who has planned, designed and constructed, knows:

(1) That in spite of the most logical volition, the decisive impulse towards co-ordination very often occurs through uncontrollable reflexes.

(2) That even in the most objective exploration of a given problem by the logical method of procedure, in nearly every case a final, one might almost say illogical, choice between different combinations has to be made.

(3) That the commanding and so to speak convincing impressiveness of really inspired construction is the outcome of an inflexible tenacity which is almost passionate, and that that passion transcends mere logic.

Perhaps the slogan: Art and technique as a new unity', which Gropius coined some years ago, most nearly expresses the idea that in the New Architecture these concepts are no longer separable.

I now come to the third dominant impulse of the Modern Movement: the relation of unbroken elements to one another—contrast. What is aimed at is *un*schematic design. Whoever supposes that our preference for flat roofs inclines us to adopt flat tops for our coffee-pots; that the cubic forms of our buildings will be echoed in our lighting fixtures; or that our guiding principle of establishing unity and a certain harmonious relation between all these things can be labelled as a 'style', has entirely misunderstood our objects. There is no hard and fast formula for doing this or that in the New Architecture. Wherever you find identical forms in different places, you can be sure it was due to the adoption of a similar solution for a similar problem. But when a cupboard begins to look like a house, the house like the pattern of a carpet, and the pattern of a carpet like a bedside lamp, you can be certain that it is not modern work in the sense that modern is used in this article.

We strive to achieve a definite design for all different elements, and we arrange them side by side without dressing them artificially for the purpose. These elements receive different forms as a natural consequence of their different structure. Their complete individuality is intended to establish a kind of balance which seems to me a far more vital one than the purely superficial 'harmony' which can be realized by adopting either a formal or structural common denominator. We reject the traditional conception of 'style' first, because it gainsays sincere and appropriate design; and secondly, because the link between quite justifiable differences in appearance produces the sort of contrast we consider is characteristic of modern life. Contrasts like house and garden, a man's working and home life, voids and solids, shining metal and soft materials—or even living organisms like animals and plants—can all be realized against the stark plain surface of a wall; also in the opposition of the discipline of standardization to the freedom of experiment that leads to its development. Such contrasts have become a necessity of life. They are guarantees of the reality of the basis we have chosen to adopt. The power to preserve these extremes without modification (that is to say, the extent of their contrast) is the real gauge of our strength.

But what about the aesthetic of the New Architecture? Its dogmas are the kind that cannot be formulated. The important thing for me is that the New Architecture exists, and that it fulfils a vital need for all of us.

WELLS COATES 1893-1958

by J. M. Richards

Wells Coates was both an architect and engineer. He was also one of the main leaders of the avant-garde, internationally connected MARS Group in England. An innovative architect such as Coates would not reveal all of himself in his work. He was a Rationalist by training and conviction (as some of his unpublished papers indicate) but he was also an intensely emotional man. This article—an extended obituary notice—by Richards is a very personal account of Coates.

A compactly built man with a Ronald Colman moustache and crisply waving hair, well dressed for all occasions with a way of switching on social charm as though it was a beam from an electric torch; a voluble conversationist whose talk was spiced with Services terminology and avant-garde jargon; ingratiatingly attentive to women, with a line of talk about places he had been to like Japan, which other people hadn't. Such was the picture too many people got of Wells Coates, from which they may have drawn conclusions that he was vain, a playboy and a fashion-monger; and since he was none of these things and is now dead, it is only just that it should be said what kind of man lay behind this deceptive exterior.

Moreover, it should be said in an architectural journal out of gratitude to him; because modern architecture owed more to him than it was customary to acknowledge and far more than the new generation of architects is likely to know—but more about that later.

First, Wells Coates the man. Underneath his elaborately social manner and his line of talk lay an intensely serious personality, with unswerving integrity about the things he regarded as important (which meant chiefly architecture) and a fighter. Why he went about in this disguise I won't go into here because this is a memoir, not a psychological treatise. Nor would the usual psychologists' explanations about over-compensation for a sense of insecurity add anything useful to our understanding of the real man and his under-used potentialities. That he was essentially a lonely character in spite of his assiduous sociability his friends already knew.

He was at his best when he felt that he was among friends who appreciated his good qualities, and one remembers him most warmly at those international meetings in which he delighted to take part, especially the periodic congresses of CIAM. On the journey to Athens and back on board SS *Patras II*, where CIAM held its first major congress in 1933, at La Sarraz, Bergamo and Aix-en-Provence and many other gathering-places, Wells was a central and energetic figure, not only in the conference sessions but around the café tables where the dissemination of ideas and the establishment of international contacts which make such congresses worth while chiefly take place. And behind the scenes as well; for he was the principal British delegate to CIAM for many years and a hard-working organizer. Many of the discussion programmes and manifestos that constituted the working papers of the CIAM congresses were drafted by him.

The international atmosphere of these congresses suited him perfectly, because he was a man of no fixed roots, with the ability of many such to seem at home everywhere. He could take his place unselfconsciously alongside the in-ternationally known figures who presided at these congresses—Le Corbusier, Giedion, Sert, Van Eesteren, Gropius—and his gaiety on these occasions was unforced as, in the hot summer sunshine, shirt-sleeved but immaculate, he busied himself with meeting after meeting or conferred with his particular intimates:

Emery, Bodiansky, Jean-Jacques Honegger and some others. It was even the same when CIAM congresses were held in England, as they were in Bridgwater in 1947 and Hoddesdon in 1951. There Wells was in the centre of everything, talking enthusiastically in French with his demonstratively Gallic accent and flourish of the hands—even to foreigners whose English required neither.

He was one of the first British members of CIAM and one of the founders of the MARS Group, its English branch. In the 1930s, when the cause of modern architecture was being sustained by arguments and manifestos until such time as opportunities of building should come along, Wells was foremost in all the groups that did this necessary spadework—work which it is easy to disparage now when all we take note of in the *Charte d'Athène* is its sententious phraseology and its too rigid adherence to functional classifications. But such statements of dogma were landmarks in their time. It was their thorough working out of theoretical principles that made it possible to put theory into practice in due course. Today's architects take for granted freedoms and opportunities that would not be theirs if it had not been for the violent propagandists of the 30s.

Wells's part in MARS and CIAM was especially directed at exploring the common ground between architecture and engineering. He was also intrigued by the common ground between architecture and the fine arts, and was one of the founders, in 1933, along with Colin Lucas, Herbert Read, Henry Moore and Ben Nicholson, of Unit One, a group designed to explore relationships between the arts and to stage exhibitions designed to clarify them.

There must have been other short-lived groups, too, because Wells, being scientifically minded, enjoyed the codification of ideas—the fitting of thoughts into a pattern—that the preparation of group manifestos entailed. But for him this was far more than the useful mental discipline it is to some people, because it gave expression to his profound belief in principles, a belief that dominated his whole working life. For him the fascination of every design problem was not the intrinsic merits of the eventual solution but the way it could be used to illustrate a principle he believed in or test out some theory. 'Search and re-search' was one of his favourite expressions and he was indefatigable in his efforts to isolate the philosophical essence of any procedure or idea, to relate the particular to the general.

Speculation of this kind, because of the polysyllabic language in which it is often expressed, easily acquires an air of pretentiousness. Such an air overhung Wells Coates's public façade; but in private, among people he knew, intellectual pretentiousness quickly evaporated, and he revealed himself as a sincere and simple character, quite humble when he was discussing his own work because then talk became only a means of explaining ideas that were their own justification.

He was also a kindly character, and in his studio flat in Yeoman's Row, London, an attentive and generous host. There he entertained his friends on cushions on the floor, informally but memorably, especially when he could be persuaded to show his skill at cooking a Japanese dinner, an attainment that dated from his childhood spent in Japan.*

His skill as a cook is worth mentioning because it illustrates that sense of craftsmanship, that sense of the importance of doing however small a thing really well, which was the essence of his character. In fact if one were asked to define Wells's contribution to the development of modern architecture one would probably begin by saying that he was one of the first to show what craftsmanship meant in relation to modern conditions and techniques. The word craftsmanship is generally associated with the products of another age than the modern one that Wells Coates was interested in, and especially with handicrafts; but Wells, trained (as he enjoyed reminding people) as an engineer, knew that artists and architects

* Where his father was a professor of comparative religion and philosophy. Japan was his home until he was 18, when he went to Canada, his mother's native country. He came to England in 1929.

could successfully come to terms with machinery only by acquiring a mastery and understanding of technique comparable with the hand-craftsman's mastery over his tools and materials. He insisted on being on these terms with his, which was evident not only in his work but in the way he lived—for example in the way he drove his vintage-model Lancia with the nonchalant air of one to whom an engine is but an extension of his own limbs.

And he insisted on every possible detail of his life being consistent with this idea—he was not only, by his nature, interested in flying but was a qualified pilot, and his service in two wars was connected with flying. Another very small but significant example: I suspect that he was one of the first to use the now ubiquitous stencilled lettering on drawings. If he was, it was typical of his discontent with the accepted ways of doing things if another way could be worked out that seemed more in accord with the whole modern trend of development.

His habit of regarding every problem as a challenge, which demanded seeing all round it and understanding it in all its aspects before anyone was qualified to set about solving it, was one of the secrets of his versatility as a designer. His pre-war Ekco radio set—one of the best-looking on the market for many years—was an example of complete integration of engineering with what would now be called styling, although it was perhaps typical that in his own studio he had a set, also of his own design, that was simply a glass case with all the works exposed, whose precision and intricacy pleased him even more. And another example of his enquiring mind at work was the time and energy he spent in later years designing a sailing boat—a catamaran of a kind—which involved not so much improving on existing models as thinking out basic aerodynamic principles in order to create a new one.

The same combination of qualities went of course into his architecture, with the addition of an equally profound habit of enquiry into the social as well as the technical functioning of his buildings. This is especially evident in the building that made his name: Lawn Road Flats, London, which he built in 1934 for Jack Pritchard. Again he was looking ahead; not catering for a present pattern of living

1 Lawn Road Flats, Hampstead, built for Jack Pritchard

but asking himself what architecture could do to facilitate the emergence of a more appropriate pattern.

In this case what he (and Jack Pritchard) were trying to do was to plan for the new type of man who likes not only to travel light but to live light (a type, incidentally, to which Wells Coates himself largely conformed), unencumbered by possessions and with no roots to pull up. For such a man the multiplication of spaces—such as the more expensive domestic architecture usually provides—is not the ultimate luxury, but the perfection of service arrangements so as to reduce domestic obligations to the minimum. Lawn Road consists of minimum-size bed-sitting rooms, each with a compact but fully equipped kitchen and bathroom—it is nearer to the *machine à habiter* than anything Le Corbusier ever designed. The building is brilliantly planned, and in spite of its thirtyish lack of crispness of finish and its concrete structure expressed in a monolithic fashion we find somewhat clumsy now, it remains unique and completely successful in practice. It was in fact successful from the moment it was built, and it must have warmed Wells's cosmopolitan heart to find that it became the home and meeting-ground of the architects and other refugees from Nazi Germany who had such a stimulating influence on English architecture in the years just before the war and were, besides, his friends.

I suppose the prototype—or it may have been the further development—of Wells Coates's one-room flat idea was his own studio flat in Yeoman's Row. It differed in that a sense of space was aimed at and achieved, but the conception of how it was to be used was the same, and it had the same minimum bathroom and kitchen tucked away round the corner, with the addition of a couple of minimum sleeping areas on balconies, reached by ladders from the studio. These are significant because they were the first example of his capacity for planning in section, which played an important part in his work afterwards and showed that he had the three-dimensional imagination of the real architect. This capacity was demonstrated in the split-level planning of his flats in Palace Gate (1938) and in his design for the National Film Theatre (put up as part of the 1951 South Bank Exhibition), where the levels were again skilfully used and the projection rooms fitted into the thickness of the balcony structure.

Other qualities in his buildings were unerring taste (even in his more elaborate designs there was no trace of the showiness that was sometimes a part of his public personality), and an ability, perhaps linked with this instinctive taste, to reduce a design to its essentials without making it merely dull or arid. But there are not enough buildings by him in existence to bring out his capacities as a designer to the full. He never had anything like the number of commissions his talents deserved. This was at least partly, it must be said, due to defects in his own temperament, for if the hackneyed phrase, 'he was his own worst enemy', is true of anyone it is true of Wells Coates.

He had little judgement about public relations and a saddening way of getting personally on the wrong side of his clients. He would, for example, harangue a board of hard-headed business men with the kind of art-jargon that made them suspect his practical ability, or turn up at a friendly luncheon with a well-disposed prospective client accompanied by his lawyer and frighten him away with sheaves of forms and contracts.

For such and other reasons his practice was always accident-prone; so much so that his friends became hesitant about asking how any project, about which they had heard him talk confidently and enthusiastically, was going, for fear of embarrassing him by compelling him to admit that the commission, like so many before it, had fallen by the wayside. This fatality pursued him to the end; after he had moved from England to Canada, the project there on which he pinned most hopes—the design for a new town of Iroquois, called for by the construction of the St Lawrence Seaway—has now been completed by other hands than his and on a different site to the one he worked on so keenly.

But he would not have had one dwell on his disappointments, for in spite of them

2

3

2 The Minimum Flat: the living room (1933)

3 The Minimum Flat: the kitchen. The design incorporated electric clothes dryer, cooker and water heater, built-in cupboard suites and draining board

4 The overall size 5 ft × 4 ft 8 in (1·52 × 1·42 m) of the kitchen belied its efficiency as a modern labour-saving space. The kitchen was exhibited at the Dorland Hall Exhibition

4

5 Cresta shopfront, Baker Street, 1932 showing the use of large 'structural' advertising lettering. The letters form the web of a truss

6 Wells Coates's own office in Bedford Place, c. 1932. The table tops were Venestra doors

5

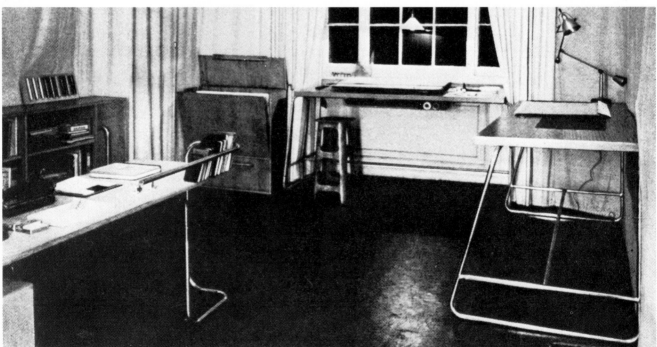

6

he remained determined and buoyant to the end of his life, and never lost his belief in the worth of what he was doing. It was especially for this bravery of spirit that his friends felt affection as well as admiration for this companionable, lonely and not very happy man. His friends were all over the world, a fact that he, with his cosmopolitan instincts, especially valued. So I end with a comment by one of them: Sigfried Giedion, secretary-general of the CIAM in which Wells played so active a part. The comment occurs in a letter Giedion wrote to Jaqueline Tyrwhitt (who had been associated with Wells in much of his later work) on receiving the news of his death.

'I think of him as I saw him first in 1933 on the ship at Athens and then, even more clearly, surrounded by young women, as I remember very beautiful ones, at a party with champagne in his house in London. This was around 1940. I lived in his Lawn Road apartment house. He had all the talents to be a gentleman with big estates behind him, and one had always the feeling that this had been taken from him, even if, in fact, it had never existed. He was one of the few people of his generation who had the talent to be lazy. But he never could. And that dichotomy between desire and necessity made him the interesting personality that he was. He was never completely at home either in architecture or in life: this may somehow explain much of the stiffness that was apparent during the year he spent at Harvard. I am sorry about him, and his death is for me as inexplicable as was his life.'

But shrewd though Dr Giedion's comment is I cannot quite end on so defeatist a note, because defeatism was altogether foreign to Wells Coates. Few of the greater spirits are happy men, and whatever faults of temperament Wells had, it is now part of history that he was one of the half-dozen men in England in the 1930s whose force of character began and carried on the grand Resistance Movement out of which modern architecture has grown. His force of character is indeed the key to Wells's achievements. For under the Hollywood charm there was a tiger of a man with a ruthless will, which he employed tirelessly on architecture's behalf.

It doesn't really matter in the long run that there are so few Wells Coates buildings for posterity to remember him by, because *all* the modern buildings we see when we look around us are collectively his memorial. The young men who find it so natural and easy to do 'modern architecture' today are the beneficiaries of his lifelong zeal, and whatever his personal triumphs and failures, his real record is a record of success because it lies in the vigorous growth of the movement to which he devoted all his powers and passions.

BERTHOLD LUBETKIN

by R. Furneaux Jordan

*Besides Wells Coates, the other key figure in British Modern Movement develop-
ments was Berthold Lubetkin, the founding father, so to speak, of the team Tecton.
Tecton's work was at the centre of a controversy over 'formalism' in the late 30s. In
this article, reprinted from* The Architectural Review *(July 1955), Robert Jordan
examines the errors of that argument and sets out Lubetkin's and Tecton's
contribution to architectural ideas.*

'The rootless cosmopolitan with hate foaming from his mouth'—the words are
Zhdanov's; the hatred is of systems, organizations and academies, cliques and
claques, hatred of men who 'get on' by smoking the right cigars in the right clubs.
Lubetkin would insist that his work is the work of Tecton. He would insist,
secondly, but more passionately, upon the intensity of his individualism, upon the
dilemma of the radical who rejects anarchy, upon the masochistic delight of
swimming against the current. And thereon he quotes Zhdanov.

Carlyle called Christopher Wren a gentleman. From Carlyle, when we remember
the ungentle heroes of his hero-worship, that may have been a qualified
compliment, a statement even of limitations. An artist, as Carlyle well knew, may
be rather less than a gentleman, but simply must be much more. The 'something
less' is mere Bohemianism; it is the 'something more' that makes the artist an odd
and, sometimes, a persecuted figure in our society.

When the inner eye, like Ruskin's famous stork and swallow leaning upon the
sirocco wind, views from afar all the crumbling cities of old Mediterranean
peninsulas, then that merely gentlemanly phase is seen for what it is—a minor
facet of a North Sea culture, as recent as the Restoration and now dead. But it does
raise the question, *tout court*: what is Art? Is it no more than a cool and careful
arrangement of spaces and proportions to a rule of taste; or is it—hand and
intellect being mere tools—is it the sublimation through sensual form of the
deepest sexual or religious passions. From the Lascaux caves to that eternal
quadrille danced by baroque saints beneath a dome in Prague, all history cries
aloud that it is the second of these things. Each cathedral was an orgasm. And yet,
somehow, that icy hand of taste fell, intent upon freezing art as a vested interest,
not of that aristocracy which had basked in the warmth of baroque form, but rather
of a new bourgeoisie bent upon petrifying form within the limits of its own
inhibitions.

But the artist in society became a dangerous figure and only after two centuries
made his reply—Blake's flaming invective against Sir Joshua. Omens of victory
came only with the Salon des Refusés of 1863 (*Déjeuner sur l'herbe*) and in England
only with the Roger Fry Exhibition of 1910. So much for painting . . . architecture,
more hopelessly enmeshed in the nature of patronage, had to wait a little longer. If
the Modern Movement was a structural and aesthetic revolution, its historic role
was to attack the system. It became a movement of the Left; forced to wait upon
events, it became obsessed with them. Its response to Hitler, to Munich, to the
Spanish War, to Unemployment and to all that, was an emotional response, also a
correct one. But that, while possibly a birth pang of a new culture, did not by itself
give us a new art form. The intellectuals of the 30s—what Betjeman might call the
vieux jeu avant garde—deprived and indeed very willing to be deprived of their
traditional milieu of Chippendale and porcelain, escaped hastily to the clean world
of the new technocrat, to share in the Pyrrhic and Wellsian victory of nineteenth-

century materialism. With the very dirty bath water of 'style' they threw out the baby of philosophic understanding. *Vers une Architecture* was their handbook.

Lubetkin, while part of all this, was more profound. Unlike his English contemporaries he had learnt the history of art; unlike the Teutonic scholars he understood the deep emotional and dynamic values lying beneath the forms and facts. Lubetkin will dilate upon those opposite poles of baroque and classic, upon the violent storm music of the former as against the spaces and composure of the latter. Lubetkin will contrast the Place Vendôme as a baroque interior—minus its ceiling—with those vast spaces between Carrousel and the Etoile around which classic buildings, like milestones, demarcate not merely space but also a more epochal change from an architecture of the single masterpiece to an architecture involving the complex of the whole city. Lubetkin will explain the sempiternal nature of the dividing line between the Invalides of Hardouin-Mansart and the Panthéon of Soufflot. Lubetkin will illuminate the transformation wrought in Petersburg when Catherine the Great—untying, as it were, the baroque knot—re-orientated those monuments at the fork of the Neva, depriving them of their inward-looking, incestuous, baroque relationship, and setting them instead to look outwards, classically, over the spaces of the River, thus converted the Neva itself into the Place de la Concorde of Russia . . . an imperial *coup d'état* based quite consciously upon a philosophy of art; something inconceivable in any other century.

To expand upon Lubetkin letting off any of these verbal fireworks could be a fascinating digression. And not wholly a digression; it would point to the springs of his own visual imagination; it would also help to explain his place in the Modern Movement, or rather to explain his detachment from it, to explain his denial of the very existence of any such thing as a 'movement' *qua* movement. Architecture, for him, is bigger than that. Lubetkin can only be understood, and his work can only be understood, when one realizes that to the structure and form of twentieth-century housing he would apply certain values acquired in Paris and Petersburg: baroque and classic values, but also—in his view—values of eternal validity. Moreover, he would say that he is not merely applying these values to structures in the modern idiom, he is also reconciling classic and baroque with each other.

It is a more imaginative and more profound attitude—as well as a more intellectual one—than can be found elsewhere in architecture today. Whether it is a possible attitude, whether it 'works', whether it is flying in the face of history, whether it is—as at, say, Priory Green or Spa Green, Finsbury—producing good architecture . . . all those things may remain open questions. To dismiss it as formalism or 'pattern-making' is too shallow; one should at least respect any attempt to imbue Western architecture with qualities that might lift it above the trivial or witty which, for all its competence, are now its main characteristics.

London, for Lubetkin, was the end of a long journey—the rootless cosmopolitan in search of his freedom. Naturally he never found it; to this day London remains an approximation. It was a long journey for a Tiflis boy. He was the son of an admiral; Choisy, Bannister Fletcher and scholarly histories of painting were part of his childhood. His architectural education, such as it was, began in Moscow of the Revolution. It was all as exciting as that, and an aura of excitement hangs around him still. The journey to Warsaw in 1923 must have been a kind of flight, not to freedom, but from chaos to order, from a sort of Slavonic *Schlamperei* to a correctitude, an insistence upon status that was Prussianic. No place for Lubetkin.

And then, after a slightly fabulous interlude studying carpets in the museums of Vienna, came Paris. Paris, as the womb of Liberty, might perhaps be different from Warsaw. In a sense it was, though even a boy from Tiflis must have known that there is nothing in the world so unassailable as that carapace of French academicism . . . the right men in the right clubs! Not that Paris was without its dividends. They were rich dividends. There was the whole backcloth: Paris itself, classic and baroque, to be going on with. That was something that the Modern

1 25 avenue de Versailles (1927) which created a storm. Lubetkin explained its horizontality as a reflection of the passing traffic

Movement had repudiated as part of a dead world; for Lubetkin it was a quarry, not of forms but of values and emotions. Paris also brought the first jobs—with J. Ginsberg—such as the apartment block (1927) at 25 Avenue de Versailles. It caused a storm. Although all that the word 'modern' then meant, 25 Avenue de Versailles is still a smooth and accomplished building, unmannered and dated here and there with only the ghost of an *art nouveau* touch. Typical of Lubetkin is his explanation of its strong horizontality, not in structural or functional terms but as a reflection of the passing traffic. It has worn well and still has a certain Parisian elegance which Lubetkin, one suspects, may have learnt to despise. Above all else in Paris was the Atelier Perret. Lubetkin, in the midst of admiration for his master, would say that he got much from him in the way of method, in the understanding of scale and proportion, very little in the philosophy of art, a great deal in the philosophy of reinforced concrete. And it was that that he brought with him to London.

Le Corbusier in Paris, Lubetkin in London. To set them side by side may be offensive and obvious, also rather instructive. Both, being intelligent, accepted their inheritance from the 'pioneers'—the not unintelligent idea that a building might be fit for its purpose. They were, in what was then popular jargon, functionalists. Both, being intelligent, could apply that credo—or whatever one calls it—to the total form of the building and the city, rather than merely using it to make new details for a new style. It was a revolution; yet fundamentally it was only negative. It was where one went from there that mattered. Le Corbusier's work has been a development of that credo; Lubetkin's a critical commentary upon it.

In some ways the Le Corbusier problem was simpler, and the impact—when it came—therefore more shattering. For 'Corb' the enemy beneath that carapace was so well defined. Against all the *vieux pompiers* of the Grand Manner in decay he had only to set the stripped precision of Hellenic and mechanized form ... and there was *Vers une Architecture* and the Pavillon Suisse; against the squalid cities he had only to set his clear geometric and schematic reply ... and there was *Ville Radieuse*. Beneath the carapace there was never a twitch, but then the carapace no longer mattered; Le Corbusier had become the god of all ateliers outside France. And now today, twenty-five years later, L'Unité has inspired another generation all over again. A most remarkable 'follow through'.

Remarkable, but not profound. Was it not a little too simple—this febrile, optimistic, Wellsian world, where two modulor men play tennis for ever and ever on a flat roof, and never think? The Lubetkin problem was, anyway, more subtle and more complicated, English society being more subtle, more complicated than French. French academicism, with its own logic, had enshrined and codified itself in institutions; English academicism had very little to do with the Academy or even with the RIBA, and it is an odd mark of Lubetkin's 'foreignness', not that he rejected Professor Reilly's efforts to bring him into the RIBA, but that he thinks that Institute important enough to be worth annoying. English society—the 'system'—was not so simple as that; it was a more subtle, tangled muddle of many mutual admiration societies, including such things as the Academy, the Athenæum or the Arts Club, but mostly unnamed and even unaware of their own existence. This philistine bourgeoisie could have no art; its only architecture was an emasculated Suedoise. To an English Le Corbusier there would have been no response. That was the England where Lubetkin—still chasing his will o' the wisp nineteenth-century radicalism—arrived about 1930. To make an impact upon all that one had to build so as to hit the solar plexus. He did. Highpoint I was an orgasm.

Meanwhile there were five years to go, and the home of nineteenth-century radicalism—as Lubetkin first saw it from the Brompton Hospital—took more than a little unravelling. Godfrey Samuel came to the rescue, bringing along five other AA boys to form Tecton. Later he brought together Tecton and the Zoo, the latter in the person of Peter Chalmers Mitchell. In addition to Samuel and Lubetkin there were Michael Dugdale, a rather amusing partner who withdrew early; Anthony Chitty; Val Harding whose death in the war was a disaster for English architecture; Lindsey Drake, who remained until in 1948 he joined Denys Lasdun, another pre-war partner, to build the Paddington scheme; and Freddie Skinner—still there, the one constant star. Douglas Bailey came in on the Peterlee episode, miraculously survived it, and is now the third partner in the present firm, the name Tecton having been dropped. No one, least of all Tecton itself, will ever sort out respective contributions, and if Tecton was meant to be a team—though a team with a captain—that is as it should be.

In the Paris of 1927 there was nothing happening beyond the fortifications that one could call architecture. Lubetkin, to whom the dynamic of space was all, hankered for those more open sites of outer London then ripe for flats and housing, jobs that might be realized in three dimensions. It was then—this move from Paris to London—not altogether unlike Palladio's move from Venice to Vicenza, an escape from the palaces of the Canal, with their single façades, to buildings with some outward expression of their volume.

It was a few years before the first of such sites—the brow of Highgate Hill—came Lubetkin's way; meanwhile the Zoo was an enjoyable and unexpected substitute. For young men with ideas there could hardly have been a more ideal field than the Zoo during the regime of Chalmers Mitchell and Huxley. A series of projects, each small and each an isolated architectural concept on its own site; each with a stringent functional programme and yet each capable of light-hearted solution... almost a series of school projects plus an enlightened client. Again and again, moreover, these Zoo jobs enabled Lubetkin to exploit all the novel plastic potentialities of concrete. It is not a far cry from the Zoo to the church at Raincy; yet how far beyond Perret did Tecton and Ove Arup take this new and peculiar art of designing concrete. The most famous of the Zoo jobs is probably the Penguin Pool; carefully designed to meet penguinian acrobatics it ended up as a kind of Max Bill abstraction—the free and loose double spiral of the diving platform being firmly enclosed by the elliptical wall of the pool itself. This motif—the highly sculptural one of the free form within the rigid frame—was neither the invention nor the monopoly of Lubetkin, but he enjoyed it enough to use it again in the less known, but not less interesting, Penguin Pool at Dudley; above all, but for the last time, in the flowing plan of Highpoint I, ground-floor set beneath the geometric rigidity of the towers. It is fair to remember that only later did other people make it a cliché, and that with Lubetkin, as with Corb, it really does spring directly from function, that is from the need to free and differentiate the ground-floor of an apartment block from the standardized upper floors.

Just because the Zoo buildings were so complex, they do perhaps tend to be strained or over-designed. In such frivolous concepts that may not matter, but Lubetkin—with all his emotional response to form—does design, as they say, 'at the top of the voice'. If it is a fault it is one that is born of a heightened imagination. It is the opposite of insipidity; it is virility.

These buildings at Huxley's Zoo,[1] plus a nice bit of sharawaggi at Dudley, were a curtain raiser to Highpoint. Highpoint I (1934), had almost everything. Lubetkin would disagree, insisting that it was no more than a bit of juvenilia ... and that even Highpoint II (1937) was only adolescence. He would say that Highpoint I was arid, schematic, the barest functionalism, a merely sculptural upward projection of a plan. He would not deny, however, that there was in those years of frustration, the years of the Goodhart-Rendel regime at the AA, a generation of young English architects to whom Highpoint I mattered. It mattered to them because 'even the slightly zooish flippancy of some of its details was unimportant beside the clarity of the building—a clarity that was both real and sculptural.'[2] It mattered because it proclaimed that their modernism really was a structural revolution, not just a style; it mattered if only as a symbol that their Modern Movement could be a reality, not a mere protest. To visit Highgate, instead of reading French, was at least an encouragement.

It mattered, of course, in other ways. It was the first of the point blocks, it was not a *Ville Radieuse*—for we had not yet got around to building new towns—but it

2 Gorilla House, Dudley Zoo (1933). These small isolated zoo buildings, although strictly functional, had a light-hearted character

3 Penguin Pool, Dudley Zoo (1934) gave almost the first full demonstration of the plastic potentialities in reinforced concrete

4 Dudley Zoo entrance (1937), a handling of reinforced concrete against brick which emphasizes their contrasting character

5a

5b

5a, b, c, d Highpoint I, exterior
views

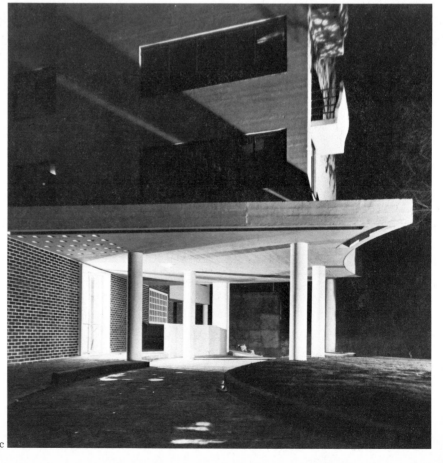

5c

5d

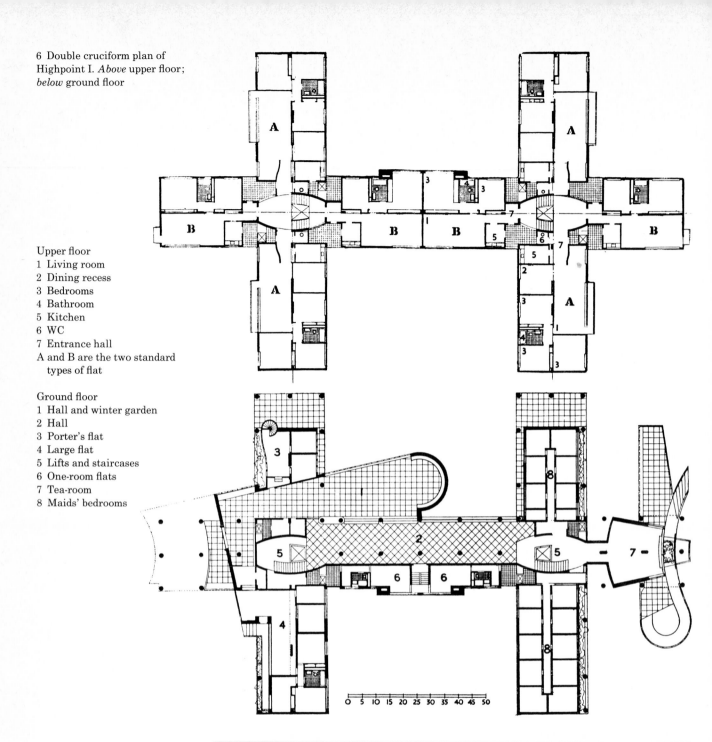

6 Double cruciform plan of Highpoint I. *Above* upper floor; *below* ground floor

Upper floor
1 Living room
2 Dining recess
3 Bedrooms
4 Bathroom
5 Kitchen
6 WC
7 Entrance hall
A and B are the two standard types of flat

Ground floor
1 Hall and winter garden
2 Hall
3 Porter's flat
4 Large flat
5 Lifts and staircases
6 One-room flats
7 Tea-room
8 Maids' bedrooms

7 Living room in Highpoint I. The living room of each flat is a long, narrow room with a window occupying almost the whole of one side and a glazed door leading to one of the cantilevered concrete balconies. This restrained rational room design proved to be adaptable to any kind of furnishing; here, period furniture, with a Queen Anne writing desk against the end wall and a William Morris table under the window

8 Highpoint II: entrance. The
synthesis: three-dimensional
patterning, concrete and brick,
foliage and sculpture

could have been a unit in a *Ville Radieuse*. It took account of a social problem, land
and population, as did no other building of its time. The flats were meant to be
enjoyed—all sunlight, sky and freedom—and were all let before the job was
finished. Le Corbusier could write:

'The building is large enough to be an example, a proof. The ground-floor here
extends like the superb surface of a lake, absorbing easily the lines of traffic. . . .
These flats possess the most important factor of all domestic architecture: sun,
space and intimacy. The building at Highgate is an achievement of the first rank,
and a milestone that will be useful to everybody.'[3]

One glance at, say, the LCC Ackroyden Estate (1954) shows this statement to be
correct.

   If, to that generation, Highpoint mattered at the time not less than the Pavillon
Suisse, they might add now that the tragedy of Lubetkin is the absence of the
'follow through'—that very remarkable 'follow through' of Corb's from Pavillon
Suisse to L'Unité. They might say that the Tecton work of today, while having its
own more obscure qualities, is emphatically not L'Unité and, even more,
relevantly, is not Highpoint I. They would be wrong, partly for confusing criticism
with their own nostalgia, partly for failing to recognize the real effort by Lubetkin
to put into his recent work those classic and baroque values—values not forms—
that are the mainspring of his imagination. He, on his side, would be wrong in
failing to recognize, what, perhaps, he never knew, that twenty years ago he gave
to the Modern Movement in England, with all its curious Domestic, Romantic and
Quaker origins, just that warmth, glamour and guts, the absence of which had
made it so 'odd' and so insular. To dine out at Highpoint I, to arrive past the
caryatids of Highpoint II just when the dark foliage is catching the lights, is still an
architectural experience. For an Englishman it is, very nearly, to recapture some
half-forgotten evening in some indefinable south; it is—as Henry James might
have put it—'to be so ineffably "abroad"'. But then glamour too, not less than
sensual form and functional fitness, is part of an architecture.

109

9a and b Highpoint II: Lubetkin's
own penthouse flat, the furniture
and decoration designed by
himself

9a

9b

Between Highpoint I and Highpoint II were three years; there was also a gap of six feet. Lubetkin would say that this gap is symbolic—symbolic of many things both in the external world of the Hitlerian jungle and the internal world of his own development. He would claim, one suspects, that the 'forward from functionalism' boys, in choosing the gay, brittle road that led to *Domus* and Brazil, failed to express their own social crisis, while he at least acknowledged the gathering mysteries and shadows, through an architecture which, while seeming to withdraw from life like some Buddha or Sphinx, did so only to look down upon it in serene comprehension. To the Anglo-Saxon this is Slavonic mysticism taken to the point of fantasy; for Lubetkin it was a conviction, almost a catharsis. Being an architect's catharsis it changed the London skyline.

Catharsis ... or the beginning of decline? Lubetkin, fierce individualist, probably doesn't care. He had after all—it was one evening at the Zoo, with Wells Coates and Connell—helped to found MARS, given it very material help and then, feeling it to be just one more 'club', resigned. He has detached himself from the Modern Movement and thinks that it is—if it exists at all—only clever-clever variations by the 'club' upon the theme of old clichés. So, decline, catharsis, self-isolation ... it hardly mattered when, into Highpoint II sixteen years ago or into Holford Square today, one had to put those indefinable things—storm music, space dynamic, repose—that Mansart or Gabriel had put into very different monuments ages ago.

It was magnificent, but it was not architecture. One cannot with impunity defy one's gods. Taking account of life and techniques, it was more noble than stylistic revival but doomed to the same cul-de-sac. The values of a Mansart or a Gabriel may mean everything to a Lubetkin ... in private; he can never share them with twentieth-century man. Highpoint II was technically an advance upon Highpoint I—in fact a technical triumph—but whereas 'Highpoint I stands on tip-toe and spreads it wings; Highpoint II sits back on its haunches like Buddha'—the Buddha that squats, not the serene, comprehending Buddha of the architect's intention. It might all be a move 'forward from functionalism', but only to formalism. It was more than a deviation of appearance, it was a deviation of aim. Anthony Cox, in his *Focus* article, stated the case when he wrote:

'It (Highpoint II) is more than an adjustment within legitimate limits; it is prepared to set certain formal values above use-values. ... As I see it there are limits of intention by which certain aspects of the vast concept "building" are emphasized in relation to the long-term development of modern architecture in an industrial economy ... If these limits of intention are changed, rather than extended (and in the case of Tecton it seems they *are* changed), it should follow that a point has been reached at which external material conditions affecting architecture have made such a change necessary and appropriate. If this point has been reached, and I cannot see that it has, the change in aim must be due to personal reasons, to a turning inwards towards private formal meanings which have no generally recognizable social basis. Is it really an important move forward from functionalism, from which development is possible; or is it a symptom of decline, an end in itself?'

The same article admits that to speak of 'legitimate limits', 'use-values' and so on, is to beg a lot of questions about the nature of modern architecture. Nevertheless, here is a young architect already, in 1938, much concerned with formalistic deviationism within the Movement. Highpoint II seemed almost a betrayal. Highpoint II was a reversal of Highpoint I, L'Unité a development of Pavillon Suisse. Highpoint II was not, however, a betrayal merely because it went beyond the limits set by 'use-values'—'use-values' themselves being indefinable—but rather because the nature of the infringement involved *private* meanings as incomprehensible to the 'club' as to the man in the street—no doubt a profound and brilliant language of the emotions, but nevertheless a private one in which Mansart and Lubetkin talk to each other across time. Perhaps Lubetkin thinks of it as some universal esperanto; perhaps he thinks that a building in the street may be as private as a painting in the studio; perhaps he is content that only the dead and himself shall understand.

Examine, for example, the Finsbury Health Centre (1938). This building, while just a little later than Highpoint II, would seem in fact to show a transition in Lubetkin's development. Like Highpoint I it spreads it wings; it spreads them witha fine clarity that is a foil to the richer complexity of the central block from which, indeed, they are almost detached. It is an albatross of a building. Here, between the wings and the central block, is an early use of the 'loose link', justified not as a cliché but as something derived from the contrasted architecture of the things linked; that architecture, in turn, being derived from 'use-value'.

Nearly all the forms of the Health Centre do in fact spring from use. The programme was stringent, but the solution almost as 'functional' as any 1938 purist could wish for. And yet . . . examine that central block: things are happening, strange convolutions and interplay of forms. The private language is at work. There is, for example, an intermediate area, a kind of terrace, above the entrance but below the lecture hall roof that is—aesthetically—common to both. Like the upper storey of Les Invalides it 'belongs' equally to the façade below and to the dome above; the eye can flick it up or down at will, making it part of either; it is the opposite of the ruled horizontality of Highpoint I. Baroque movement is playing like a beam over an otherwise functional façade. It does not displease, it merely lacks it full flavour until the cook explains. Real baroque flavours get through to us because the 'punctuation' of the baroque vocabulary emphasizes them. Moreover we read them knowing the idiom will not be our own and this adds the indefinable piquancy of historical sentiment. Modern architecture can get through to us only in our own language. True, to an eighteenth-century mind it may not have much to say, but the little there is should at least be comprehensible to the sort of people who use the building.

Lubetkin, needless to say, would disagree and has his own explanation of the 'private language', of this baroque basis for modern building—this formalism both of Highpoint II and of his more recent work. With the Cartesian dualism that entered seventeenth-century society the old domination of the Church was broken; Mind and Matter came under separate authorities, thus opening the way not only for the scientist but for specialization as such. The single masterpiece of the classic, as opposed to the unity of a baroque group, symbolized this specialization, this fragmentation of the monistic baroque world, until we end with the architecture of capitalism, the architecture that says to the common man— 'Keep Out!'

One cannot return to a baroque world any more than to a baroque art. Can one— and this is the question posed by Lubetkin—restore that communion between building and onlooker? Can one make the large housing block a single object, a *trompe-l'œil*—as, say, was Les Invalides—and thus set up in the passer-by an emotion or at least a reaction—for even bewilderment is reaction of a sort.[4]

But of course the world beyond one's building remains the same chaos of fragmentation. And so one isolates one's own statement . . . one is not resigned to this, it is an interim necessity. The blank end wall, the shadowed base (whether achieved by piloti or otherwise) and the penthouse under the flat roof—all these combine to isolate and to frame in that inward-outward looking façade that is to set up that reaction in the passer-by.

If we had an 'integrated society' then our building could respond to and look towards other buildings—baroque-wise. Meanwhile the architect must make his own statement, an aesthetic statement but also a social protest.

This analysis of how—at Highpoint II in 1937—formalism entered like a bacillus into the bloodstream of modern architecture, makes unnecessary any full analysis of Tecton's post-war housing. That Gestetner owners of Highpoint and typical glamour client of the 30s—should be replaced by the Borough of Finsbury is normal. That, at any rate, means that the tragi-comic story of getting Highpoint II

10a and b Finsbury Health Centre (1938). The simplicity of the wings is a foil to the richer textures and modelling of the centre

10a

10b

past the local authority won't happen again.

The formalist controversy today is not very different from sixteen years ago, although three new elements may be said to have entered the arena. One, the conceptual building; two, façade patterning and, three, social realism.[5] The main stream—the Modern Movement—has advanced, at least in theory, beyond the mere upward projection of a plan in terms of functionalist elements. The building itself must now state, in a single *coup d'œil*, the 'idea' underlying it; it must be a concept capable, like, say, a medieval cathedral or a Farnsworth House, of being visually grasped and enjoyed, fondled almost, as if it were a Ming pot. Is this an advance? Does this conceptual building now invalidate the very intention of formalism, of the private language, of saying something that 'arid functionalism' could never say? Has the Modern Movement, in its Mies phase, now found its own answer in its own terms to the problem Lubetkin tried to solve so long ago?

Formalism, on the other hand, faced with the terrific problem of humanizing groups of vast[6] slab blocks, has meanwhile added to its vocabulary. That baroque beam still plays over Spa Green (Rosebery Avenue), and Priory Green; upper stories and penthouse still ingeniously recede, shadows still ingeniously detach the building from the ground; there is still the nod across the centuries. That is just a carry-over from Highpoint II and the Health Centre into our own era—an era wherein the strictest economies have robbed these baroque values of the suavity and finish without which the whole thing becomes almost nonsense—misplaced sophistication.

In any case this interplay of masses on large buildings could not be enough; classic had to come to the rescue of baroque, with its façade treatments, its scale-giving elements, its divisions and subdivisions. Windows, panels between windows and brickwork below, all come into play—like entablatures and orders—to make of the façade an all-over pattern ... like a carpet in a museum in Vienna.[7] Less important than the criticism that—as at Bishops Bridge Road[8] for instance—the pattern forces the window into the corner of the room, is the fact that this is not, not here and now, a viable architecture. Lubetkin would reply that Family Smith, Family Jones, etc, are each given their due expression, their own unit of the pattern within the containing frame of the building. This is not strictly true. It was not, moreover, a form of self-expression for which the wealthier and more individualistic tenants of Highpoint had ever hankered unduly; they were content, like aristocracy in terrace housing at Bath or Nancy, to live in an architecture of distinction.

That third new element in the arena—social realism—is irrelevant here except that by analogy, or by antithesis rather, it points to the sophistication and difficulty of formalism. For that abstruse language it would substitute catchy tunes, marching songs and folk tales. After great revolutions and national wars there comes eventually a moment when liberation and victory give vent to an architecture. That is the moment when the classic dynamic of space takes over from the baroque, when the Crillon, Chambre des Députés and the rest become points of demarcation around an area. It is the space, not the building, that proclaims the nation. That is the moment when even bad buildings serve to set off, as it were, the incredible spaces and flights of steps in the new Stalingrad. That dynamic of space is one thing, the architecture is another. That the western baroque chosen by Peter the Great for his new westernized capital upon the Gulf of Finland should be the basis of a modern revival is explicable but, at least to a 'modern' mind, odd. It is perverse, not only socially and technically, but aesthetically, since an architecture of rich textural surfaces is lost in space—destroyed by its own foreground. Baroque qualities that are admirable inside the Place Vendôme would be wasted on the Champs Elysées. The calm classicism of the white cliff that is the Rue de Rivoli, the grouping of separate buildings leading on from space to space—as Gabriel leads one on from the Quai d'Orsay to the Madeleine—that, or rather its equivalent in a technically modern idiom, was the answer to the great spaces of Russia's new cities.

This is not a digression. It points the error both of social realism and of formalism. Social realism, in its anxiety to find a popular language, revives a style—baroque—that was intended for quite different social purposes and for quite different spaces—for piazzas, courtyards and little German parks.[9] Formalism makes the opposite error. Lubetkin understands aesthetic values and spatial relationships and handles them with superb facility and erudition; he cannot interpret them through a generally comprehensible architecture. It is all rather sad. Social realism and formalism are heresies against the 'Modern Movement'—as seen by, say, CIAM—and in intention at least, both are nobler, than the catholicism they offend. Both, while prepared to grant the merits of English legislation, Italian craftsmanship, Scandinavian detail and so on—do, more and more, find that Modern Movement nervous, bright, papery and fundamentally trivial—which indeed it is.

One day the tragic story of Peterlee may be told. Whatever else the plan did or did not do, it did not make the primary blunder that will haunt the other New Towns for years. It did not fail to make an unambiguous centre and to make it at the start. It did not regard that centre as a mere market-place group of communal and commercial buildings; it conceived it in strong architectural terms. At the centre of Peterlee were to be three very high buildings—not an undue proportion of high against low for the town as a whole—and these three towers were to be disposed at the points of a triangle—ie, classically—demarcating space with such clarity that market groups, cinemas and all the rest of it would inevitably, because naturally, be born between and beneath them. The outer rings of the tree trunk would then form themselves later, in the right order. If England had emerged from war in a more triumphant or self-confident mood, the bureaucratic scandal of Peterlee might have been overcome and one new town at least would have had a true dynamic born of architecture conceived spatially. The concept was accepted at the highest level in the country; it was only lesser fry who first muddled and then postponed it to the Greek Kalends, and all in favour of pink cottages beyond the true Peterlee boundary. Lubetkin and Bailey resigned. They had been commissioned to design the town, not to murder it.

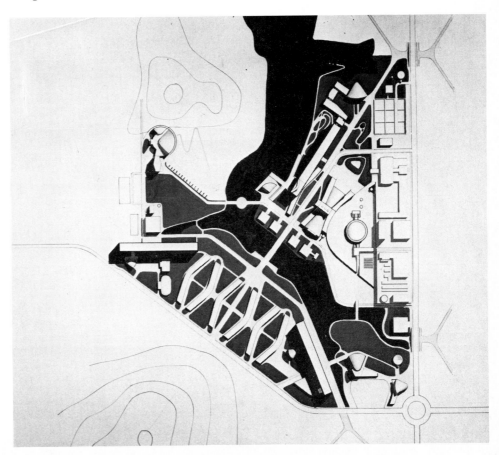

11 Plan for Peterlee New Town

When Lubetkin says of the Peterlee plan that, in the sense that its three key buildings demarcate space, it is a 'classical' concept; or of Priory Green that, in the sense that its patterned façades look inwards to enclose space, it is a 'baroque' concept, he may seem far-fetched. But he means it. It is, admittedly, a nostalgic statement, the statement of an emotional being reading into the rather humdrum architecture of today, dreams peopled with ghosts from the Neva, the Danube and the Seine. It is, admittedly, an attempt to rationalize in the form of an architectural theory, the products of a deep imagination. That does not invalidate it. This passionate feeling for space, the dynamic of space, the definition of space, the architecture of space, is the golden thread running through Lubetkin's career. Going beyond current arguments about formalism and the rest, it may not set Lubetkin above his colleagues, but it does differentiate him. It explains his genesis as an architect; it explains the move to London; it explains the sculptural nature of the Zoo projects; it explains the exploitation of the brow of Highgate Hill; it explains the post-war planning; and it explains Peterlee.

He is a technician—Highpoint II set a new standard in its own field, and so did the Health Centre. And he is a decorator. His own Penthouse at Highpoint speaks for itself, but even there the throwing forward, as it were, of the room towards the long window and panoramic view, is a spatial thing far more important than the ephemeral decor.

Individualism, imagination, humility and artistic erudition makes a curious amalgam. To link such strands of character with the ultimate product—in this case an architecture—is the fascination of all biography. In the 30s it was individualism, whether of the Left or the Right, whether of a Lubetkin or, say, of a Baker, Cooper or Blomfield, that held the stage. The Modern Movement in England was as much an affair of individuals as was the academicism of the Right ... and had been ever since the Red House. So Lubetkin, at that time, had found almost what he was looking for. In the post-war world where men sink their individualism in organizations—organizations such as Hertfordshire or the LCC—to produce good architecture ... can there be a place for the Lubetkins? There must always be a place for the artist and technician, but to 'belong', to be on the band-wagon, is the eternal problem of the Leftist who has seen his dreams come almost true. It is why, sometimes, old revolutionaries disappear.

Are individualism and humility a contradiction? The humility of the artist is humility in face of his art ... not self-effacement. Turner, with all those big blazing canvases, could steal any show anywhere; before the god of sunsets he was prostrate with humility. When Lubetkin, in 1935, designed a building to steal the show there was no arrogance, no réclame; it was a three-dimensional statement about structure and life, an honest and therefore humble statement about convictions honestly held. When the author of this article was Principal of the AA School he heard many criticisms of students; most of them cancelled each other out; Lubetkin's comment went home—that too many students designed to their own glory. There are, however, others besides students; to seek applause from the 'right people' for the wrong reasons, to rob one's work of real architectural content, only to fill the vacuum with nice sentiment, is the quintessence of conceit ... an assurance of architectural death since there is no *architecture* to live. Lubetkin's work—specially in recent years—is often bewildering and as difficult to understand as are his own explanations; sometimes it is self-assertive or even over-designed. It is never guilty, however, of prettiness, triviality or nice sentiment; it is on the contrary packed with very real architectural content, and is thus assured of survival.

NOTES

[1] The condition of these Zoo buildings today is a scandalous reflection upon the present regime at Regent's Park; it also invalidates any comment upon a colour treatment that has long since disappeared. (Written in 1958—Editor.)

[2] Anthony Cox in *Focus* 2, winter 1938.

[3] Le Corbusier in *The Architectural Review*, January 1936.

[4] The autocratic basis of baroque in no way excludes this communion with the on-looker; with its outward drive into avenues

and public spaces it demands a reaction. The reaction demanded may be 'awe', but, unlike Capitalist architecture, baroque does not exclude the onlooker.

[5] The 'new brutalism' is not a fourth element—only a conceptual building in a private language. Lubetkin talks across time to the great masters; the Smithsons talk only to each other.

[6] 'Terrific', 'vast'? London, as seen on a clear day from the Senate House tower, shows that the new housing of the inner boroughs—a fair proportion of it Lubetkin's—is changing the skyline more than any equivalent event in our architectural history. The Gothic Revival (Westminster, St Pancras, South Kensington, etc) is the only rival.

[7] It is significant that Lutyens, in his tenement blocks for the Westminster Estate, arrived at a comparable patterning. He was en route from baroque style, Lubetkin en route from baroque values.

[8] This big Paddington scheme began in the Tecton office, its layout taking shape there. It has been executed and developed by Lasdun and Drake in a manner which, superficially at least, would seem in its breezy self-assertion, to be rather more Lubetkin than Lubetkin.

[9] The buildings of the Ring in Vienna are also classical milestones demarcating great areas, and yet are often baroque. Each, however, while playing its part in the spatial conception is, on approach, found to have its own immediate baroque setting. Vienna is an interplay of the two scales.

NB Some of the biographical facts Jordan includes are inaccurate: Lubetkin studied architecture in Warsaw, continued his studies in Paris, and before arriving in London in 1931 went to Moscow from Paris.

The Italian Rationalists

by Bruno Zevi

The distinguished Italian historian and editor Bruno Zevi investigates in his specially commissioned contribution to this book the confusion over the term Rationalism in modern Italian architecture. He refers in particular to the unpublished 'Manifesto of Futurist Architecture' drawn up by Boccioni but suppressed by Marinetti. The article was translated by Giorgio Verrecchia.

As far back as 1933–4 the uncompromisingly anti-fascist critic, Edoardo Persico, lashed out at the compromises and at the muddled thinking of his rationalist friends. He wrote: 'The fact is that Italian Rationalism didn't arise out of a deep need, but grew either from amateurish stands like those of the fashionable Europeanism of "Gruppo 7", or from practical pretexts lacking ethical backbone. And so, the point about their lack of style is certainly justified: their arguing only led to confused aspirations, without contact with real problems, and without any real content. The battle between "Rationalists" and "traditionalists" boiled down to an empty and inconsistent dialogue, in which the opposed parties showed the same lack of theoretical preparation and the same inability to conjure up an architecture made up of more than just sterile show'. And went on: 'Italian Rationalism is necessarily unable to share in the vigour of other European movements, because of its intrinsic lack of faith. And so, the Europeanism of the first Rationalism is pushed, by the cold reality of practical situations, into the "Roman" and the "Mediterranean", right down to the last proclamation of corporate architecture . . . The history of Italian Rationalism is the story of an emotional crisis'.

These rather severe judgements were explained by the thinness of the socio-cultural background. With a much later process of industrialization than in the other, more advanced, western countries, the development of nineteenth-century engineering was rather rickety: Alessandro Antonelli, in his astounding domes in Alexandria and Turin, tried, paradoxically, to rival metal constructions with brick and mortar. Giuseppe Mengoni in his magnificent Galleria Vittorio Emanuele in Milan of 1865, set against the luminous vaults, grey, classical buildings, dressing up the fronts with triumphal arches. There was, besides, no corresponding movement to the English Arts and Crafts.

The neo-medievalism and Art Nouveau found anaemic followers in the eclectic personalities of Raimondo D'Aronco in Udine, Ernesto Basile in Palermo, Giuseppe Sommaruga and Gaetano Moretti in Milan. Italy had missed a century of history and has to pay the consequences of her backwardness and her swaggering nationalism. Persico fully realized that, under fascist rule, it would prove impossible to regain the time lost. The new architecture, without a genuine social ideology, could not help becoming corrupted, by coming to terms with the leaders of the academic monumentalism—Gustavo Giovannoni and Marcello Piacentini.

Italian Rationalism was born, officially, in 1926, when a group of seven young architects, in a series of articles, championed a new architecture. Their statements were vague and cautious: 'the new generation announces a revolution in architecture, a revolution set to organize and build—sincerity, order, logic and, above all, a great clarity—these are the real features of the new spirit'. The seven had the naive conviction of being able to avoid a frontal conflict. In 1928, they organized the first exhibition of 'Rational Architecture' and found MIAR (Movimento Italiano per l'Architettura Razionale). The compromise did not last

Antonio Sant'Elia: Milan 2000 (1913–14)

119

for more than three years. In 1931, the second exhibition, characterized by the 'Table of Horrors' displaying the works of fascist academics, caused a big scandal and the demise of MIAR—and inglorious end of trying to marry dictatorship and modern architecture. The defection of three of the original seven left only Luigi Figini, Gino Pollini, Adalberto Libera and Giuseppe Terragni, while many other MIAR members succumbed to Piacentini's offer of Commissions for Rome's University complex. The collapse of MIAR was not the complete end of Rationalism. In fact, Florence Railway Station and the new town of Sabaudia in the Agro Pontino, were built after 1931. But the decade immediately preceding the Second World War was dominated by the Monumentalists. To the Rationalists was left the small peripheral area centred on the Milan Triennale and the magazine *Casabella*, edited by Giuseppe Pagano.

Before we consider the works of this period, we should mention that the basic mistake of the Rationalists was their failure to link up with the Futurist avant garde as their only valid precedent. A still little-known episode should size up for us this failure. In 1975, among the unpublished papers of Umberto Boccioni, was discovered a 'Manifesto of Futurist Architecture' dating back to the end of 1913 and the beginning of 1914. Filippo Tommaso Marinetti knew of it, but kept it in the dark so as not to steal the show from the young Antonio Sant'Elia, killed in the First World War. Boccioni's text is so illuminating that it deserves at least partial reproduction here:

'The cube, the pyramid and the rectangle, as the general line of building, must be eliminated: they freeze the architectural line. All lines must be used in any point and by any means. This autonomy of the parts of the building will break the uniformity . . . and utility won't be sacrificed to the old and useless symmetry. Like an engine, the spaces of a building should reach peak efficiency. Because of symmetry one gives light and space to rooms that don't need it, at the expense of others that have become essential to modern living. . . . So, the front of a house can go up and down, in and out, join and divide according to the degree of the needs of the spaces that make it up. It is the outside that must serve the inside, as in painting and sculpture. The outside is always a traditional outside, while the new outside, achieved through the triumph of the inside, will inevitably create the new architectural line. . . . We said that in painting we shall put the observer at the centre of the painting, making him the centre of the emotion rather than a simple spectator. The urban habitat is changing: we are surrounded by a spiral of architectural forces. Until yesterday, buildings ran along panoramic perspectives, house followed by house, street by street. Today the habitat grows in all directions: from the luminous basements of the big stores, from the multi-level tunnels of the Underground, to the giant rise of the American cloud scrapers. . . . The future is preparing for us an endless vista of architectural skylines'.

Though written in a hurry, forgetting a few grammatical rules, the text is surprising for its not only Futurist but also Cubist and Expressionist elements, anticipating the analytical syntax, later devised by De Stijl in 1917, and Wright's concept 'from the inside to the outside'. During his stay in Paris, Boccioni had realized that (*a*) the Futurist theory of movement wasn't enough to support an architectural language; (*b*) the Cubist lesson remained of basic importance, in spite of the fact that, without the Futurist dynamism, it was running the risk of getting caught in a tangle of static rules, anti-Beaux Arts but, at the same time, showing attitudes similar to it; (*c*) Expressionism had the extraordinary ability to shape matter into gushing, explosive forms. As we know, together with Guillaume Apollinaire, Boccioni planned a joint front for the three movements, in his 'Manifeste-synthèse' (*Le Figaro*, June 29, 1913), signed by Marinetti, Picasso, Boccioni, Max Jacob, Carrà, Delaunay, Matisse, Braque, Severini, Derain, Archipenko, Balla, Palazzeschi, Papini, Gleizes, Laurencin, Léger, Kandinsky, Strawinsky, Duchamp and many others. The Rationalists did not have access to Boccioni's 'Manifesto of Futurist Architecture' because Marinetti had prevented its diffusion. But they could have found inspiration in much of his other writings, particularly those on 'plastic dynamism'. Instead, they completely ignored the Futurist precedent and its Expressionist component. They took in Le Corbusier and the Bauhaus, and, only minimally, De Stijl. In fact they emphasized the intrinsic dangers of Cubism: many of the Italian Rationalist buildings were symmetrical, box-like with little or no invention in the external and internal spaces; in short, they were leaning towards the classical. In Italy the dogmas of proportion, of regulating lines and assonance still prevailed along with the picturesque of the Mediterranean. Futurism entered the mainstream of European avant garde groups; the Rationalism of 'Group 7' and of MIAR remained an often provincial sideshow.

Three figures stand out from the general dimness of Italian Rationalism: Giuseppe Terragni on the creative level; Edoardo Persico as a critic and Giuseppe Pagano, promoter and leader of the campaign moving from architecture to civil rights.

Terragni was born in Como in 1904 and died in 1943, broken by the Russian front. Persico, from Naples, died at 36 in 1936. Pagano, born in Parenzo in 1896, was a determined fascist. When he realized his mistake he joined the resistance, taking command of a partisan brigade. He was taken prisoner and tortured but managed to escape and to start many other partisan initiatives. In the end, he was murdered in Mauthausen. As usual in Italian history, it is the best few who pay for the dull majority.

More than thirty years after his death Terragni has become the object of intensive studies by, among others, Peter Eisenman, the intellectually more able of the New York 'five architects'. What is the reason for this interest? The fact that he was, perhaps, the first complete 'mannerist' of the Modern Movement.

He started with the project for a Gas Works, shown at the Monza Biennale of 1927, influenced by Russian Constructivism. Then the Novocomum, a compact and blocky building that, with its glass corner cylinders, goes back to a solution attempted by Golosov in the Zujev Club in Moscow. In 1932 he began the construction of the Fascio House, the best-known work of Italian Rationalism.

1 Giuseppe Terragni: Novocomum, Como (1927–8)

2 Giuseppe Terragni: the Fascio
house, Como (1932–6)

Giving up Constructivism, using a square plan and a structural cage of square
moduli in the frontal part, he fitted the roof garden with the perimeter of the
volume, like Le Corbusier, employing regulating lines based on the golden section.
But, having started with a cubic shape, he didn't cover it with surfaces without
depth and didn't use pilotis and 'free façade'. The cube wasn't cut by skin-deep
continuous windows, but perforated and sculpted in such a way as to emphasize
the concrete pillars and beams. In the façade on the square, the relationship
between flat plane and structural frame wasn't bidimensional; the flat plane
carried on round the corner, becomes volume, unbalancing the composition; the
other three façades each have their own identity, characterized by the implosion of
the plastic cavities. In the interior, in spite of a certain classical solemnity, we find
faultless details and mouldings of confident originality. After the war, the Casa del
Fascio became a Casa del Popolo fitting perfectly the new democratic shoes.

Terragni's most successful work was the nursery school Antonio Sant'Elia:
planning freed from geometrical elementarism, a dominance of the horizontal,
expressed functionally by partitions, either clearly defined or veiled by structural
netting, linear play in the transparent overhanging projection, a symbiosis
between classrooms and open spaces. It is a smiling and happy language that filters
with its spontaneous quality, the programmatic strictness of the Casa de Fascio. In
the Villa Bianca at Seveso, Terragni explored another tool of the time—the
separated slabs of De Stijl and Mies van der Rohe, as is shown by the plan, whose
flat planes do not extend beyond the corners so as to avoid becoming volume. As
the building is a box-like parallelepiped, the play of the slabs cannot cut through the
main construction, but departs from it in the ramp, in the balcony and, above all, in
the roof terrace with the flat planes thrown towards the sky with a moving and
almost metaphysical lyricism. In his last works, especially in the block of flats
Giuliani-Frigerio in Como, Terragni unbalanced the volume with projections,
junctions and contrasts between the ribbon windows and the deep cavities,
between the casing and the structural cage.

Terragni's mannerism has its roots, first in Russian Constructivism, then in Le
Corbusier, Gropius, Mies, deriving from them an original and incisive linguistic
code. Starting from a study of the contents, he brought them out by using the

3 Luigi Figini, Gino Pollini: villa-studio in the park of Milan Triennale (1933)

4 BBPR Studio (Gianluigi Banfi, Lodovico Barbiano di Belgiojoso, Enrico Peressutti, Ernesto Nathan Rogers): heliotherapic colony, Legnano (1936)

5 Cesare Cattaneo: villa in Cernobbio (1940)

6 Ignazio Gardella: TB dispensary, Alessandria (1936)

3

4

5

6

asymmetric and dissonant features of the plan, rejecting the vision of a central perspective in order to fulfil its tridimensional dynamism, cut up the building into slabs to avoid the box, and made use of every architectural recipe in his structural game. A good proof of all this is the project for the Palazzo dei Congressi, entered for the World Exhibition that should have taken place in Rome in 1942. What is lacking in his linguistic contribution is a genuine consciousness of space-time, creativity in the field of spatial images and the ability to reintegrate the building into the continuity of land and city. In fact, the Italian Rationalists had not yet grasped the genius of Frank Lloyd Wright.

The strongest group was the one formed in Lombardy, led and inspired by Terragni, Persico and Pagano. Its best-known members were Figini and Pollini with their delightful villa-studio, in the park of Milan Triennale (1933), and then with the Olivetti Factory in Ivrea; the Office of BBPR (Gianluigi Banfi, Lodovico Barbiani di Belgiojoso, Enrico Peressutti and Ernesto Nathan Rogers) with the heliotherapic Colony in Legnano (1936); Cesare Cattaneo from Como, particularly with his villa in Cernobbio (1940); Piero Bottoni, with his town planning that was to materialize, after the war, in the QT8 district in Milan; Ignazio Gardella with the TB clinic in Alessandria, grafting Scandinavian feelings on to the Rationalist severity; Giuseppe Pagano with his Faculty of Physics in Rome (1934) and Bocconi University in Milan (1936–42) and also his projects for 'Green Milan' (Milano verde) and the 'Horizontal City'. Edoardo Persico himself tried his hand at building in partnership with Marcello Nizzoli: the Gold Medal Room at the Milan Aeronautics Exhibition (1934) was an endless cavity, uprooted from any kind of context, with the rhythmic dissonance of its black and white (square section) thin bars: an abstract, Kafkian atmosphere explored further by Franco Albini in his museographical productions. As in literature, hermetism proved to be a good weapon to sabotage the vulgar fascist monumentality.

Turin can boast of an incunabulum: the Fiat-Lingotto Works (1914–26) by Giacomo Matté Trucco, reproduced by Le Corbusier in *Vers une Architecture*. The spiral ramp for motorcars and the testing track on the roof give a micro-urbanistic character to this structure, emphasized by the internal 'road' about 1 km long. The Turin Exhibition of 1928 swings between Art Deco and Futurism, with painters like Prampolini, Depero, Fillia taking part in designing rather inferior pavilions. Pagano and Gino Levi-Montalcini carried on with Rationalism in the Palazzo Gualino, while Luigi Carlo Daneri represented the renewing force in Genoa that was to, eventually, culminate in the grandiose serpentines of Forte Quezzi (1960).

In 1933, in Florence, a group of young Tuscans led by Giovanni Michelucci, won the competition for the new railway station. Apart from the meaning acquired in the furious polemic let loose by the conservatives it remains an ageless piece of work. Opposite the apse of Santa Maria Novella a low volume of pietraforte, with its horizontal plane emphasized by the cantilevers, leans like an arcade towards the town with the glassy waterfall of the main entrance; inside, a sequence of narrow roofings of masterly design heads into the contracted space of the main gallery, underlined by the clever use of light and fittings. Balanced between Rationalism and the organic, the station merges the plastic cavities with the walkways and fits, by its very dissonance, into the urban landscape.

This creative 'ease' followed Michelucci in his later work: the Borsa Merci in Pistoia (1950), grafted sober geometry onto the medieval context; the small and moving church of Collina where he attempted to rescue the anonymous language and the continuity between cottage and land in the peasant world; the Cassa di Risparmio in Florence, a sort of gallery or covered street in the town centre; the church of the Autostrada del Sole of 1961 where the Expressionistic vein pushes and modifies the crowded space of structural webs.

The whole of Michelucci's 'school'—Italo Gamberini, Leonardo Ricci, Leonardo Savioli, among the rest—was at odds with the 'Renaissance' leftovers of purist Rationalism, knowing their high cost in social and poetical terms. The situation in Rome was not so clear cut, heavily mortgaged as it was, to the Mussolinian

7

8

9

7 Guiseppe Pagano: Faculty of
Physics, Rome (1934)

8 Guiseppe Pagano: Bocconi
University, Rome (1936–42)

9 Edoardo Persico, Marcello
Nizzoli: the Gold Medal Room at
the Milan Aeronautics
Exhibition (1934)

10 Giovanni Michelucci, Nello
Baroni, Pier Nicolo Berardi, Italo
Gamberini, Sarre Guarnieri,
Leonardo Lusanna: railway
station, Florence (1936)

10

academics. In 1932 the Fascist Revolution Exhibition of Adalberto Libera showed a come-back, in a decorative vein, of the Futurist themes; he followed it with the compromise of the Palazzo dei Congressi for the 1942 exhibition, the villa Malaparte in Capri and, after the war, the horizontal Unité d'habitation in the Tuscolano district of Rome while Mario Ridolfi, whose imaginative flair was already evident in the Tower Restaurants project and in the post office of Piazza Bologna, channelled his craft-like skill on to Rationalist tracks.

The same applied to Giuseppe Vaccaro and Luigi Moretti, known respectively for the Youth Colony at Cesenatico and the Fencing Academy of the Foro Italico in Rome.

The south of Italy had much less to offer—in Naples, Luigi Cosenza working with Bernard Rudofsky; in Palermo, Giuseppe Samona who, after the war, was to run the Venice school of architecture, introducing radical new trends in teaching.

11 Adalberto Libera: Villa Malaparte, Capri (1940)

12 Mario Ridolfi: post office in the piazza Bologna, Rome (1932)

13 Giuseppe Vaccaro: marine colony, Cesenatico (1938)

14 Luigi Moretti: Fencing Academy at the Foro Italico, Rome (1936)

11

12

13

14

The figure of Pier Luigi Nervi rises well above the national boundaries. His masterpieces are represented by the hangars of Orbetello (1936), with the extraordinary weightless trellis of the roof vault and, above all, the 'cavities' (more shelter than enclosure), and the profiles, the wonderful angular plastic solutions. Reinforced concrete finds here an exceptional artistic synthesis, while, later, his daring structural inventions are often conditioned by a classical sensitivity: a new technique at the service of outdated spatial schemes. Rationalism had no chance to grow on the urban scale, where the fascist regime ruthlessly disembowelled historic centres—among the major crimes were Brescia, Via Roma in Turin, San Babila in Milan, Via della Conciliazione and Piazza Augusto Imperatore in Rome—replacing them with buildings in the rhetorical and classical manner. The towns in the Agro Pontino are either ridiculously monumental, like Littoria (today's Latina), or pseudo-vernacular, like Aprilia. Sabaudia is the only exception, whose competition was won in 1933 by Luigi Piccinato, Gino

15 Pier Luigi Nervi: hangar at Orbetello (1936)

16 Franco Albini: Baldini and Castoldi Library, Milan (1947)

17 Luigi Piccinato, Gino Cancellotti, Eugenio Montuori, Alfredo Scalpelli: Sabaudia (1933)

15

16

17

Cancellotti, Eugenio Montuori and Alfredo Scalpelli. A satellite nucleus in human scale, inspired by the centres of the Ruhr, the Russian Autostroy and Wright's ideas on the crisis of the metropolis, it became the pivot of a vast farming complex on reclaimed land. Piccinato looked back to the medieval urban organization, articulating community life in a series of separate squares, finely adjusting the visual echoes and fitting the open shape into the landscape of Lake Paola. We must not forget the contribution of Adriano Olivetti, prime mover in the setting up of the Val d'Aosta regional plan, conceived together with Figini, Pollini, Bottoni and the BBPR Studio.

The range of figurative tendencies got wider and richer with the years; Alberto Sartoris's axonometrics are typical of the 20s, while Carlo Molino's 'ripples', especially in Turin's Riding Club, are characeristic of the 30s and a prelude to the post-war organic developments.

But this evolutive process stopped short in 1938, during the preparations for the World Exhibition of 1942. Rationalism was completely outlawed. Lining up with Nazi Germany meant a grotesque orgy of false arches and false pillars, with the best—goose pimpling—symbol in the so-called 'Square Colosseum', clearly visible in the Eur district of Rome, with its reinforced concrete structure dressed by fat arches of travertine. Faced with these obscenities the whole of the avant garde realized that the problem had moved from architecture to political and civil rights. All hopes of fighting fascism from the inside had gone. Those who believed in modern architecture had to leave the drawing board and join the resistance. The writer Elio Vittorini said that only in revolutions politics coincide with culture, and the Rationalist architects verified the truth of that statement with their lives. As we saw, the price had been very high, and after the Second World War, Italy was without most of her leaders: Terragni, Persico, Pagano, the critic Raffaello Giolli, the architect Gian Luigi Banfi of the BBPR group and Giorgio Labo, shot by the Germans in Rome.

The Italian Modern Movement started again, but cruelly mutilated. It is not by chance that the first post-war work was the Monument to the Fosse Ardeatine, celebrating the sacrifice of more than three hundred Romans, murdered in a Nazi reprisal: a moving homage to the glory of Rationalism.

BIBLIOGRAPHY
Zeno Birolli (ed), *Umberto Boccioni: Altri inediti e apparati critici*, Milan, Feltrinelli, 1972. Includes the text of the Manifesto of Futurist Architecture. See also Bruno Zevi, 'La profezia di Umberto Boccioni', in *Il linguaggio moderno dell'architettura*, 2nd ed, Turin, Einaudi, 1974
Michele Cennamo, *Materiali per l'analisi dell'architettura moderna—La prima Esposizione Italiana di Architettura Razionale*, Naples, Fiorentino, 1973
Peter Eisenman, From Object to Relationship II: Giuseppe Terragni. Casa Giuliano Frigerio, Casa del Fascio, in *Perspecta*, the Yale Architectural Journal, No 13, 14, 1971
L'ereditá di Terragni e l'architettura italiana, in *L'architettura—cronache e storia*, No 163, May 1969
Giovanni Fanelli, *Architettura moderna in Italia 1900–1940*, Florence, Marchi and Bertolli, 1968
Raffaello Giolli, in *L'architettura razionale*, ed Cesare De Seta, Bari, Laterza, 1972
Giuseppe Pagano Pogatschnig: Architetture e scritti, *Domus*, Milan 1947
Enrico Mantero, *Giuseppe Terragni e la citta del razionalismo italiano*, Bari, Dedalo, 1969
Omaggio a Terragni, special issue of *L'architettura—cronache e storia*, No 153, July 1968
Luciano Patetta, *L'architettura in Italia—1919–1943: Le polemiche*, Milan, Clup, 1972
Ernesto Nathan Rogers, Testimonianza sugli architetti del ventennio, in *Casabella-continuitá*. No 269, October 1962
Cesare De Seta, *La cultura architettonica in Italia tra le due guerre*, Bari, Laterza, 1972
Giula Veronesi, *Difficoltá politiche dell'architettura in Italia 1920–40*, Milan, Tamburini, 1953
Giulia Veronesi (ed), *Edoardo Persico: Tutte le opere (1923–1935)*, 2 vols, Milan, Comunitá, 1964
Bruno Zevi: *Spazi dell'architettura moderna*, Turin, Einaudi, 1973
Bruno Zevi: *Storia dell'architettura moderna*, Turin, Einaudi, 1975. With a complete bibliography on Italian Rationalism
More recently a new work has been published *Il razionalismo e l'architettura in Italia durante il fascio*, edited by S. Danesi and L. Patteti (Venice, 1976) (Editor's note)

Towards a rational aesthetic

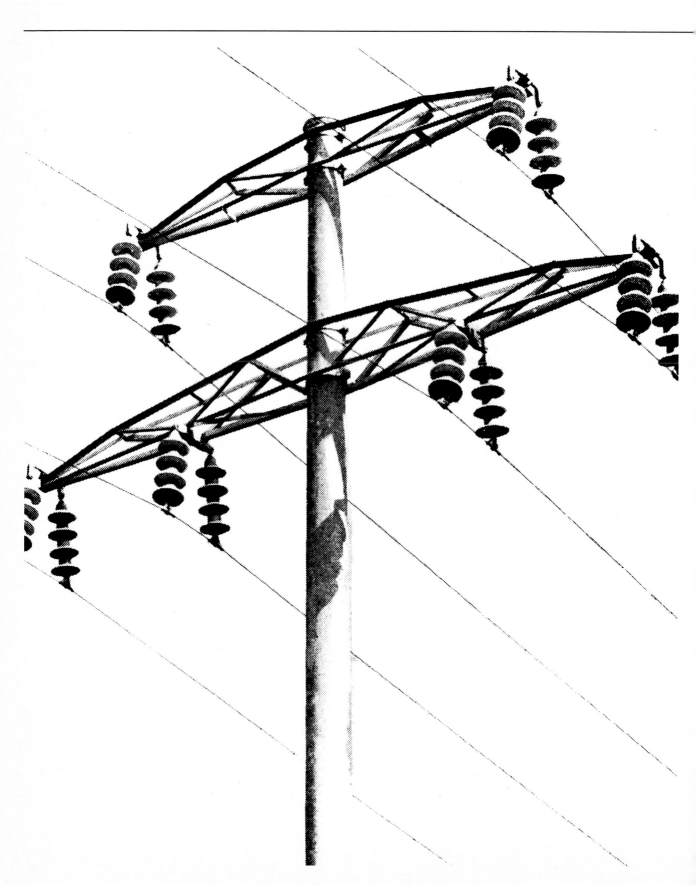

by J. M. Richards

In this important British essay (from The Architectural Review, *December 1935), J. M. Richards examines the characteristics of modern design with particular reference to the influence of the machine and machine production. He saw the machine aesthetic as developing unselfconsciously as part of what he called 'the progressive impersonalization of design'. This, he argued, placed a new emphasis on the product rather than on the process and led to the discovery of the abstract aesthetic virtues of machines themselves.*

'The real problem is not to adapt machine production to the aesthetic standards of handicraft, but to think out new aesthetic standards for new methods of production.' Herbert Read: *Art and Industry*, introduction

'Face to face with these new machines and instruments, with their hard surfaces, their rigid volumes, their stark shapes, a fresh kind of perception and pleasure emerges: to interpret this order becomes one of the new tasks of the arts.' Lewis Mumford: *Technics and Civilization*

'By beauty of shapes I do not mean, as most people would suppose, the beauty of living figures or of pictures, but, to make my point clear, I mean straight lines and circles, and shapes, plane or solid, made from them by lathe, ruler or square. These are not, like other things, beautiful relatively, but always and absolutely.' Plato: *Philebus* (quoted in the catalogue, *Machine Art*, of the Museum of Modern Art, New York)

'Standardization is not an impediment to the development of civilization, but, on the contrary, one of its immediate prerequisites. The standard can be defined as that simplified practical exemplar of anything in general use which embodies a fusion of the best of its anterior forms.' Walter Gropius: *The New Architecture and the Bauhaus*

The factor which dominates contemporary life is power production. I say particularly power production, not machine production. The use of machines or tools as weapons in man's constant effort to improve his environment is a characteristic of almost every period; in fact, in varying degrees, of every period. Machines have been used throughout history as an extension of handicraft—for saving labour and performing new operations within the framework of the handicraft order. With the advent of power production the machine acquired new values, as something more than an implement, in the sociological, industrial sphere; and it is these values which make the new order, the machine age, different in kind, not merely in degree of utilization of machinery, from any previous age.

Gropius has summed up this essential change, as seen in manufacture, in saying that 'the difference between industry and handicraft is due far less to the different nature of the tools employed in each than to subdivision of labour in the one and undivided control by a single workman in the other'. That is the key to the difference between the products proper to the handicraft age, which persisted in its own right until the beginning of the nineteenth century (and persisted beyond in the shape of resistant movements and reactions against a changing order), and the products proper to the machine age, which is the present one.

The changed conditions of which this difference is symptomatic are gradually bringing about, as a reflection of the order that determined it and as a criterion of our success in assimilating the machine, a new machine aesthetic, un-

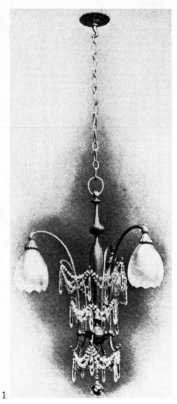

1

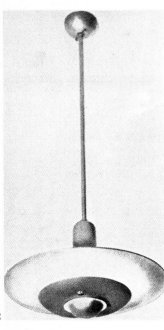

2

1, 2 Typical of the products of the Modern Movement, 2, as distinct from those of the previous generation, 1, was reliance on simple shapes deriving from the machine instead of on superimposed ornament derived from an earlier handicraft epoch. The two light fittings are from Best and Lloyd's 1916 and 1935 catalogues

selfconsciously developing, not being imposed from without. To this new aesthetic the opportunities of rationalization that the machine brings, the progressive impersonalization of design, the new emphasis on the product rather than on the process of making it and the discovery of the abstract aesthetic virtues of machines themselves have all contributed. The difference is, in brief, that which lies between a humanistic aesthetic and an abstract one.

The search for order

It might be asked why the necessity for a new aesthetic, which almost implies a new philosophy, should arise from the mere application of power to industry. What fundamental change does power production imply that goes beyond even the material and sociological issues referred to? The answer is that the application of power to industry is itself only one material manifestation of a fundamental historical process—the application of science to life. The foundations of the new order of civilization were laid, as Lewis Mumford points out in his book *Technics and Civilization*, by the school of natural philosophers of the seventeenth century. Descartes, Galileo, Newton, Pascal first saw the universe as a system in which order predominated over disorder. They made a search for the underlying order the function of experimental science, and they established the technique of laboratory research which is the foundation of scientific progress. Without the conviction of an underlying order none but a purely empirical thought is possible.

The emergence of a sense of order or routine is indeed the basis of technological evolution, together with the application of scientific thought to succeeding branches of knowledge. For the origins of this revolution in thought we must go back still earlier; to the dawn, in fact, of the objective consciousness. As Mumford suggests, the elementary factors were the development of the sense of time and space. The routine of the monastery was probably the first manifestation of a sense of time as a repetitive progression. With that routine the invention of the clock is linked, and it is significant that throughout subsequent history the clock as a piece of mechanism is nearly always more perfect than any other contemporary contrivances. 'The monasteries', to use Mumford's own words, 'helped to give human enterprise the regular collective beat and rhythm of the machine; for the clock is not merely a means of keeping track of the hours but of synchronizing the actions of men. . . . It dissociated time from human events and helped create the belief in an independent world of mathematically measurable sequences: the special world of science'.

The other essential stage in the approach to the new intellectual curiosity was concerned with the sense of space. To the medieval mind space and time were unrelated. Quoting Mumford again:

'The word anachronism is meaningless when applied to medieval art: it is only when one related events to a co-ordinated frame of time and space that being out of time or being untrue to time became disconcerting. Because of this separation of time and space, things could appear and disappear suddenly, unaccountably: the dropping of a ship below the horizon no more needed an explanation than the dropping of a demon down the chimney. Objects swam into vision and sank out of it with something of the same mystery in which the coming and going of adults affects the experience of young children, whose first graphic efforts so much resemble in their organization the world of the medieval artist. The connecting link between events was the cosmic and religious order. . . . Between the fourteenth and the seventeenth centuries a revolutionary change in the conception of space took place in Western Europe. Space as a hierarchy of values was replaced by space as a system of magnitudes. One of the indications of this new orientation was the closer study of the relations of objects in space and the discovery of the laws of perspective and the systematic organization of pictures within the new frame fixed by the foreground, the horizon and the vanishing point. . . . The measured space of the picture reinforced the measured time of the clock. Within this ideal network of space and time all events now took place. . . . In

3

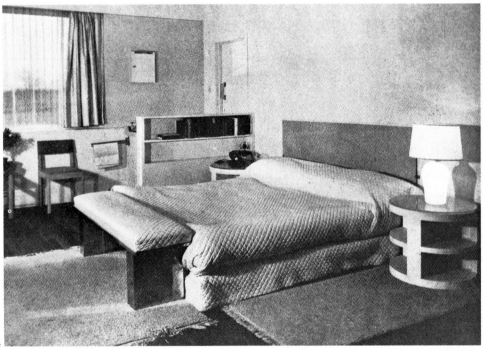

3, 4 Besides the simplicity that came from machine processes, modern conditions demanded a background of simplicity as a relief from the perpetual succession of stimuli in everyday life. Simplicity of surface also brought out the intrinsic qualities of materials that elaboration destroyed. *Above* a typical late Victorian bedroom; *below* a 1930s bedroom (architect, Guy Morgan; furniture designed by J. Duncan Miller)

4

Renascence space the existence of objects must be accounted for: their passage through time and space is a clue to their appearance at any particular moment in any particular place. . . . The very existence of such an order was an incentive to explore it and fill up the parts that were unknown'.

It is not necessary to trace the whole growth of this emergence of order and detachment through several centuries, by way of the development of commerce and finance—themselves dependent on order; by way of the military arts—in which are found the earliest manifestations of orderly planning and of the manipulation of a number of identical units; or through the study of astronomy— the identification of a mechanical system, serving as an incentive to the creation of system in everything; all leading up to the philosophic conception already referred to of the whole universe in terms of system. The first steps having been taken the rest follows; but these first steps are the keys to the whole contemporary way of thought and activity. The basis of the modern aesthetic is knowledge and system, from which spring all its characteristics of clarity and exactness and its refusal to be content with what is only approximate or ill-defined.

The problem of assimilation

What is known as the industrial revolution was a material application of that world of scientific order that was defined by the school of natural philosophy, made possible by the mechanical discoveries that concentration on the factual aspects of existence led to. The important contemporary factor is, as I have suggested, power production, which is a further step in the establishment of an absolute system. The machine, instead of being an extension of his own faculties becomes, for man, a mechanical equivalent of nature; a physical manifestation of the world of order and scientific thinking, giving him a sense, in inventing power machinery, of himself contributing to the orderliness of the universe. The machine itself becomes organic—and coincident with this realization, it is interesting to note, is the disappearance of organic or naturalistic form from the machine and its products.

At the same time power enabled the machine, through the process of specialization of labour observed in Gropius's definition, to make its other great contribution to civilization—the technique of co-operative enterprise. The products of the machine are no longer, as with the handicraft machines, the result of a single operation (or of several closely related operations), but the complex result of a whole co-operative industrial system, in which interference by the personal factor, after the first creative or selective impulse, is reduced to a minimum.

A quality common to all periods of good design is that which Herbert Read has called 'a certain community of feeling and imagination'; a kinship between the parts and the whole prevailing order. Present-day chaos in the province of manufactured objects, of architecture as well as the everyday things for which architecture is the setting, is due simply to the absence of this underlying consistency. The more the complicated organization of modern society approaches the calculated rhythms of a machine the more unbearable are the examples of non-conformity of parts of the new order with the whole. The problem today is to bring about a new co-ordination of the arts, manufacture, architecture and planning as well as of social conditions and politics in terms of the new machine order, which we have just established as the basis of the contemporary system. Neither the intellectual renaissance of the seventeenth century nor the industrial revolution of the nineteenth will be complete until this re-synthesis has been achieved.

Modern characteristics

Conformity with a new set of conditions—with a new world of experience—means the adoption of a new aesthetic. The nature of this machine aesthetic is perhaps best defined by examining the typical qualities of such objects and designs as have already been produced to conform with it; the common characteristics, in fact, of modern design, particularly in the way they differ from those of handicraft design; the new vocabulary of the Modern Movement.

First of all, by a machine aesthetic is not intended, of course, an aesthetic admiration for machines as substitute works of art. It implies appreciation of those qualities that have been introduced into art by the machine. It means perception of the machine art-forms and acceptance of the modification of the handicraft art-forms brought about by the machine. It means a changed vocabulary in conformity with the new unity of values.

What are the characteristic terms of this new vocabulary? The first is simplicity. Simplicity is almost a prerequisite in modern design for several reasons. One, the least important, that we are undergoing a reaction against the elaborate ornamentation of the nineteenth century—a subjective and ephemeral reason for simplicity which would only have importance if the Modern Movement were being interpreted as a new style, similar in kind to the many conflicting styles of the nineteenth century, instead of as the natural outcome of a new scale of organization. Secondly comes the growing complication of modern existence, resulting in our being subjected to a perpetual succession of stimuli, to counteract which a negative rather than a competitive environment is essential. The products

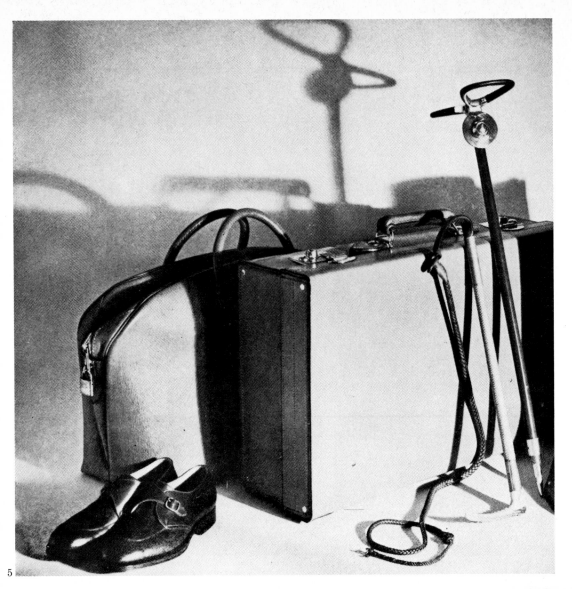

5

6

7

8

9

5 The characteristics of modern design were apparent in many objects in the everyday environment. Their designer concentrated on the economical, logical use of the appropriate material and their forms reached aesthetic perfection by the progressive modification of a type over long periods. Such objects as these, had considerable influence in forming a typical contemporary idiom. A collection of leather goods (by courtesy of Fortnum and Mason) in which standards of finish and craftsmanship create their own aesthetic values

6 Laboratory glass by Chance Brothers

7 Porcelain laboratory vessels by Doulton and the Worcester Royal Porcelain Company: ideal examples of the aesthetic advantages of standardization

8 A portable griller, exemplifying the design influence of practical household equipment

9 A strong-room door by John Tann: the beauty of mechanical precision

10

11

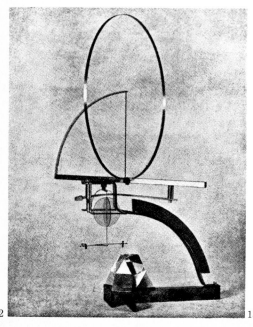

12

13

136

of handicraft were designed to hold interest; those of machines to distribute it. Thirdly, the effect of our greater knowledge of materials. Knowledge of materials means interest in materials for their own sake, and greater respect for them. Simple surfaces, of a nature appropriate to mechanical processes, take the place of applied ornament, which destroys the integrity of the material. Finally, probably the most important cause of simplicity in modern design is an even more immediate result of the application of power to industry—of the source of energy being divorced from the control of it: the loss of the virtue that attaches to complication in execution. In the handicraft period technical virtuosity, resulting in elaboration of forms and detail, was an expression of the personal skill of the worker. With emphasis transferred from the worker to the work done the urge to virtuosity disappears. The machine has destroyed the belief that a thing is more beautiful because more expertly made or because more difficult to make. It has not destroyed the virtue of craftsmanship. It has liberated the craftsman from the routine of production, and transferred his special qualities from the process to the object.

Given that the present rather purist phase of modern design is still one of transition between the handicraft and the machine aesthetic, it is natural to ask whether the disappearance of ornament is only temporary. There is no reason why a vocabulary of machine ornament should not emerge, though ornament in the sense of elaboration is hardly compatible with the compulsion to simplicity. It is more likely to take the form of emphasis and variation of surface provided by an incidental machine process—taking as a precedent textiles rather than, say, carvings—together with refinements of colour and surface. Finely finished colour and surface can be their own ornament.

Those English designers of the late nineteenth century, who are now regarded as pioneers of the Modern Movement, Voysey and Mackintosh, and Van de Velde and the leaders of the *Kunstgewerbe* movement on the Continent, saw the need for the new simplicity, but pursued it by returning to the primitive or vernacular instrument or method rather than in the perfection of the machine method.

The machine as precedent

The abandonment of the craftsman's own personal part in execution, as distinct from his influence on design, leads us to the second modern characteristic: emphasis on the impersonal. Modern design concerns itself with generic types rather than with *ad hoc* products. The search for the standard or type form is the paramount task of the modern designer. This characteristic is, of course, closely bound up with the question of standardization—the factual corollary of mass production—the most typical contribution of the industrial revolution to everyday life. The impersonal nature of modern design has, however, other causes than the impersonal nature of the machine process. The chief of these is the example, as a design precedent, of the machine itself. That an efficient machine is *ipso facto* a work of art is a belief, that of pure functionalism, that cannot be seriously sustained. Many machines (including in that category works of engineering) are also works of art, owing probably to unconscious selection of alternative solutions for aesthetic reasons on the part of the designs; but if machines generally are not works of art their nature underlies modern works of art. Study of machines as objects and analysis of their several beauties have added many qualities to the designer's vocabulary; among these is an appreciation of the formal, abstract relationships of machine forms. There is no need to point out the debt to the machine owed by certain schools in the so-called 'fine' arts, notably the Cubists and the Constructivists. Both the machine and the artist have been engaged in resolving the organic world into its essential geometrical elements. The constructions of such artists as Pevsner, Gabo and Moholy-Nagy are in fact machines that happen to be non-utilitarian in the purely productive sense. The possibility of their existence, incidentally, points *per contra* to the weakness of the 'beauty out of pure function' theory. So many of the formal values of the machine have little connection with the machine in operation. The distinction has to be maintained between the machine as an aesthetic object and the machine as a source of aesthetic form. Literal functionalism claims the validity of the former—given practical efficiency—although, as Geoffrey Scott has worded it (ironically enough, in *The Architecture of Humanism*): 'Forms impose their own aesthetic character on a duly sensitive attention, quite independently of what we may know, or not know, about them'.

In rejecting the simple philosophy of pure functionalism, modern design also avoids the functional exhibitionism that is its aggravated form: the conscientious display of the means, and the unnatural emphasis on characteristic forms. The misleading phrase, 'to express its purpose', is made the excuse for a new, a historical brand of stylization.

A sharpening of our perception of abstract formal relationships, through the observation of machines and machine-made things, is accompanying the disappearance of the handicraft quality—the personal contribution of the skilled workman. Design, as with culture, is becoming abstract rather than humanistic.

Standardization

The admirable definition of standardization made by Gropius is quoted at the beginning of this article. Elsewhere in the book in which the definition appears, *The New Architecture and the Bauhaus*, he points out that the tendencey to reduce unlimited variety to a number of type forms is typical of a high standard of civilization in most periods. Power production and its equivalent in terms of work, mass production, have made standardization applicable to almost every sphere of design.

It cannot be too often repeated that standardization, a word that is often misapprehended, does not mean monotony or sameness. It means, rather, a liberation of objects with certain intrinsic formal characteristics from accumulations of the ephemeral and the inessential. Standardization is a pre-requisite of mass production and mass production is typical of power technique, but examples of standardization—even of mass production—are by no means unknown in the handicraft era—quite apart from the fundamental standardization of goods in the form of money. The commonest example is, of course, in printing, the printed page being a perfect mass product. The military arts produced the earliest examples of mass production in industry in the same way that they were the birth centre of much technical invention. Mumford cites the military uniform as the first large-scale demand for absolutely standardized goods, and the mass production of muskets at the end of the eighteenth century (including the standardization of interchangeable parts) and the even earlier assembly of wooden ships out of standardized units by Bentham and Brunel as important innovations. He also instances the parade ground itself as the prototype of modern industrial organization, with its tendency to turn the individual into an impersonal unit, personal determination on part of which is a hindrance to efficient action instead of an aid to it. Indeed, many characteristics of the modern aesthetic existed separately in various phases of the historical periods; for example, the tendency towards dehumanization and mechanization of labour in Egypt, and the Hellenic impulse towards clarity coupled with a progressive geometrical refinement.

Allied with the implications of standardization is what might be termed the aesthetic virtue of regimentation: the appreciation, typical of the machine age and deriving from machine forms, of the series or the group of identical units. The search for order already referred to is reflected in the delight taken in the regularity of sheer repetition. This addition to the aesthetic vocabulary has probably been increased by air travel and high building—by the bird's-eye view, in which such repetition of identical forms commonly ocurs, and which gives a toy-like quality to organic objects repeated to a minute scale that conduces again to the typical objective vision.

New appreciation

The quality of exactness demanded of modern design has already been referred to as a further reflection of the new order which is based on system, the search for knowledge and order having resulted in dissatisfaction with what is approximate and indefinite. The appeal of vagueness and of the picturesque gives place to the aesthetic satisfaction of the mathematical equation. This characteristic of exactness is also the product of the machine itself, whose intrinsic beauties have added to our vocabulary of beauties, and to the high degree of mechanical exactness possible with machine technique. The increased use of machines has, further, increased our appreciation of both their formal and functional virtues. As an example of the latter, the satisfaction to be obtained from driving an efficient motor-car is without doubt partly aesthetic. The surgeon's praise of 'a beautiful operation' is by no means the misuse of the word 'beauty' it might appear to be. The demand for the same aesthetic sensations elsewhere has encouraged qualities of precision and economy in modern design. In architecture theatrical effects of mass, weight and so on, give way to effects of poise and lightness. Accurate structural elimination is the contemporary virtue instead of imposing structural solidity.

This question of solidity brings us to the consideration of the 'factor of safety'. Our greater knowledge of the limitations and capabilities of materials enables us to use them with greater economy and accuracy. There is no longer need for oversizing to allow for ignorance. We no longer believe that exact sizing is not worth the labour of exact calculation. For this advance the refinements of aeroplane design amongst other things have been greatly responsible.

Our whole attitude to the right use of materials has also undergone a certain amount of change. Previously we knew about materials in terms of our own experience with them; we had handled wood and stone—even steel—on a small scale, and knew instinctively when their substance was adequate on a larger scale. In the case of the new synthetic materials, of which reinforced concrete is typical, their properties are not within the bounds of common experience and have to be taken on trust: a new influence in the impersonalization of design. This change does not mean that knowledge of structural properties can be a substitute for visual satisfaction with their adequacy. Geoffrey Scott's reservation from 'The Mechanical Fallacy', already quoted, is still valid; but we have to adapt our perceptions to the abstract values of new materials to the extent that they differ from the handicraft values of the old.

Exactness, cleanness, precision of form and finish are the representative modern qualities. They are present in machines themselves as conditions of the machines' functional efficiency. They are present in the products of the machine, partly because the processes of machine manufacture produce these qualities, and partly also in imitation of the machine, from the use of those art forms which study of the machine has contributed. The prevalence of 'streamlining', for example, is an illustration of the influence of a mechanical idiom; its influence being seen in stationary objects where aerodynamic considerations are quite irrelevant.

The distinction must here be made between this influence, which is the unconscious assimilation of an idiom common to our mechanical surroundings, and the deliberate application of a so-called 'modern' idiom: the stylization of modernity producing the *moderne* or 'modernistic', wherein the building or object has applied to it (or is forced into) certain shapes for eclectic or decorative reasons. The result is, of course, no more modern, in the true sense, than my foot—in fact, a good deal less. In the same way that abstract art, directly it loses what might be called the tension or concentration that gives it its aesthetic significance, becomes empty pattern-making without vitality, the vitality of the modern machine product depends on its retaining some of the formal significance of the machine, not on its imitating a few superficial characteristics.

In the nineteenth century this preoccupation with superficial style, this habit of capriciously varying the shape or colour of an object entirely apart from any attempt to improve it, either in economy or efficiency, was a typical instance of refusal to accept the new order of the machine. It provided an alternative avenue of escape to that of the antiquarian and the student of the primitive and the vernacular. It made design the slave of fashion, from which its antithesis, standardization, now releases it. At the same time recovery from the partial anasthesia which the prevalent ugliness of the nineteenth century induced in the senses should result, in time, in the sharpening of our sensitivity to simple relationships and proportions, to take the place of the connoisseur's unaesthetic interest in variation of style.

Changing values

Certain qualities belong essentially to the handicraft age. One of these is rarity. The advent of the machine has devaluated rarity. The craftsman produced single objects; the craftsman-designer now produces objects as patterns, to be reproduced in infinite numbers to the same standard of workmanship. Along with rarity goes antiquity, like rarity the concern of the connoisseur, whose appreciation is based primarily on historical knowledge and education. To antiquity we prefer newness; not for its own sake because it will embody the latest fashion, but because it will embody the most complete solution and the latest technical improvements. The machine is responsible for the purification of aesthetics from the irrelevances of archaic taste.

The disappearance of the false romanticism of the antique, with which is associated the cult of the curio, does not mean that romanticism as a spiritual or intellectual quality is incompatible with mechanization. Romanticism as preached by William Morris and by Goethe, and as practised by many Arts and Crafts movements, as an alternative to the machine, no longer has the same appeal. The impulses that provoked it, as an action of escape, are catered for in our broadening machine aesthetic. Turner first saw the possibilities of romance in the world of machinery, though he tried to translate them into terms of his predecessors' interest in the merely picturesque. Kipling, much later, revealed the same possibilities in literature.

When it signifies achievement of aesthetic satisfaction through the exact allocation of means to function an essential modern virtue is economy. It is the quality that pure engineering has in common with architecture. But when it signifies the smallest cost for which an object can be produced it is aesthetically quite irrelevant; though it is a common fallacy that cheapness as a virtue is somehow concerned with aesthetics. It often happens, however, that the necessity for cheapness compels the designer to discard the handicraft qualities of technical virtuosity; thereby giving the product aesthetic merit as it were by mistake, and it often happens that high cost in an object is an indirect criticism of its mechanical integrity, though it may also be an indication of its designer having aimed at an absolute rather than an economic standard of quality.

The designer

The various characteristics of machine design outlined above demand two qualities in the designer: the objective outlook of a mind unprejudiced by a stock of ready-made solutions, and a sympathy with the whole technological order that will give to his work the necessary community of direction with this order. In addition to these are, of course, the craftsmanship qualities of familiarity with his materials, machines and processes. It might be felt, with the constant reference above to an aesthetic dominated by the machine, that the design itself was determined by the machine: that a machine aesthetic tended to substitute technology for art. The answer is twofold: first, that the machine itself is a human product, undergoing a constant process of humanization; secondly, that the designer's primary function is the civilization of technology, with the machine as a means to an end; in this complicated era, an end of order and equilibrium.

In machine design the original pattern is everything; the rest an automatic process. The whole responsibility rests, therefore, on the designing room. This

14

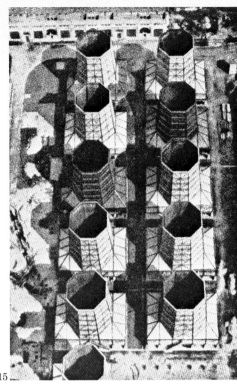

15

14, 15 The typical modern virtue of regimentation, the aesthetic value of the serial repetition of identical forms, is displayed in 15, an air-view of a battery of cooling towers. The photograph also suggests the extent to which the development of air-photography assisted the appreciation of this quality. 14 shows the same quality to a smaller scale, apparent in the pattern value of the keys of an accounting machine, by the National Cash Register Company

becomes less a studio, in which paper designs are evolved on a capricious basis of appearance, than a laboratory of research in which the methods of scientific analysis are employed (but employed by a scientist under the influence of aesthetic sensibility) in the apt utilization of the machine and the perfection of standard forms.

Gropius says: 'Handicrafts and industry may be regarded as opposite poles that are gradually approaching each other. The former have already begun to change their traditional nature. In the future the field of handicrafts will be found to lie mainly in the preparatory stages of evolving experimental new type-forms for mass-production'.

The world men carry in their heads

The aeroplane is a representative modern product. The average piece of architecture, furniture or household equipment is not. To say that the furniture should be more like the aeroplane is so incomplete a statement as to be misleading in its implications: but it should have an affinity with the aeroplane, as the argument of this article sets out to show, because of its dependence on the same conditions of machine production. It can be examined in the light of the same aesthetic, and it has its own duty of contributing to the unity and common direction of the contemporary environment. It must reflect the real, essential world of scientific order that underlies our civilization: the 'world men carry in their heads', of which the aeroplane is a typical inhabitant.

The business of the Modern Movement is to bridge the gulf, as Marcel Breuer has expressed it, 'between appearance and reality'. This gulf is only widened by the make-believe of historical escapade, by the trite formulae of period styles, or by efforts to perpetuate the obsolescent culture of an earlier epoch. We have to start with power and the machine, which dominate our existence. 'Our capacity to go beyond the machine', to quote Mumford once more, 'rests upon our power to assimilate the machine. Until we have absorbed the lessons of objectivity, impersonality, neutrality, the lessons of the mechanical realm, we cannot go further in our development toward the more richly organic, the more profoundly human'.

The rational and the functional

by Geoffrey Broadbent

Geoffrey Broadbent outlines the development of the word 'rational' and contrasts it with the use of 'function' and 'functional'. Setting out clearly the history of rational ideas, he then questions the validity of a number of Modern Movement buildings as 'functional' solutions to their programme.

Most of us have reasonably clear ideas as to what we mean by 'rational' and 'functional'. A rational person is someone who thinks things out, coolly and clearly before acting. He will apply logical thought to every situation, often at the expense of spontaneity, intuition, feeling or other 'human' impulse. He will be a scientist rather than an artist. A functional object on the other hand will be one which serves its purpose, simply and directly. The efficiency with which it does its job certainly will not have been compromised for the sake of appearance, although if it has been designed properly, it will undoubtedly *look* functional. In an ideal world, of course, 'rational' designers would produce 'functional' objects, and indeed, much that has happened in the development of architecture and architectural theory can be seen as attempts to make it more 'scientific', more rational and *therefore* more functional.

Banham actually argues that the idea of functionalism was by no means 'significantly present' in the minds of those who developed modern architecture in the 20s. Indeed, he suggests that the first person to use it 'consequentially' was Albert Sartoris in his *Gli elementi dell'architettura funzionale* of 1932. Initially Sartoris had intended to use another title; possibly *L'architettura razionale* but Le Corbusier suggested the alternative to him in a letter which Sartoris reprints as a preface to his book:

'The title of your book is limited; it is a real fault . . . to put the word *Rational* on one side of the barricade, and leave only the word *Academic* to be put on the other. Instead of Rational, say *Functional . . .*'.

Towards the end of his life, however, Le Corbusier was to repudiate all that. He says in some most revealing records made at the end of his life (1965):

'Functional architecture? That's a journalist's gossip . . . It is a redundancy. Architecture *is* functional. If it isn't functional, then what is it? Rubbish!

Yet as Hitchcock and Johnson showed in the exhibition and book by which they launched the term 'International Style' (1932, probably at the suggestion of Alfred Ban) a very recognizable functionalist attitude to architecture *had* emerged in the 1920s. In the section of their book actually entitled 'Functionalism' they discuss the question of function versus aesthetics:

'Leading European critics, particularly Sigfried Giedion, claim with some justice that architecture has such immense practical problems to deal with in the modern world that aesthetic questions must take a secondary place in architectural criticism. Architects like Hannes Meyer go further. They claim that interest in proportions or in problems of design for their own sake is still an unfortunate remnant of nineteenth-century ideology. For these men it is an absurdity to talk about the modern style in terms of aesthetics at all. If a building provides adequately, completely, and without compromise for its purpose, it is to them a good building, regardless of its appearance'.

Laugier's primitive hut (1753) showing the columns, beams and pedimented roof which for him constituted the whole of architecture

They go on to say:

'Since the works of the European Functionalists usually fall within the limits of the International Style, they may be claimed among its representatives ... Naturally these doctrinaires achieve works of aesthetic distinction less often than some others which practice the art of architecture as assiduously as they pursue the science of building'.

And certainly within four years of this Nikolaus Pevsner was quite clear that the *one true* style of modern architecture was founded 'in science and technology, in social science and *rational* planning' (my italics). He and Giedion were quite clear that the first example of this functional architecture was the office building that Gropius and Meyer had built for Karl Benscheidt's Fagus factory at Alfeld an der Leine in 1911.

It was 'Functional' in Pevsner's view because it was simple, rectangular and flat roofed and also because, as he put it 'for the first time a façade is conceived in glass. The supporting girders are reduced to narrow bands of steel ...'. None of this is true as I have shown elsewhere. Pevsner was describing what he *thought* the building should have been like; as I have also shown elsewhere this *image* became, for most of us, the basis of functional architecture.

Having thus defined what functional architecture should be, Pevsner then directed his attention to its opposite, that wilful indulgence on the part of architects which he called Expressionism. As Pevsner put it:

'Expressionism was a short interlude, following early Gropius and preceding the mature Gropius of the Bauhaus buildings at Dessau, the mature Le Corbusier for the villas of the mid twenties, and the mature Mies van der Rohe of the German exhibition pavilion at Barcelona. We are now in the middle of a second such interlude, the one for which Le Corbusier (with such recent buildings as the Pilgrimage chapel at Ronchamp) and the Brazilians are responsible. Like Gaudí between Sullivan and Behrens, Loos and others after 1900, like expressionism between the Fagus and the Bauhaus buildings, so late Le Corbusier and the structural acrobatics of the Brazilians and all those who imitate them ... are attempts to satisfy the craving of architects for individual expression, the craving of the public for the surprising and the fantastic, and for an escape out of reality into a fairy world'.

In Pevsner's view clearly, this is thoroughly irrational, and it could not be more unfunctional, but when it comes to actual buildings one cannot help feeling that Pevsner attaches the word 'Functional' to an *appearance* of buildings, rather than to the ways in which they actually perform.

Indeed it is surprisingly difficult to find a coherent and consistent definition of 'Functionalism' in *any* of the writings which refer to it as a phenomenon of modern architecture, although as we shall see Alfred Roth comes close. We ought, in any case, to go rather further back, for as De Zurko shows the functionalist idea is of ancient origin. For it is well over 2000 years ago that Plato recorded a dialogue between Aristippus and Socrates, in the course of which the latter asks the fundamental question:

'You think, do you, that goodness is one thing and beauty another? Do you not understand that things are beautiful—and good—in accordance with the same criteria. Virtue is not "good" in relation to certain things and "beautiful" in relation to others ... men's bodies look beautiful—and good—according to the same things, namely in respect of those things for which they are useful'.

Most of us these days, I suppose, would agree with him—that a well-built, suntanned, obviously active body is more beautiful than a pale, gross, flabby and slothful one. Yet Rubens, obviously, took quite a different view; and indeed the ideal of human beauty has varied greatly from place to place and from time to time in history. Beauty in this case obviously is in the eye (and brain) of the beholder; it

1 Gropius and Meyer: Fagus works office building, Alfeld an der Leine (1911)

is something we learn for our own place and time.

But Socrates was using the human body to make a general point: that the beauty of any object can be measured directly in terms of its efficiency. This worried Aristippus who thought he could persuade Socrates to rethink his proposition by taking it to a logical conclusion:

'Is a dung basket beautiful then?'

Which is exactly what Socrates had been hoping for; he replied:

'Certainly, and a golden shield is ugly if the one is well made for its purpose and the other badly made'.

For Socrates therefore a general principle of functionalism applied to the human body, to dung baskets and golden shields, so it is hardly surprising that he extended them also to architecture, or rather to the house, of which he said:

'To summarise, the most pleasurable and the most beautiful house is that in which the owner can find pleasant retreat in all seasons (of the year) and can (also) protect his possessions'.

It is interesting to note the criteria which Socrates applied in judging the effective functioning, and therefore the beauty, of a house. He looked for two kinds of physical protection: comfort for the owner and also security for his goods. I have suggested elsewhere that protection from the external climate (environmental filtering) is perhaps the first and most important function of all building, although, of course, it is by no means the only one. We shall consider it within a broader context later, but it will be interesting for now to compare Socrates's prescription for architecture with another one from classical architecture, namely that rather more comprehensive and more widely quoted definition of Vitruvius, which is familiar to most English-speaking readers in Sir Henry Wotton's version: 'Well building hath three conditions: Commoditie, Firmenes and Delight'. The building must contain appropriate accommodation, it must stand up and must delight. Vitruvius himself was careful to point out that delight was far more than merely a visual matter; good building would also help us keep warm in winter, cool in summer, provide us with good acoustics, and so on.

Vitruvius's prescription for good, functional architecture of course has reverberated through history. The medieval cathedrals were based on it (Frankl, Conant); so were, not only the buildings of the Renaissance, but also the treatises of the Renaissance on architecture, such as those by Alberti, Palladio and most of their successors, up to and including the present day. The crucial point here is not so much any detailed interpretation as the intention to build 'well', that is to make architecture which functions according to Vitruvius. In an ideal world obviously, one would produce 'functional' architecture by designing 'rationally', but what in this context is rational?

While the beginnings of rationalism obviously are to be found in ancient Greek philosophy, the founding-father, for our purposes, can be taken as René Descartes (1596–1650), the French philosopher who says (1631) that he found himself one day as a soldier in the Bavarian army, meditating inside a great stove. It was warm in there and free from interruption. His thoughts began to run on certain problems of architectural design, of which he says:

'. . . one of the first thoughts that came into my mind was that there is often less perfection in what has been put together bit by bit, and by different masters, than in the work of a single hand. Thus we see how a building the construction of which has been undertaken and completed by a single architect, is usually superior to those that many have tried to restore by making use of old walls which have been built for other purposes'.

Clearly Descartes had little respect for team working, nor had he much eye for picturesque irregularity. He goes on:

'So, too, those old places which, beginning as villages, have developed in the course of time into great towns, are generally so ill-proportioned in comparison with those an engineer can design at will in an orderly fashion that, even though the buildings taken severally often display as much art as in other places, or even more, yet the disorder is such with a large house here and a small one there, and the streets all tortuous and uneven, that the whole place seems to be the product of chance rather than the design of men who use their reason'.

So in town planning also, Descartes preferred the new, fortified towns such as Nancy (1588) and Charleville (1605), conceived as they had been by the mind of one engineer, to medieval towns, such as Chartres or Laon where the twisting narrow streets present evidence to this day of growth and change over the centuries. But Descartes did more than speculate. He took this imaginary model—of the architect in firm control of a unified design—and tried to apply the designer's methods, or what he conceived to be the design method, to the ordering of his own thoughts. He worked out a set of rules, by which his own thoughts might be disciplined. They are as follows:

'The first rule was to accept as true nothing that I did not know to be self-evidently so: that is to say, to avoid carefully precipitancy and prejudice, and to apply my

OF
THE ELEMENTS
OF
ARCHITECTVRE.

The I. part.

N *Architecture* as in all o-
ther *Operatiue* Arts, the
end muſt direct the *Ope-*
ration.

The *end* is to build well.

Well building hath three Conditions.
Commoditie, Firmenes, and *Delight.*
A common diuiſion among the De-
liuerers of this *Art,* though I know not
A   how,

judgements to nothing but that which showed itself so clearly and distinctly to my mind that I should never have occasion to doubt it.

The second was to divide each difficulty I should examine into as many parts as possible, and as would be required the better to solve it.

The third was to conduct my thoughts in an orderly fashion, starting with what was simplest and easiest to know, and rising little by little to the knowledge of the most complex, even supposing an order where there is no natural precedence among the objects of knowledge.

The last rule was to make so complete an enumeration of the links in an argument and to pass them all so thoroughly under review, that I could be sure I had missed nothing'.

But the problem, of course, is to decide exactly what shows itself 'so clearly and distinctly to (the) mind that (one) should never have occasion to doubt it'.

In his meditations Descartes describes the 'methodology of doubt' by which he tested all his former opinions. 'Now truth', he says, 'seems to have come to me hitherto, either directly or indirectly, from my senses. But the senses in my experience, are sometimes deceptive; and it is but prudent not to trust entirely to those who have once deceived us'. The nature of these deceptions was such that, at times, he found it impossible to distinguish between what was 'real' and was 'unreal'; what was actually happening and what only seemed to be happening. As he put it:

'How often has it happened to me to dream at night that I was here, in this place, dressed and seated by the fire, when all the time I was lying naked in my bed . . . and when I reflect upon the matter more closely, I see clearly that there are no conclusive signs by which to distinguish between our waking and our sleeping moments, that I am dumbfounded, and my confusion is such that I can almost believe myself at this moment'.

But whether he was asleep or not, the objects he saw bore certain constant resemblances to each other; eyes, hands, heads or whole bodies existed in reality: the illusions he saw in sleep were merely coloured representations of them. They could not be formed in any other way, for however bizarre a painter's representation may be, the only thing he can do is to make new assemblages of things which he knows already, having seen them in real life. He still uses the colours of reality. Colour, therefore, is a universal entity, so is everything in 'corporeal' nature: the shapes or figures of objects, their quantity, size and number, the space in which they exist, the time through which they endure, and so on. Sciences such as arithmetic and geometry, deal with simple and universal truths such as relationships between objects, rather than with the objects themselves. Such sciences therefore possess a number of manifest truths; two and three *always* make five, a square *always* has four sides, a triangle three. Such facts therefore are universal and indubitable.

'When, for example, I imagine a triangle, although perhaps there is not, and never has been, any place in which it can exist outside my mind, yet this triangle possesses a nature, or form, or essence, which is immutable and eternal, which I have not invented, and which in no way depends on my mind. This follows from the fact that it is possible to demonstrate various properties of the triangle, as that its three angles are equal to two right angles . . . even though, when I first imagined the triangle, I had no thought of these properties, which cannot therefore have been invented by me'.

It could be suggested, as Descartes says, that the *idea* of a triangle reached him through his senses; that from time to time he has actually seen triangles, or bodies which were triangular in form. But he finds that explanation inadequate:

'The fact is that I can conceive a mass of other figures, about which there can never be any suspicion that they have come under the observation of my senses, but of which I can demonstrate various properties touching their essence as I can in the case of the triangle'.

If he can *conceive* such properties without ever having seen such objects, then that must be true of other things. He has a right to believe that anything he knows 'clearly and distinctly' therefore must be true.

The basic rationalist belief therefore is that things exist, and can be known to exist, without any evidence whatever from the senses. The senses are unreliable, may be deluded (of course that is true as we very well know, if only from the range now available of optical illusions). The only truths therefore are those which one *knows* deep down within oneself. Once formed, of course, they can be developed by logical and mathematical processes. Thus much more elaborate truths are formed—one knows that these also are correct because the logical processes which went into their formulation were consistent.

The rival stream in philosophy of course has been empiricism which, like rationalism, goes back to Greek roots, although for our purposes it will be useful to identify the founding-father as John Locke (1632–1704), whose chief work on the subject, the *Essay Concerning Human Understanding* was published in 1690.

All ideas, he says, are based on information received by the senses and subjected then to reflection. The only 'ideas' a child can bring into the world at birth must be those relating to physiological necessities: hunger, thirst, warmth and possibly pain. These form the bases on which all subsequent ideas are built up; as Locke puts it:

'Let us . . . suppose the mind to be . . . as . . . white paper, void of all characters, without any ideas; how comes it to be furnished? Whence comes it by that vast store, which the busy and boundless fancy of man has painted on it . . .? Whence has it all the materials of reasons and knowledge? To this I answer, in one word, from experience: in that all our knowledge is founded . . . Our observations, employed either about external . . . objects, or about the internal operations of our minds, perceived and reflected upon by ourselves, is that which supplies our understandings with all the materials of thinking . . .'.

We see, hear smell and otherwise sense things, on which basis we recognize objects and build up concepts such as 'yellow, white, heat, cold, soft, hard, bitter, sweet' and so on. Having perceived objects outside ourselves and observed such qualities, we learn what words are attached to them by those around us. Once our ideas have been formed, we are able to operate on them by such processes as thinking, doubting, believing, reasoning, knowing, willing and so on, which help us to build up our understanding.

Of course there is much more to empiricism than that, but from our point of view, the fundamental difference from rationalism is that empiricism relies primarily on the evidence of the senses, rather than on what one 'knows' to be true.

The battle between rationalism and empiricism has raged over the past 300 years. Each has taken on new guises from time to time—phenomenology and behaviourism are the more recent versions. There have been attempts such as Piaget's to reconcile them. He points out, rightly, that they are both inadequate because they both confine themselves to the level of mental process.

But bodily functions are also crucial to our understanding of how as separate entities, we 'fit' into the world. We find that by pushing them in a particular sequence we can *cause* other objects to move, thus we begin to learn the bases of logical processes and causality. But Piaget does not and cannot produce a synthesis and it is doubtful if anyone ever will. The dialogue between them in any case is so fascinating, so revealing of things about ourselves, that the dialectic between them is well worth preserving.

I suggested in my *Design in Architecture* that the first architecture of empiricism was that which we call picturesque, and that a second has been emerging recently out of environmental physics, physiology and psychology, with their emphases on sensory comfort, satisfaction and even delight. The architecture of rationalism of course is quite a different matter.

Descartes's ideas were translated into architectural terms by a number of theorists in the middle of the eighteenth century, including the French Abbé Laugier, whose *Essai sur l'Architecture* was published in 1753. Laugier tried to establish the fundamentals of architecture by thinking back, by rational procedures, as to how architecture *must* have started:

'Let us consider the man in his first origin, without any other help, without other guide than the natural instinct of his needs. He needs a dwelling place. He perceives, near a gentle stream, a green turf, the growing verdure of which pleases his eye'.

Thus Laugier envisages man in an Eden-like environment, enjoying the fruits of nature and at perfect peace with himself. His every desire is met for a while, but then nature begins to turn hostile. First 'the sun's heat scorches him' and he seeks shelter in a nearby wood; but then 'a thousand vapours raised by chance' gather together and 'a frightful rain hurls itself down as a torrent upon this delightful forest'. He has to find shelter, and makes for a cave but this proves dark, dank and 'unhealthful', so he resolves to build a hut and once the storm has subsided, he finds torn-off branches from the trees on the floor. So:

'He chooses four of the strongest (tree trunks) which he raises perpendicularly and disposes in a square. He lays four others across these, upon which he raises others sloping up from both sides. The roof thus formed is covered with leaves placed together so that neither the sun nor the rain can penetrate; man finally is lodged'.

We know now that this was not true; the earliest buildings took many and varied forms, none of which matched Laugier's vision. But as a true rationalist Laugier was concerned with what they *ought* to have been, rather than what they actually were.

Having imagined this origin for architecture, Laugier then erects a magnificent, logical, self-consistent structure of what architecture should be. The tree trunks of course became columns, the horizontal branches became beams or entablatures, inclined ones became the pedimented roof. These became for him the *essential* features of architecture; any other parts—including walls—could only be added by 'licence'. Columns must be detached, perpendicular and round; like tree-trunks, they must have diminution but no base. Above all they must be *seen* to carry the entablature. Thus attached columns, pilasters or antae were not merely licences, they were actual defects. The pediment, similarly must form the front of a roof, and should not be used for mere decorative effect to mark an entrance or balance a composition.

The nearest Laugier could find to this ideal was the Greek Doric temple which, having been approved by 'informed opinion' through the ages, must therefore represent a kind of architectural perfection. Unfortunately, in Laugier's eyes, the temple itself was compromised for after all it had walls. These in turn lead to further abuses such as the doors, or even windows, antae and other licences made necessary. Thus the Doric temple itself is by no means pure, although it was nothing like so bad as the architecture which followed with its arches, arcades, vaults, domes, pedestals, attics and so on.

Laugier himself attempted, as he said, to 'reduce architecture to almost nothing'—a thoroughly rationalist aim. Naturally it was criticized: J. N. Durand for instance thought the primitive hut a quite unsuitable model for, open as it was on all sides, it could hardly offer man that protection from the environment at all. And what was the purpose of any building if it failed in that most fundamental of purposes? Yet in spite of this strange aberration Laugier did present the fundamental clue that architecture originated and could only originate in *necessity*. If this clue were followed to its logical conclusion, the resulting architecture would give pleasure with efficiency of a thoroughly platonic kind.

'If you lay out a building in such a way that is suited to its function, surely it will differ appreciably from one with another function? Will it not naturally have character, and what is more, a character of its own? If the various parts of the building, which have a different purpose, are arranged each as they should be, then will not these parts necessarily differ from each other, and the building will have variety, and, since the eye will be able to take in the maximum number of parts at once, the building, if laid out in the most economical, that is to say the simplest, fashion, will seem as large and as magnificent as possible, where is the necessity of running after all these parts of beauty?' (Durand 1802–5).

He goes further to suggest that far from being essential, decoration is positively harmful. A certain building strikes one as beautiful so, in an attempt to beautify another, one transposes the decorative details of the first to the second. But they may be quite unsuitable, so in striving too hard to please, architecture makes itself ridiculous. The architect, therefore, should concern himself solely with *arrangement*, and:

'The exercise of architectural talent, should . . . be confined to the solution of two problems; in a private building to produce the most suitable one possible with the money specified: in a public building, its purpose being stated, to produce the least expensive one' (*ibid*).

Durand's ideas on a rational functionalism of course were highly seductive. Based as they were on concern for materials, construction and methods, they provide the architects of post-Napoleonic Europe with an intelligible set of design principles.

They were taught, for instance, in Berlin, at the Bauschule which David Gilly founded. One of his most notable pupils was Karl Friedrich Schinkel (1781–1841) whose Classical work displays very clearly the 'simplicity, convenience and economy', so characteristic of the Laugier-Durand tradition. Nor was Schinkel by any means the last link in this particular chain, for Mies van der Rohe went on record as saying that he learned everything in architecture from Schinkel's *Altes Museum* in Berlin. There is a direct line of rationalist thinking in architecture from Laugier to Schinkel and hence to Mies, although Schinkel was by no means a rationalist in everything he did. But one has only to look at, say, Crown Hall, Mies's 'Architecture Building' for the IIT campus in Chicago, to see the strength of this connection.

2 Schinkel: Altes Museum, Berlin (1822–30). Architecture is almost reduced to Laugier's columns and beams

Mies himself acknowledged it in a radio interview. Discussing his own development as an architect, he said:

'I learned the most from old buildings ... Schinkel was really the greatest representant (sic) in Berlin. The Altes Museum ... a beautiful building. You could learn everything in architecture from that and I tried to do that ... in the Altes Museum ... he separated the elements: the columns and the walls (the windows) and the ceilings ... I think that is still visible in my much later buildings'.

At this level, Crown Hall literally is a reworking of the Altes Museum, with I-section columns in place of the Schinkel's Ionic ones. But there is more to it than that. With Crown Hall and similar buildings, Mies literally fulfils the programme which Laugier had worked out some 200 years before and what is more he does so with greater precision than anyone else who attempted to do so, including Schinkel himself.

Thanks to the technology which had become available, by then, he was able finally 'to reduce architecture to almost nothing'. He even realized Laugier's ideal of an architecture without walls, consisting only of columns and beams, and by simply closing the gaps between his columns with windows of glass, he was able to eliminate virtually all of Laugier's 'licences'—windows, pilasters, antae, although even he could not quite overcome the necessity for doors.

So with Crown Hall and his other large-span structures, Mies designed literally the most rational structures in the entire history of architecture. But the question, of course, is were they also functional? That depends on what one means by functional.

As a first check let us match Crown Hall against Socrates's criteria for functional architecture. Does Crown Hall afford 'pleasant retreat in all seasons'? Not really, for the problems of solar heat gain, heat loss, glare, distraction, noise penetration from outside, noise penetration within the building and so on have become quite notorious over the past twenty years or so. Does it 'protect (the owner's) possessions'? If by 'owner' one means those who use the building, again, not really, for its basic open plan in fact offers no security whatever for students' equipment, materials and other personal effects. It seems therefore that Socrates would not have found Crown Hall particularly pleasurable, functional or therefore beautiful.

So what about Vitruvius? Does Crown Hall offer his requisite Commoditie, Firmenes and Delight? If Commoditie means providing spaces to serve a set of needs then the answer again is not really. Crown Hall, of course, is a two-storey building. The upper floor consists of a single open 'shed' which is used largely as a drafting studio for students of architecture but the basement rooms also are drafting studios for the Institute of Design. The architecture floor, of course, is flooded with light (not to mention solar heat and so on) around the edges, rather darker towards the middle, but the Institute studios, being two thirds buried into the ground, receive daylight only from narrow clerestory windows up against their ceilings; given such vastly different conditions it is obvious that if either of the two floors actually provides a 'correct' working environment for design students, then the other cannot.

Mies himself expressed certain views on the 'fit' of space to activity in the interview quoted above. As he put it:

'Flexibility is in my opinion about a necessity (these days) ... What Sullivan said: "Form follows function"—I think that has changed in our time, very much. The function is very short-lived today, and our constructions last much longer. So it only makes sense to make the plan very flexible'.

One can see his point, but design students—and particularly his own design students—spend a great deal of time at their drawing boards. Surely there is *some* responsibility for providing them with 'pleasant retreat' for that particular kind of work. Nor do the deficiencies of Crown Hall stop at daylighting. Another necessity

3a

3b

3c

in design education obviously is the tutorial: group or individual. Yet Crown Hall, with its vast open architecture space and comparatively low screens, affords no acoustic protection whatever for each tutorial grouping from the others.

As for firmness, naturally after years, some of the glass is cracked but that perhaps is less serious than the problem of the roof which, with its beams exposed for reasons of architectural expression, was replaced in 1975 at a cost of \$1·5 million. As for Delight? Well, as we have seen in the case of the human body, that depends on how you look at it, on the eyes (and brain) with which you are looking.

So checked against those two ancient prescriptions for 'functional' architecture, Crown Hall obviously does not do very well. But they in themselves seem a little suspect these days. They cannot cope adequately with the range and complexity of buildings which we seem to have found necessary in the twentieth century.

There have been several attempts to define what functionalism in architecture really means. Until recently the most comprehensive probably was that of Alfred Roth, whose *New Architecture* was published, in a trilingual edition, in Zurich in 1940. He chose what seemed to him the twenty most significant buildings of the 30s, ranging in scale from Owen Williams's Boots Factory in Nottingham (1930) to Le Corbusier's tiny vacation house at Mathes (1935). Apart from these, the two best remembered buildings probably are Aalto's Library at Viipuri (1932) and the Broadcasting House at Hilversum by Merkelbach and Karsen (1932). Roth reviews his selected buildings under four headings: Spatial Planning, Technical Considerations, Economic Factors and Aesthetic Aspects. Of these, the most complex undoubtedly are his technical considerations which, as he says, were 'constantly branching off into special domains which must be partly worked by specialists (building statics, heating, airing, electrical and sanitary plants, sound insulation etc)'.

Roth's grouping seems to me remarkable for the fact that, unlike others in his time, he identifies aesthetic aspects as a 'function' of buildings in much the same way that spatial planning, technical considerations and economic factors undoubtedly are. The value attached to Roth's approach perhaps is indicated by the fact that 36 years later, in 1976, his book was reprinted for the fifth time and yet it seems to me that like others before him—back to and including Vitruvius—he made a category mistake.

That particular mistake finally was avoided by Bill Hillier, of the RIBA's research unit who in 1972 offered a very clear distinction between what a building does (how a building functions) and what it *is*, including how it is constructed, by asking one simple question: What *irrespective of the designer's intentions* will be the effects of constructing this particular building? He answered it as follows:

'First, a building is a climate modifier, and within this broad concept, it acts as a complex environmental filter between the inside and the outside, it has a displacement effect on external climate and ecology and it modifies, by increasing, decreasing and specifying the sensory inputs into the human organism.

Second, a building is a container of activities, and within this it both inhibits and facilitates activities, perhaps occasionally prompting them or determining them. It also locates behaviour and in this sense it can be seen as a modification of the total behaviour of society.

Third, a building is a symbolic and cultural object, not simply in terms of the cognitive sets of those who encounter it. It has a similar displacement effect on the culture of society. We should note that a negatively cultural building is just as powerful a symbolic object as a positively (ie intentionally) cultural one.

Fourthly, a building is an addition of value to raw materials (like all productive processes) and within this it is a capital investment, a maximization of scarce resources of material and manpower, and a use of resources over time. In the broader context of society, it can be seen as a resource modifier'.

I have since found it helpful for certain purposes to separate the first of these into

3a Mies van der Rohe: Crown Hall, Illinois Institute of Technology Chicago (1956). Having learned 'everything in architecture' from the Altes Museum, Mies 'reduced' architecture even further than Schinkel had done (see the view illustrated on p. 69). Here, in these views, reality takes over for, with its cracked glass, windows which cannot be cleaned in the corners, and incipient ivy, Crown Hall seems to have lost that abstract perfection which is the true raison d'être of Rationalism (b) and (c) The 'firmenes' of Crown Hall: broken steps and ceiling repairs being carried out after damage to the roof

153

two parts: the building as climate modifier (the first function) and the building as that which has a displacement effect 'on external climate and ecology' (a fifth function) in terms which are now obligatory in certain North American states—a description of its environmental impact.

Given the four functions of Hillier's models, we could start with any of these. Now obviously this omits a factor which many will see as vital, that which Vitruvius calls Firmness, and which Roth embodies in his technical considerations. But that is quite deliberate. Asked to describe the functions of a jug, one would probably say that in the first place, it held water, milk or some other liquid. Pressed further one might add that a good jug would be easy to pick up, and that when one wanted to pour the liquid, it should be easy to do so, without spilling. Pressed further still, one might go on to say that, of course, the jug should store its liquid without leaking, that the handle—if it had one—should not fall off, and so on. In other words, one would take its firmness for granted as something one had a right to expect and which should not need spelling out.

It is true that the roof of Crown Hall proved unfirm, but the defects arising from this condition obviously would be picked up if one looked in detail at its performance as a climate modifier (it let in the rain), as a container of activities (it failed to contain them properly), as an addition of value to the raw materials (they deteriorated and thus lost their value), and so on.

Those are obvious points by which Crown Hall can be checked against the four (or five) function model, but there are many others. Its value as a tool perhaps can best be demonstrated if you make the analysis yourself, for Crown Hall and a range of other buildings. One fact emerges consistently, that the more rational a building in this strict, Cartesian/Laugierian sense, the less well it will function, against criteria such as these. How could it, when the essence of rationalism is the pursuit of an abstract perfection, which has nothing to do with 'reality' which not only ignores but deliberately flouts the empiricist view that our experience of the world around us—including buildings—is based on the evidence of our senses.

The fundamental point is that the only way to achieve an architecture which has any pretensions whatever to being functional is to approach it empirically. An empirical architecture will satisfy the human senses in terms of its environmental filtering capacities, will afford the spaces in which real live human beings can gather together as necessary, will even be structurally sound. But what will this empirical architecture be like? Let me take an extreme example, one whom Pevsner has called, specifically, an anti-rationalist: Antoni Gaudí. Let us even take his most extreme building which, for certain Gaudí scholars, epitomizes all that he stood for: the chapel, or rather the crypt, which is all that was built of the Colonia Guell at Santa Colomma. Gaudí's approach, naturally, was highly complex but certain facts are known. His original sketch, for instance, shows the chapel as consisting externally of a cluster of pinnacles, much like his design for a mission in Tangier and for the Sagrada Familia itself as indicated by his sketches and models in that cathedral's museum. These pinnacles were to be supported by a system of parabolic arches, the curves of which were determined for Gaudí by his famous suspension model in which the structure itself was represented by wires and strings in tension with bags of lead shot for the loads.

One cannot describe this as a rational approach to design, for, based as it was on experiment and observation, it was specifically empirical. But at least it was sensible. Having determined the overall form in this way, Gaudí proceeded to the detail. Even at crypt level, the columns supporting his parabolic arches had to slope inwards a little, the degree of slope naturally being determined by the model. But what about their actual form? Gaudí determined this by using a favourite device of his, the drawing of visual analogies with forms from nature, in the belief that as natural forms are inherently sound, they may be safely translated into man-made ones. The source which Gaudí chose for his visual analogy for the columns and also for the roof they supported again was a favourite one—the human skeleton, which had been photographed for him in a variety of positions in front of a mirror device.

4 The only part of Gaudí's Colonia Guell Chapel to have been built was the crypt

5 Antoni Gaudí: initial sketch for the Colonia Guell Chapel (1898–1914)

6 Catenary (pragmatic) model for the structure of the Chapel in which inverted arches of string and wire were loaded with bags of lead shot in scale with the weight of the masonry—a thoroughly empirical approach to design

4

5

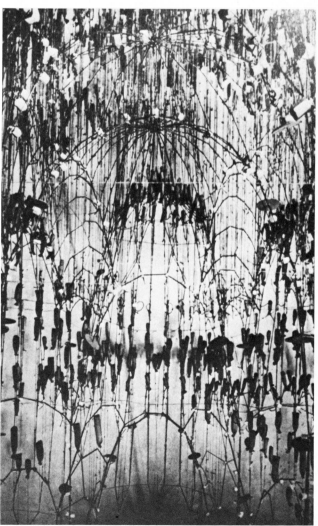

6

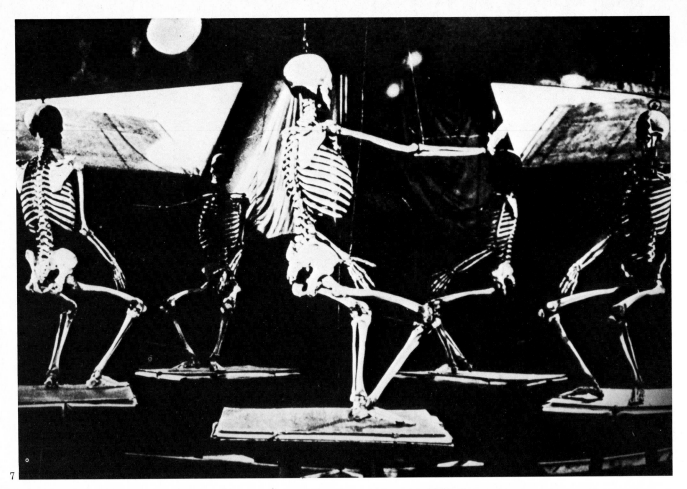

7

7 Skeleton set up on a mirrored
drawing platform by Mantamala.
Used by Gaudí as a visual source
for his own skeleton-sculpture
and also for the roof of the crypt

8 John Ruskin, drawing of the
'perfect' window at Dunblane
Abbey near Edinburgh

8

156

9 Colonia Guell Chapel; Gaudí's hooded windows bear a close visual resemblance to Ruskin's

The columns, then, are tibia-shaped while the roof resembles a rib-cage, a particularly appropriate form for the Catalan vaulting in which it is constructed. This vaulting depends on the adhesion of a rapid-setting cement (rather like plaster of paris) which enables a tile to be 'stuck' in the corner of a room or other compartment, followed by another and another round the walls of the compartment so that a vault is gradually formed from successive rows of tiles, *with no supporting centring at all to support it* during construction. Obviously by dividing his roof into small compartments with his ribs, Gaudí made the process of Catalan vaulting even quicker and easier than usual.

The windows too have a curious logic behind them. We know that Gaudí was an avid reader of Ruskin although we cannot be certain as to which texts impressed him most. But there is a passage in the Edinburgh lectures in which Ruskin expounds the virtues of a particular window in Dunblane Abbey. Ruskin was fascinated by this window, partly, no doubt, because of its vertical or almond-like shape which for Ruskin, no doubt, had what we should call today specifically Freudian connotations!

Whether or not he knew this passage from Ruskin, Gaudí adopted that same form for his windows in the Cripto Guell. The grilles which cover them externally also merit attention in that they are made by welding together waste spindles from Guell's cotton factory.

In all of these decisions and in very many of the others which he took in designing the crypt, Gaudí displayed direct, common-sense attitudes of the kind which, as I suggested at the beginning of this chapter, most of us think of as 'rational' And if one checks his design against the four-function model it performs remarkably well; it seems particularly well-suited in terms of space enclosure to the demands of the Catholic liturgy, its thick wall construction is excellent as environmental filtering offering both protection from external noise and a thermal insulation effect within the wall itself. Its relatively small windows, shaded from the Spanish sun, also work well by admitting enough draught, yet with no problem at all of solar heat gain. It is a magnificent cultural symbol, one of the most potent in the entire history of the twentieth century and while we have no record of its costs, Gaudí's structure, inherently, is an economic one.

And so, in a sense, we have come full circle. A building which at first sight looks about as irrational, and as unfunctional as a building can possibly be, proves on examination to perform extraordinarily well in functional terms. It also seems to have been conceived in a thoroughly 'rational' manner. Of course, this tells us a lot about architecture, but it tells us even more about those architects and critics, who, for their own ends, over the past fifty years or so, have to a quite extraordinary extent abused those quite straightforward words, rational and functional.

BIBLIOGRAPHY

L.-B. Alberti, (trans. J. Leoni 1726) *Ten Books on Architecture*, 1965 edn, ed J. Rykwert, London, Tiranti

Reyner Banham, *Theory and Design in the First Machine Age*, London, Architectural Press, 1960

L. M. Blanco, *Bovedas Tabicadas*, Madrid, Ministerio de la Gobernacion, Direccion General de Arquitectura, 1957

Geoffrey Broadbent, *Design in Architecture*, Chichester, John Wiley, 1973

Geoffrey Broadbent, Estructuras profundas en la Arquitectura, in T. Llorens (ed) *Arquitectura, historia y teoria de los signos*, Barcelona, Colegio Oficial de Arquitectos de Cataluna y Baleares

Geoffrey Broadbent, The Present State of Design Method Studies, in *Perspecta 15, The Yale Architectural Journal*, 1972

G. R. Collins, The Transfer of Thin Masonry Vaulting from Spain to America, *Society of Architectural Historians*, vol. 27, 1968

K. J. Conant, *Cluny: les églises et la maison du chef d'ordre*, Cambridge, Mass, Medieval Academy of America, 1968

K. J. Conant, The After-life of Vitruvius in the Middle Ages, *Journal of the Society of Architectural Historians*, no. 27, 1968

René Descartes, *Discourse on Method*, 1637 (trans A. Wollaston) Harmondsworth, Penguin, 1960

René Descartes, *Meditations on the First Philosophy*, 1641 (trans A. Wollaston) Harmondsworth, Penguin, 1960

R. Descharnes, and C. Prevost, *Gaudí the Visionary*, Cambridge, Patrick Stevens, 1971

J. N. L. Durand, *Précis des leçons d'architecture données à l'Ecole Polytechnique*, Paris, 1802–5

P. Frankl, Secrets of the Mediaeval Masons, *Art Bulletin* 17, March 1946

Sigfried Giedion, *Space, Time and Architecture*, Cambridge, Mass, Harvard UP, 1940, (1962 edn consulted)

Walter Gropius, *The New Architecture and the Bauhaus*, London, Faber, 1936

W. R. G. Hillier, J. E. Musgrove, and P. O'Sullivan, Knowledge in Design in M. J. Mitchell, (ed), *Proceedings of the 3rd Environmental Design Research Association Conference*, University of California, Los Angeles, 1972

W. J. Hipple, *The Beautiful, the Sublime and the Picturesque in Eighteenth Century British Aesthetic Theory*, Carbondale, Southern Illinois University Press, 1957

H. R. Hitchcock, and P. Johnson, *The International Style: Architecture since 1922*, (1966 edn consulted) New York, Norton, 1932

Marc Antoine Laugier, *Essai sur l'architecture*, Paris, 1953, reprinted Farnborough, Gregg Press, 1966

Le Corbusier, Recorded interview with Hugo Desalle, Paris, Réalisations Sonores, Collection Hommes d'Aujourd'hui, 1965

John Locke, *An Essay Concerning Human Understanding* 1690; (ed J. W. Yolton), London, Dent, 1961

R. Mainstone, *Developments in Structural Form*, Cambridge, Mass, MIT, 1975; Harmondsworth, Allen Lane, 1975

C. Martinell, *Gaudí, his Life, his Theories, his Works* translated from the Spanish by Judith Rohrer, edited by George R. Collins, Barcelona, Blume, 1975

Mies van der Rohe, interview with Graeme Shankland, London, BBC, 1960

Andrea Palladio, *Four Books of Architecture*, New York, Dover Publications, 1965 (a facsimile reprint of Isaac Ware publication of 1738)

Nikolaus Pevsner, *Pioneers of the Modern Movement*, London, Faber, 1936 republished as *Pioneers of Modern Design*. Harmondsworth, Penguin, 1960

A. Roth, *The New Architecture*, Zurich, Girsberger, 1940

John Ruskin, *Lectures on Architecture and Painting*, London, Allen, 1905

A. Sartoris, *Gli elementi dell'architettura funzionale*, Milan, Hoepli, 1932

H. Weber, *Walter Gropius und das Faguswerk*, Munich, Callwey, 1961

H. Wotton, *The Elements of Architecture Collected from the Best Sources and Examples*, London, John Bill, 1642; reprinted Farnborough, Gregg Press, 1969

Xenophon, *Memorabilia and Oeconomicus*, London, Heinemann, 1932 (trans E. C. Marchant)

Rationality in architecture and in the design process

by Henryk Skolimowski

In this chapter[1] Professor Skolimowski enquires into the conceptual underpinnings of the design process. Rationality, he argues, is the backbone of the conceptual framework within which design occurs but it is found to be a changeable phenomenon. It is not a set of permanent abstract principles but a semi-permanent structure which may differ from culture to culture and from epoch to epoch.

He argues that we are now witnessing a clash of two rationalities. We are in the process of transition from the older 'objectivist' rationality (which is the backbone of the scientific technological system) with its insistence on economics, technical expertise and the 'form follows function' principle, to the new evolutionary rationality which is to be found in the emerging new concept of architecture based on the criterion of 'quality of life' and on the dictum 'form follows culture'.

There is no one timeless form of rationality

Rationality is a subject as old as civilization. And so is architecture for that matter. But the two are hardly ever discussed together. Is there a special reason for discussing them together now? Perhaps there is. Architecture is in a state of crisis. This crisis is above all the crisis of the criteria of validity. We no longer seem to know what counts as valid architecture, indeed what counts as architecture as such. The crisis of the criteria of validity is ultimately the crisis of rationality.

Rationality has a noble heritage, but it has endured many transformations during the last 2500 years. It came into being with Anaxagoras who declared that *nous* (reason) is the cornerstone of the universe. Since his times the structure of thought of western man was to comply to the criteria of rationality and reason. In the eighteenth century rationality and reason were appropriated by the ideologists of the Enlightenment. In their scheme of things, rationality was made a weapon directed against the Church and all religion. In the nineteenth and twentieth century rationality was made a handmaiden of science and technology so much so that what was 'scientific' and technologically efficient was deemed rational; a far cry from the conception of rationality of the early Greeks, who would despise our criteria of efficiency.

Nowadays rationality is a much abused term. It has so many meanings that at times it seems meaningless. It would appear that when architects use the term they often do not know what they are talking about. In present-day architectural discussions, rationality has been woven into quite different contexts, and consequently made subject to quite different criteria. I shall argue that the predominant form of rationality (objectivist, or scientific or technological) is a strait-jacket which more often than not inhibits our best creative efforts and produces, in terms of human habitats, dull and deadly built environments. In short, I shall attempt to demonstrate that the decay of our environments is exactly the result of the decay of our reason and our rationality, which, put in the constraining grid of science and technology, produce marvels of technical virtuosity which, however, are suffocating and crippling from the social and human points of view. And I shall simultaneously argue that a way out of the predicament is not to introduce yet another technique, but to change the entire idiom of thinking, thus of our rationality, and of the criteria of validity.[2] Unless we change our paradigm of thinking, reasoning and action, the present conceptual strait-jacket will compel us to produce inhuman environments which are all right technologically and economically, for technology and economics do not have human needs.

The old objectivist rationality v. new evolutionary rationality: a skyscraper in New York and a part of Paolo Soleri's Arcosanti project, Arizona

My enterprise is therefore conceptual and philosophical in nature: it attempts to reconstruct the ultimate principles of thinking which motivate and justify our thought and action, particularly in the design process. One of the conclusions that follow from my argument is that so-called new rationalisms in architecture and design, announced in recent years, are neither new nor particularly rational, for they are merely variations on the theme of the Brave New World—a salvation through new techniques and technology; they are mere epicycles of objectivist rationality. It also follows from my argument that the Marxist approach to the subject, as seen for example in *Architecture and Utopia* by Manfredo Tafuri (MIT Press 1976), which denounces with great gusto the pseudo-rationality of capitalist architecture (and claims, quite rightly, that rationalism reveals its own irrationality) is itself not immune from the same charge because Marxism and its rationality are based on the apotheosis of science and technology, and therefore share all the shortcomings of objectivist rationality, which I shall analyse at some length.

Before I go to the central issue, let me briefly consider the problem of meaning in architecture which is as baffling as it is important. What is the relation of rationality to validity and to meaning in architecture? We are very muddled about this relation. Meaning in architecture can be defined in at least three different ways: as significance in the most general sense; as function, that is, as related to the uses of architecture; as semiotics, that is, as the relation between the sign and what it signifies; architecture is then treated as a system of semiotic inscriptions.

This last interpretation of meaning has been quite influential in recent times, in my opinion much to the detriment of both semiotics and architecture. For treating architecture as if it were but a semantic system, rather than as a system of constructions performing an extraordinary variety of functions and satisfying an extraordinary variety of needs, is a rather fanciful and arbitrary way of redefining architecture.

Function in and of architecture has always been important. However, when function is deified and begins to rule like a tyrant, then a conflict arises between architecture in its total significance and its one defined aspect. We have often seen this conflict in the twentieth century.

Of the three definitions of 'meaning' in architecture, meaning conceived as significance in most general terms comes closest to what I should like to call rationality in architecture, by which I mean reason for existence. This at once satisfies the traditional notion of rationality (something justified by the appeal to reason) and, what is crucial for architecture, the existence of physical constructions.

What about validity? There are at least two contexts in which the term is used.

Technical: validity is limited to technical aspects, structural and engineering aspects above all. A valid design is one which satisfies the criteria spelled out in the handbooks of structural engineering, physics, etc.

General: validity is used almost synonymously with rationality, for we are concerned not only with technical aspects, but also with, for example, whether a given building makes sense in a given social context, and whether it will have positive or negative effects on the environment at large. Whenever I use the term 'validity' interchangeably with 'rationality', it is this meaning that I have in mind.

To summarize: rationality conceived as the reason for existence converges with validity in the general sense and also with meaning as significance.

Rationality and the system

To say that rationality is the reason for existence is a very rough definition, really the first approximation. Taken literally, it can lead to surprising paradoxes, for it seems to follow that there must have been some reason for everything there is, and therefore whatever exists is rational, and what does not exist is not rational. On the strength of this logic, such monstrosities as Battersea power station and Los Angeles are rational merely because they exist. So, obviously, when we ask for a reason for existence, we ask for more than the mere assertion of existence; we ask indeed whether this existence is justified by legitimate reasons. These reasons, taken together, constitute what we call 'rationality'.

Are there any such reasons which are universal and thus valid for all times? Whenever we ask for a definition or at least an explanation of rationality, we invariably expect to find such universal reasons, but they are extremely hard to come by. My contention is that there are no universal criteria applicable to all times and to all architectural systems.

Rationality is not a set of timeless abstract principles, which we apply to our thinking to make it 'valid'. Rationality differs from epoch to epoch. We alter the assessment of our visual perception of built environments in accordance with the shifts in our conception of rationality. Rationality (of a given time) is built into our eyes. Just ten to fifteen years ago the tower point was just 'right', an expression of the rational order in the realm of architecture. And the geometrical type of city planning, which resulted in lifeless neighbourhoods, was considered progressive and rational.

Nowadays we are beginning to *perceive* the tower point as a monstrosity; the linear geometric city planning as a fundamental mistake; and we find the arguments in their favour, which were so convincing and undoubted just a decade ago, quite facile and based on unwarranted assumptions. What has happened? We have changed (or at least are changing) the basis of our rationality. Rationality is no longer tied to simple geometry and to economic sub-optimization. We now recognize that the most congenial forms of human habitats are irregular, indeed often a maze of irregular planes and spaces. It is in such mazes that life happens, and the quality of life can be assured; while the simplified geometric cities, and their epitome, the tower point, are lifeless and in the final analysis anti-human. As the result of this shift in our criteria of rationality, *our perception of built environments has changed*. We can clearly see that our eye follows our mind: our perception is guided by our criteria of rationality. Rationality is a changeable phenomenon. It is our culture that ultimately justified the changes in both our perception and our conception of rationality. As I have argued elsewhere: *Form follows culture.*[3]

The realization of the subtle but a necessary connection between culture, rationality, our modes of perception and predominant forms of architectural thinking is simply missing in the present debates. Take for example an opinion of a well-known architectural critic who maintains that 'there is only one realistic way to get a pleasant environment and that is to replace bad architects with good ones'. This contention is as simple as to appear a truism. But it is erroneous. It is not bad architecture that messes up our environment, but our assumptions about what the environment ought to be and what kind of habitats should be created. Equally unsatisfactory is the opinion of Frank Tindall who says: 'I find that only a handful of architects seem to be aware of what is next to their site. Mostly, they design buildings in a vacuum'. It was of course one of the dogmas of technological (objectivist) rationality that *we make the environment*, imposing on it our criteria concerning how things ought to be, rather than our following the environment. At the bottom of many disastrous mistakes are the opinions and credos of the Corbusiers and the Mieses. To quote a memorable passage from Le Corbusier:

'We must have the courage to view the rectilinear cities of America with admiration. If the aesthete has not so far done so, the moralist, on the contrary, may well find more food for reflection that at first appears.
The winding road is the Pack-Donkey's Way. The straight road is man's way.
The winding road is the result of happy-go-lucky heedlessness of looseness, lack of concentration and animality.
The straight road is a reaction, an action, a positive deed, the result of self-mastery. It is sane and noble'.

What Corbusier postulated as sane and noble we now consider insane and ignoble.

Intoxicated by the image of technology triumphant, and with the slogan 'form follows function', we have made our rationality and our perception of the built environment a slave to industrial efficiency. In the process we have deluded ourselves in various ways. For example, we insisted that the Modern Movement was 'doing more with less', while, when we carefully look at the actual record, we may come to a surprising conclusion that *we have been doing less with more:* with more technology, more know-how, more new materials, we have created architecture which is less memorable than any created before. Having at our disposal the best means, we have created the worst architecture in history. For if we compare ourselves with former epochs the conclusion is inevitable: they built splendid things with slender means; we have built shoddy things with splendid means. The verdict 'doing less with more' is a just one. One of the expressions of the pseudo-rationality of the former epoch is that it squandered our resources while leaving little behind of lasting value, that is in terms of the monuments that will be cherished in a century or a millenium. We have simply not built for the next millenium. We have only built for today. Built-in obsolescence is another manifestation of the pseudo-rationality of the Modern Movement.

The architects who escaped the tentacles of the crippling rationality of the Modern Movement, such as Frank Lloyd Wright and more recently Louis Kahn and Paolo Soleri did so because they tacitly accepted a much broader concept of reason. They are the transcendentalists for whom the forms of the built environment do not follow from most recent technological inventions or simple economic calculations of what comes cheapest, but who attempt to respond to the needs of man which are beyond immediate physical, biological and economic. They are the transcendentalists for they hold a certain transcendental conception of man, and it is this conception that guides their action and is at the basis of their rationality.

The only way for present architecture to get out of its present impasse, the only way to reconstitute the scope of new rationality in architecture, is not by indulging in the eclecticism called post-Modern Movement, which Charles Jencks does with great verbal skill but with lamentable lack of new content, or by indulging in new terminology by calling present architecture 'the period of diversity', which Christian Norberg-Schulz does in his *Meaning in Western Architecture*, while his examples of diversity are but epicycles of technological rationality, but by recreating a new scope for human reason and by creating on this scaffolding the architecture which is rooted in the quality of life criteria. In so far as life has an extraphysical dimension, in so far as architecture attempts to fulfil the full scope of human needs, including spiritual needs, our concept of rationality in architecture must be transphysical.

Now, as I have mentioned, rationality in architecture is relative to the architectural system within which we think, build, and design. Such a concept of rationality is not exclusively limited to architecture and design. I suggest that rationality, whatever its manifestation and whatever the field of its application, is always relative to the system which is governed by it.

Every reasonable self-contained system tends to generate its own rationality which, so to speak, sanctifies the order that is peculiar to the system. Rationality is thus generated by the system and it in turn attempts to preserve the stability and integrity of the system by fending off intruders and by ruling out as irrational, unreasonable, or simply unacceptable those elements which jar or clash with the system. Such a conception of rationality enables us to discuss the rationality of architecture and even of art on a par with the rationality of science; for schools and idioms in art are self contained systems governed by their peculiar rules which spell out the reason for their existence. Perhaps I am not saying anything new: perhaps we have always known, if only by intuition, that there is a rationality governing even such movements as Dadaism, Surrealism, or abstract Expressionism.

Rationality, unrelated to a system, is a platonic ideal, in our search for which we dream of permanent, absolute, unchangeable forms. Then we discover that our successors, in pursuing the same ideal, dream up different forms, which only proves that such forms are not unchangeable or absolute at all.

The idea that rationality is relative to the system may appear strange at first. Yet this is the only way we can talk rationally about rationality and its vicissitudes in architecture. The point is that it is only after we grant that rationality, and thus validity, is relative to a given system that we can comprehend and accept the fact that different types of architecture, expressing different architectural systems, may be equally valid and rational, particularly if the two systems belong to different historical epochs: the validity of Gothic architecture in no way undermines or annihilates the validity of Renaissance architecture, and vice versa. But if there is one rationality underlying all systems, then the acceptance of one system would automatically invalidate other architectural styles and systems; this only proves that there is no one absolute system.

The preponderance of the physical

Unless we grasp the meaning of the concept of 'system' our understanding of rationality as relative to systems will be only tenuous. What is its central meaning in reference to architecture?

Let us start with the most rarified and refined concept of the system as it is used in formal disciplines. By 'systems' in logic and mathematics (that is, by formal systems) are meant abstract and idealized languages which serve as the means of analysing the concept of deduction. The rationality of formal systems is that which accounts for the peculiar order of these systems, which is the logical order. The universe of formal systems consists of formal (that is, logical) relationships, and since its raison d'être is logic, logicality then equals rationality and vice versa. Because formal systems are so hermetic, idealized, and abstract, their perfection is never really attainable by those systems which embrace the physical and the human world.

The system of physics governs the universe of physics. Its rationality is that which accounts for the peculiar order of this system and explains the furnishing of this universe, its form and content. But to say that the rationality of physics is the set of principles that account for its peculiar order seems almost tautological. What is not tautological is the fact that the rationality of physics (that is, the rationality governing its universe) has become the rationality of all science, and moreover the prevailing rationality of our western civilization. What is characteristic of one system has become the paradigm of all knowledge and of all understanding. Mechanistic and physical explanations came to be regarded as paradigm cases of explanation. Phenomena peculiar to physics and inter-relationships that occur among them came to be regarded as the basic stuff of the universe. For the last two centuries, we have deliberately structured our knowledge to comply with the system of physics and we have deliberately conditioned our understanding to conform to that understanding which is peculiar to physical phenomena, so that the structure of our current rationality is the mirror image of the rationality of the physical system.

The quest for the illusory definiteness of science has caused us to reduce complex phenomena to the level of the simplified models of science. Scientific reason has suppressed in us the general faculty for reason and judgement. Scientific reason has become the demon who has possessed us and has made us worship the idols of precision, quantity, measurement, and number, so that we try to measure what is unmeasurable, and we try to quantify what can only be assessed on the scales of our soul.

Physics has conquered us, not because it has found physical explanations of all phenomena (it has not), but because it has imposed on us its structure of rationality and has persuaded us to accept this rationality as universal. We have to free ourselves from the spell of scientific rationality if our civilization is not to undergo a further eclipse.

In this general predicament of our civilization, architecture has more than its share. The field of design and architecture has been inundated by systems analysis and operational research; scientific management and behaviourism; computerized models and set theory; structuralism and instrumentalism. Architects and designers accepted these doctrines with charming naivety, thinking that such borrowings enriched their understanding, while in fact they were being brainwashed.

The point is that, in spite of the apparent diversity of these borrowings, most of them are united by one common denominator: they serve the cause of the ideology of modern science. They all perpetuate the cult of objectivity, of factuality, of quantity and number. Their origin is in classical empiricism developed under the inspiration of Locke and Hume. The latter advocated that we purge our libraries of all those books that are not concerned with matters of fact or quantity or number. But what is architecture without its ties with human needs, human passions, transcendent aspects, and sordid dilemmas?

Empiricism received a new lease of life in the early twentieth century when it allied itself with formal logic and became logical empiricism. Then it perfected its tenets and conquered the world. Its rejection of all metaphysics (whatever was beyond physics was, of course, considered metaphysics), its tough mindedness and narrow factualism, and its criteria of meaning, otherwise known as the criteria of validity, slowly penetrated social science and finally the sphere of design and architecture, causing ultimately enormous harm in human terms. Why? Because these empiricist misconceptions gave rise to specific courses of action. Empiricist schemata, pushed to an extreme, 'objectivize' the world so completely that they leave very little room for human elements, and harm is caused simply by default. We arrive at architecture purged of the human element, often mistakenly called 'rational' architecture.

This ruthless objectivist tendency has a variety of idioms. One of them is the philosophy of logical forms, which is based on the assumption that no distinction should be made between architecture, engineering, and industrial design because 'the logical nature of the act of designing is largely independent of the character of the thing designed' (Alexander). Though its achievements fall short of its aspirations (to be really logical and independent of the character of the thing designed), the philosophy of logical forms is in perfect conformity with scientific rationality and is another manifestation of a system at the service of the ideology of modern science.

The technological system

The technological system may be considered as a manifestation of the physical system. But to stop at this level of interpretation is to miss entirely the devious and machiavellian, if not diabolical, nature of technology, which has its own rules, its own raison d'être, and, one might even say, its own supreme plan. For if we analyse technology historically, and if we treat the totality of technologies in their development, then certain striking tendencies of this development emerge and justify us in attributing to the technological system an autonomy of its own. The pervading tendency of the system, manifested through its various tributaries, is constant increase of efficiency. The rationality of technology lies in this incessant and relentless drive. Even when technology unites with science, it usually undermines science so deviously that science then serves the cause of efficiency and becomes in fact a servant of technology and of technological rationality.

Jacques Ellul, in his influential book *The Technological Society*, defines technology as the totality of techniques rationally arrived at and striving toward absolute efficiency. Ellul suggests that this relentless drive is universal and that the technological system, slowly but inexorably, is taking over, submitting everything and everybody to its imperative. Ellul's story is a fascinating one, though perhaps a bit chilling. He demonizes (perhaps needlessly) the evil he wants to exorcise and attributes to it more power than it in fact possesses. But even if

1 The Gropius locomotive design of 1909

2 'The bullet-train to nowhere'

Ellul's story is exaggerated, his point should be well taken, namely that the technological system does exhibit a remarkable tendency toward increasing efficiency at whatever cost. This is the crux of the matter: efficiency is conceived in the technological system in economic terms and in relation to the yield we obtain from the transformation of physical materials. What, then, are the other costs at the expense of which the technological system occasionally increases its efficiency? Human costs, social costs and, at a more intangible level, the disruption of the equilibrium of nature.

The price the USA has had to pay for its material progress (through the increased efficiency of its technological system) has been, in human terms, quite appalling. And what are the devastation of the environment and the subsequent ecological crisis if not the result of the relentless pursuit of the technological system? Efficiency had to be increased on a more and more global scale and in fierce competition with other competitors, all of whom considered economic profit through increased efficiency to be the highest imperative. And the cost is the disruption of the equilibrium of nature. This is no longer a matter of emotional attitudes and romantic gestures. It is simply absurd and frivolous to accuse people concerned with the ecological crisis of emotionalism, panic, and empty gestures. There is a relentless logic in technological development, for the rationality of technology demands an ever greater increase of efficiency.

All this affects deeply architects and designers. The tentacles of the technological system are so extensive that they reach into innumerable realms of our experience. We follow relentlessly the rules of logic, of science, and of technology, and we disregard the nature and the character of the thing designed and of the person for whom we design. We fulfil the canons of the objectivist system and stop at this point. We can prove 'objectively' that we are rational and we think that we are rational, though the effects of our allegedly rational activities are sadly anti-human. Is it not obvious that the rationality of the objectivist system represents a perversion of reason?

The disease of a civilization sets in when the variety of the forms of human experience and the multitude of responses to the world are eclipsed and suppressed by one form of experience and one interpretation of the world. Such a disease in the western world has been brought about by the growth and development of science, which has undermined the multitude of our non-physical relationships with nature and with other people.

Rationality man-rooted
It is abundantly clear that our present dilemmas in the realm of design lie in the constraints of the systems which we have adopted as valid but which in fact strangle us. Under the auspices of physical science, we have subconsciously tried to mould our architectural systems so that they resemble the alleged perfection of physical systems. But the point is that, though we may incorporate a great deal of science and technology into the architectural system, this system transcends science and technology and can never be reduced to them. For it has a different function, thus a different reason for existence, and thus a different rationality.

Following Bertalanffy, we can make a distinction between open systems and closed systems. A system is closed if no materials enter or leave it. A system is open if there is inflow and outflow and therefore change in the component materials. Physics and chemistry are exclusively concerned with closed systems. Biology, on the other hand, is concerned with open systems. And so are architecture and design if they are meant to be for living human beings.

Moreover, biological systems are hierarchical: understanding of the organism lies in comprehension of its functions, and, even more important, in comprehension of its hierarchy. Similarly hierarchical are architectural systems. Physical systems, on the other hand, are linear: the model for their understanding is the clock, with its mechanically interlocking parts. Biological systems, as well as architectural systems, are connected with other systems, whereas the physical system (at least as conceived of within classical physics) is isolated.

It is obvious that if architectural systems are meant to be for living human beings, they must meet the demands of living systems. The living organism is wise and thus rational if it successfully adapts itself to the environment. If it follows the rules of logic and perishes in the process, it is stupid, unadaptable, and irrational. The rationality of the living organism lies in its adaptability and is relative to that system which enables it to adapt optimally to the environment.

What about human beings? Each and every system of rationality must enable human beings to adjust to the environment—natural, man-made, social, and the environment of the mind—and to cope with life in general on human terms. Those systems which disturb our equilibrium with the environment and with life in general are anti-human and thus anti-rational.

If there is a universal rationality applicable to all systems (a kind of supra-rationality, or transrationality), it is if and only if there is one supra-system which contains all sub-systems and is governed by a set of homogeneous principles that are applicable to all sub-systems. If there is such a system, it is for the time being beyond our grasp and comprehension.

An opponent might still argue that rationality, as the term is currently used, implies an objective referent 'out there'. This contention is yet another expression of the platonic dream, that there must be some constant, unchangeable forms. This dream or the mathematical ideal of rationality must not be confused with the rationality of open systems, which are in dynamic equilibrium. The rationality of formalist systems represents an extreme end of the spectrum of our knowledge and experience. Their abstract perfection is so perfect because they are so abstract. The actual systems in which man lives and dies are of a different nature, and are characterized by a different kind of relationship: they are open, hierarchical, and heterogeneous, and in a dynamic equilibrium. Man is a biocognitive animal and he has no choice but to view the entire universe through the prism of the knowledge of the race. And it is this knowledge, tacit and explicit, that favours certain patterns which, in the long run, are life supporting and thus species supporting. These patterns are the essence of human rationality. Rationality is thus a sanctification (on an abstract level) of the order that supports us. *Rationality is a formalized repository of the wisdom of the species.*

For these reasons, we must limit rationality to the human scope; not to man as such, but man in his development. For man evolves, develops, and changes, and so change his needs, his forms of interaction with the environment, with other people, with himself. The caveman had little time and aptitude for refined conversation and even less for transcendental meditation. Our concept of rationality must combine the anthropocentric character of all rationality and the evolutionary character of man. In this way, we arrive at evolutionary anthropocentric rationality.

Valid architectural systems must embody this concept of rationality and must be permeated by it, for rationality is the reason for existence. The reason for the existence of architecture is man, not the individual man, but man as the species which is constantly evolving: as Balzac said, 'architecture is the register of human history', or, in Guy de Maupassant's words, 'across the centuries architecture has received the privilege of symbolizing every period, of summing up by means of a very small number of typical monuments the way of thinking, feeling, and dreaming of a race and of a civilization'. Inadvertently, Mies van der Rohe expressed the very same idea when he said, 'architecture wrote the history of the epochs and gave them their names'.

The valid architectural system must embody all the achievements of man and must provide the potential conditions for his further development. For nothing less is worthy of man; and nothing less is rational. We must not run away from man's transcendental aspects (because this is what we have been doing under the auspices of empiricism), for man is a spiritual creature. He shares many characteristics with other living organisms, but he also possesses some

3

4

characteristics which, as far as we know, other organisms do not possess: his self-consciousness, his art, his spirituality. A truly rational architectural system must include man's spiritual aspects. Whoever sees this as a paradox does not grasp the importance of architecture in enhancing the spiritual aspects of human nature, for, to quote Victor Hugo this time, 'Architecture is the book of human history'.

Though I have discussed at length the dangers inherent in the pursuit of scientific rationality, or more generally of objectivist rationality, I have not given its defining characteristics in contrast to those of evolutionary rationality. They are as follows.

1   Objectivist rationality accepts one rigid conceptual framework which is physical in nature and treats it as if it were absolute. Evolutionary rationality, on the other hand, accepts a flexible framework, or rather a variety of frameworks, all of which are ultimately related to man as the point of departure or arrival. From the standpoint of evolutionary rationality, our behaviour, thought, or action must be seen and assessed as rational or anti-rational within a specific framework and within the relationships characteristic of this framework.

2   Whereas objectivist rationality is a priori (based on rules), evolutionary rationality is a posteriori (based on feedback). When our action, thought or behaviour produce consequences which are negative or undesirable, then it is a sign that we have to rethink the existing relationships and the validity of our framework.

3   Whereas objectivist rationality is based on rules which, if followed, will render our action consistent and thus rational, evolutionary rationality is based on the idea of feedback, and in particular negative feedback. Regardless of how consistently we apply the rules of logic and science, if the outcome of our conduct has detrimental consequences, then this conduct is not rational.

4   Whereas objectivist rationality concerns itself with relationships that are very clearly defined, the universe of these relationships is very limited. Evolutionary rationality, on the other hand, deals with relationships which are not always clearly—let alone mathematically—defined, but the universe of these relationships is very extensive. The contrast here is essentially between the poverty of connections and relationships which are well defined against the richness of connections and relationships which are not so well defined.

5   Whereas objectivist rationality concerns itself with homogeneous phenomena which are usually physical in nature or reducible to physical ones, evolutionary rationality deals with heterogeneous phenomena and establishes various kinds of orders across these various kinds of phenomena.

6   Whereas objectivist rationality is linear, evolutionary rationality is hierarchical. Objectivist rationality forces us to make judgements on the basis of abstract computation within one system. Evolutionary rationality allows us to make judgements by referring to a hierarchy of systems and to the importance of the particular element in the system.

7   Whereas objectivist rationality presupposes the system that is isolated, evolutionary rationality is conceived for those systems that are connected.

8   Whereas objectivist rationality assumes that the behaviour or action of large and complex systems is the result of the behaviour of its particular parts, so that total behaviour equals the sum of its parts, evolutionary rationality recognizes that the behaviour or action of many large and complex systems cannot be explicable by the behaviour of the constituents of the system; total behaviour equals more than the sum of its parts.

9   Whereas objectivist rationality strives toward maximal simplicity in its result, evolutionary rationality strives toward the satisfaction of the aesthetic, moral, and transcendental aspects of man which are inherent in his nature and must find an outlet.

It would be wrong to imply that architects are totally unaware of the existence and importance of evolutionary rationality. There is a great deal of tension within themselves and a great deal of confusion in their thinking. On the one hand, they

3 Konrad Wachsmann, Mobilar Structure: a system of construction for hangars of varying sizes developed for the US Air Force in the 1940s

4 Ralph Erskine's Byker estate in Newcastle-upon-Tyne

are confined within the terms of objectivist rationality, which dictates to them what is valid and thus rational in scientific terms; and on the other hand, they are intuitively aware that there exists another kind of rationality which alone makes their work truly (that is, humanly) valid.

Architecture and design are rational if and when they meet the demands and requirements of man in a given historical epoch. Ours requires and demands that man's habitat is considered within the total environment hierarchically conceived. Or, as Vincent Scully put it, 'the human act of architecture is the construction of the whole human environment, and the entire constructed environment is architecture'. This must be the basis for new rationality.

Conclusion

The new rationality of architecture we seek will be a function of the architectural system we adopt, and vice versa. We can adopt a semi-formal system as our basis, as we have so often done in the past, and find ourselves imprisoned in it. Or we can adopt a system in the measure of man, the transcendent creature who defies the confines of mechanistic, physicalistic, and logical systems. The fundamental co-ordinate of the architectural system is man in evolution. Systems which omit man as the fundamental co-ordinate are either subhuman or superhuman. In the former case, they of necessity distort and impoverish us as human beings. In the latter case, they are beyond our human grasp. So the criteria of rationality must be anthropocentric and above all evolutionary: what may be deemed rational in the context of the caveman is not necessarily rational for man in industrial society. Furthermore, what may be deemed rational for industrial man may turn out not to be so for post-technological man.

Indeed, we must evolve a new rationality in architecture for post-scientific and post-technological man—for post-scientific man who accepts the enlightenment science provides, but does not become the slave of scientific reason; and for post-technological man who accepts with gratitude the material abundance technology provides but does not become obsessed by the means of technology and the idea of material progress, who is aware that modern technology signifies the end of the period of scarcity, but who is also aware that the present distribution of material goods provided by technology (which is, after all, the property of all humanity) is unfair and unjust.

For such a man we must design and build. And in relation to such a man we must evolve new criteria of rationality. For the first time in human history, we can take science and technology for granted and use them for creating conditions which in previous epochs would have been called a utopia on earth, but which for us are simply necessity. It is our historical mission to create these conditions. We must do so for one fundamental reason: in order to survive as a civilized society. It is thus not only a choice but an imperative. And this imperative must be followed.

Architecture has always been a servant to man. During the last few decades we have made it a servant to the mechanistic man. With the introduction of evolutionary rationality as the basis of our design, the rationality which is related to and rooted in quality of life criteria, we return to the great tradition of architecture in which it served the transcendent aims of man; and only such architecture can survive the test of time and become a part of the cherished historical heritage.

NOTES

[1] Parts of this chapter are derived from a paper presented to RIBA, London.
[2] For further discussion of the criteria of validity in architecture and in design, see Henryk Skolimowski, Space, Quality of Life and Architecture, *Architecture: Achievement and Opportunity*, RIBA Publications, 1977.
[3] *ibid.*

Mannerism and modern architecture

by Colin Rowe

Two papers by Colin Rowe, published in The Architectural Review *in 1947 and 1950, have proved to be of lasting value and are constantly under discussion. His 'Mathematics of the Ideal Villa' (AR, March 1947) has been reproduced in recent anthologies. This article takes up some of the points he made in the earlier 'Villa' piece but in addition it provides a valuable insight into Le Corbusier's ideas.*

The villa built by Le Corbusier at La Chaux-de-Fonds, his first considerable work to be realized, in spite of its great merits and obvious historical importance, finds no place in the collection of the *Oeuvre Complète*. This building, in a sense, is out of key with his later works, and by its inclusion, the didactic emphasis of the collection might have been impaired; but the omission is all the more unfortunate, in that six years later, the design was still found sufficiently serious to be published as an exemplar of proportion and monumentality.[1]

The house is of nearly symmetrical form, and in spite of a general lightness deriving from its concrete frame, its conventional character is fairly emphatic. The principle block is supported by flanking wings; and a central hall, rising through two storeys and crossed by a subsidiary axis, establishes for the plan a simple, balanced, and basically cruciform scheme. Externally the appearance of these same characteristics of restrained movement and rational elegance seems to invite appreciation in Neo-Classical terms. Thus the elliptical windows are part of the stock furniture of French academic architecture; and while the lack of ornament with the simplified cornices suggests the influence of Garnier, and the expression of the concrete frame in the flanking walls indicates an obvious debt to Auguste Perret, the building as a whole, compact, coherent and precise, is an organization which the late eighteenth century could have relished, and work towards which a Ledoux, if not a Gabriel, might have found himself sympathetic.

One may, it is true, admit innovation in the simplification of elements, although adequate Austrian and German prototypes could be suggested: one might also perceive in the two bedroom suites of the first floor a premonition of later spatial complexity; but having made these observations, in plan and in three façades at least, there is little to be found, which detracts from a conventional, conservative excellence. But the fourth and entrance elevation presents quite distinct problems of appreciation. Behind its wall, the presence of a staircase continued to the second floor has led to an increase in height, which somewhat detaches this part of the building from the rest; and this elevation affects a severe and obvious distinction from the mass behind, with which on superficial examination it seems indeed scarcely to be related. Its succinct, angular qualities are foreign to the curvilinear arrangements of the block, and its inclusive, rectilinear, self-sufficient form seems to deny the type of pyramidal composition, which reveals itself from the garden.

The flat vertical surface of the two upper floors is divided into three panels. The outer ones, narrow and vertical, are pierced by elliptical lunettes, while the central one, elaborately framed, comprises an unrelieved blank, white surface. It is towards this surface, accentuated by all the means within the architect's control, that the eye is immediately led. The low walls, screening service rooms and terrace, are curved inwards rising towards it; two entrance doors prepare the duality to be resolved; the projecting marquise with its supporting columns completes the isolation of the upper wall, where the composition is to be focused; the emphatic elliptical windows in the outer panels increase the demand for a dominant focal

The villa by Le Corbusier at La Chaux-de-Fonds, built in 1916. It was omitted from the *Oeuvre Complète*, presumably because 'the didactic emphasis of the collection might have been impaired' by its inclusion. The formal ambiguity it displays, with the remarkable focus on a blank, framed panel, provides an interesting comparison with some designs of the sixteenth-century Mannerists in Italy

1 The use of the blank panel to provide central emphasis is illustrated here and in 2. The so-called Casa di Palladio at Vienna, 1572, a subtle exercise in the inversion of classical rules, bears an obvious relationship to the villa at La Chaux-de-Fonds

2 Zuccheri's casino at Florence (1578): the design of this house remained in the repertoire of academic architecture for a considerable time. Both the elder Wood of Bath and Sir John Soane comment on its rustication and both too are aware of its symbolism

point; and with the mind baffled by so elaborately conceived an ambiguity, the eye comes to rest on the immaculate rectangle and incisive detail of its brick frame.

Contemplating this façade for any length of time, one is both ravished and immensely irritated. Its mouldings are of extreme finesse, lucid and complex; the slightly curved window reveals are of considerable suavity: the contrast of wall above and below the canopy is permanently exciting; the sharp and dogmatic change of texture refreshes and soothes; but the blank surface is both a disturbance and a delight. The masses and the modelling impel the eye towards it, but it is the activity of emptiness, which the intellect is called upon to enjoy.

Since this motif was presumably intended to shock, its success is complete, for it imbues the façade with all the qualities of a manifesto. In this abrupt composition, if nowhere else in this villa, there appears a tension which seems to foreshadow the later development; and it is the panel with its intensifying frame which establish for other elements of the façade—columns and canopy—their apparent precocity. Distinct and deliberate, drawing attention to itself, and yet without apparent content, at once distributing attention over the rest of the house; by its conclusiveness the whole building gains significance; but by its emptiness it is, at the same time, the problem in terms of which the whole building is stated. Thus, as an apparent outcome of its systematically opposite values, there issue a whole series of disturbances, of which it is both centre and periphery.

Behind the panel lies the staircase, the lighting of which can only be impaired, and one must assume that an architect as apt as Le Corbusier could, had he wished, have chosen some alternative and functionally more satisfactory organization; while even if it were to be supposed (improbable as it appears) that the frame was intended to receive some fresco or inscription, it is still a motif sufficiently abnormal and recondite to stimulate curiosity and encourage a hunt for possible parallels. The most probable and certainly the most rewarding field of investigation seems to be Italian; not that with Le Corbusier any direct allusion could be expected, but that in general terms he so frequently appears to be descended from the architectural traditions of Renaissance humanism.

In early Renaissance loggia and palace façades, sequences of alternating windows and panels do not appear to be uncommon. In such more frequent sequences from the sixteenth century, panels and windows acquire almost equal significance. Panels may be expressed as blank surfaces, or become a range of inscribed tablets, or again they may form the frames for painting; but whatever their particular employment may be, the alternation of a developed system of panelling, with an equally developed system of fenestration, seems always to produce complexity and duality of emphasis in a façade. This quality must have given considerable pleasure to the generation of architects subsequent to Bramante; and in the pages of Serlio, for instance, panels occur in an almost embarrassing profusion.[2] Sometimes they are to be found in the typical alternation, or on other occasions absorbing entire wall surfaces; in elongated form they are used to intersect two whole ranges of windows, or they may appear as the crowning motif of a triumphal arch or Venetian palace. It was probably Serlio who first employed the panel as the focus of a façade. In some cases he has groups of windows arranged on either side of this reduced but evocative form of central emphasis; but it also seems likely that in only two instances does the panel make a central appearance within an elevation so restricted as that at La Chaux-de-Fonds. Although comparisons of this sort are frequently tendentious and overdrawn, the so-called Casa di Palladio at Vicenza and Federico Zuccheri's casino in Florence do show a quality sufficiently remarkable to permit their interpretation as sixteenth century commentaries upon the same theme. Dating from 1572 and 1578 respectively, small houses of a personal and distinctly precious quality, it would be pleasant to assume that they represented a type, a formula for the later sixteenth century artist's house.

Palladio's building is apparently generated by the combination of a domestic façade and an arcaded loggia, which in its ornaments assumes the role of a

3 A house in Suffolk Street, London. Palladio's building has here been elevated on a normal London ground floor, and the 'panel' conventionally glazed. Misunderstanding is complete

triumphal arch. Unlike the conventional triumphal arches of antiquity, in this instance a developed Corinthian superstructure is included; and although on the ground floor the two functions of the loggia as part of a house and as part of a triumphal arch are closely integrated, in itself the arch is even more intimately related to the panel formed by the Corinthian pilasters above. The breaking forward of the Ionic entablature about the arch provides a direct vertical movement through the two orders, emphasizing their interdependence, so that the panel retains the focus developed by the arch below, but seems otherwise to read as an intrusion projected upwards into the *piano nobile*. Its anomalous character is further increased by details which suggest a respect for the functions of the domestic façade; and thus such a feature as the balcony rail of the windows, which emerges from behind the pilasters to appear in the panel as a continuous string course, only serves to exaggerate, as it was presumably intended it should, an already inherent duality.

It need scarcely be pointed out that we are here in the presence of a formal ambiguity of the same order as that which Le Corbusier was to provide in 1916; although in lucid, academic dress, the disturbance is less perceptible and perhaps more complete. Palladio's inversion of the normal is effected within the framework of the classical system, whose externals it appears to respect; but in order to modify the shock to the eyes, Le Corbusier's building can drawn on no such conventional reference. Both state the problem of their complex duality with an extreme directness and economy of means, which by comparison, causes Federico Zuccheri's essay in the same composition to appear at once redundant and bizarre.

His approach is altogether more violent, his building a *jeu d'esprit* conceived as part of a programme of personal advertisement, and illustrating his triple profession as painter, sculptor, and architect. Unlike Palladio, his two elements of focus, the void of the entrance below, and the solid of the panel above, are not placed in direct relationship; but each, as the dominant interest in strongly contrasted stone and brick surfaces, appears set within an arrangement of incident, which both diminishes and accentuates its importance. Two triangles of interest are established. That below is formed by the three tablets with their reliefs of mathematical instruments, and has as its apex an heraldic cartouche. That above is organized by windows and niches about the central panel, in this case, as in the Palladio house, intended to receive a painting. This diffused incident, which is still concentrated within the strictly triangular schemes, establishes a form of composition different from Palladio's, so that with Zuccheri, the particular ambiguity of the panel is of less importance, when compared with that of the entire façade.

The composition of the lower wall is framed by rusticated pilasters, which seem to restrict its detail between quite rigid boundaries; but these pilasters receive no downward transmission of weight. Two advanced surfaces in the upper storey carry a form of triglyph or bracket, which seems to suggest for them a function of support; but they are displaced by niches from the position above the pilasters, which reasonably they might be expected to occupy; while the insertion within them of elaborately framed windows invalidates still further their apparent function. The niches in themselves, on first examination, seem to expand the interest of the upper wall and create there the appearance of an organization as open, as that of the wall below is compressed; but, within this organization, it becomes clear that the different elements—niches, windows and panel—are crushed in the harshest juxtaposition, so that on second analysis, the contrast compels one to attribute to the supposedly compressed basement an almost classical directness and ease.

The complexities and repercussions which such schemes provoke are endless and almost indefinable, but patience perhaps exhausts itself in the explanation. It would seem to be abundantly clear that it is a dilemma of dual significance, a distinction between the thing as it *is* and as it *appears*, which seems to haunt all these three façades; and if Zuccheri's building by comparison with the more lucid expositions seems to be something of an exercise in genre, its second-hand qualities perhaps enhance its value as a document, almost as a text-book illustration of deliberate architectural derangement.

The two examples from the sixteenth century are characteristic late Mannerist schemes, the most apt registers of that universal *malaise*, which in the arts, while retaining the externals of classical correctness, was obliged at the same time to disrupt the inner core of classical coherence.

In so-called academic, or frankly derivative architecture, the recurrence in 1916 of a form of composition, which at first glance appears intrinsically Mannerist, need perhaps cause no undue surprise; but, occurring as it does, in the main stream of the Modern Movement, it is remarkable that this motif at La Chaux-de-Fonds should not have aroused more curiosity. It is not in any way suggested that Le Corbusier's use of the blank panel is dependent on the previous instances, and it is not imagined that a mere correspondence of forms necessitates an analogous content. Such a correspondence may be purely fortuitous or it may be of some deeper significance.

Apart from Nikolaus Pevsner's article *The Architecture of Mannerism*[3] and also Professor Blunt's lecture at the RIBA, in its accepted sense as a style Mannerism has been the subject of no popular discussion. Such discussion must obviously lie beyond the scope of this present essay, which for a frame of reference relies to a great extent on the article and lecture already cited. In the most general terms, works produced between the years 1520 and 1600 are to be considered Mannerist, and it is hoped that the particular analysis of two sixteenth-century schemes has provided some illustration of types of ambiguity that are characteristic.

An unavoidable state of mind, and not a mere desire to break rules, sixteenth-century Mannerism appears to consist in the deliberate inversion of the classical High Renaissance norm as established by Bramante, to include the very human desire to impair perfection when once it has been achieved; and to represent, too, a collapse of confidence in the theoretical programmes of the earlier Renaissance, which it is able neither to abandon nor to affirm. As a state of inhibition, it is essentially dependent on the awareness of a pre-existing order: as an attitude of dissent, it demands an orthodoxy within whose framework it might be heretical. Clearly, if as the analysis of the villa at La Chaux-de-Fonds suggests, modern architecture may contain elements analogous to Mannerism, it becomes essential to find for it some corresponding frame of reference, some pedigree, within which it might occupy an analogous position.

Among sources for the Modern Movement, the characteristic nineteenth-century demand for structural integrity has rightly received greatest emphasis. Dependent to some extent on the technical innovations of industrialism, this demand was unexpectedly reinforced by the Revivalists, both Gothic and Greek; and it was they who transformed its original rational basis and imbued this structural impulse with a dynamic emotional and moral content. In this possibly fallacious form, the structural tradition has remained one of the most crude, indiscriminate, and magnificently effective forces which we have inherited from the nineteenth century.

But it remains apparent that a system of architecture cannot enjoy a purely material basis, and that some conception of form must play an equal and opposite role. Although formal derivations for the Modern Movement often seem to impose too great a strain on the imagination, at a time no more remote than the later nineteenth century, it is noticeable that advanced architecture from the seventies onwards belongs to one of two discernible patterns.

The programme of the first is certainly closest to our sympathy, and its outlines clearest in our minds. It was the heroic process of simplification, representing an intense and consistent aesthetic effort, the direct assault upon nineteenth-century pastiche of a Philip Webb, a Richardson or a Berlage, and it would seem that the central tradition of modern architecture does proceed from the personal conflict, which such individuals experienced between the authorities of training and reason. Obedience to the nature of materials, to the laws of structure, consecrated by the theorists of the Gothic Revival and everywhere recognizable in the products of contemporary engineering, seemed to offer an alternative to purely casual picturesque effects; and from within such a framework, it was felt that an architecture of objective significance might be generated. For architects of this school an inevitable tension is clearly experienced between a pictorial education and the more purely intellectual demands which a structural idealism imposes. Trained in pictorial method, but insisting on an architecture regulated by other than visual laws, their forms frequently bear all the marks of the battleground from which they had emerged.

The alternative tendency apparently owes nothing to this dialectic; but equally concerned with the rational solution of the mid-nineteenth-century impasse, it found in physical attractiveness its architectural ideal. Without either the former school's consistent vigour or narrow prejudice, the architects of this second school look down the perspectives of history with a liberal eye and are anxious to coordinate its suggestions. From an analysis of function, there emerges a discipline of the plan; and from the impressions of a visual survey, that research into architectural composition which has engrossed so many subsequent theorists. Adhering to no distinct formula of revival, there is willingness in this second school to combine motifs from several different styles, and in the resultant amalgam, they appear as 'telling' features in a composition, rather than for any further significance which they might possess. Thus we find Norman Shaw is able to support late Gothic effects of mass with detail from the school of Wren; and concerned chiefly with broad effects of movement, mass, silhouette and relationship, architecture is valued more completely as a source of visual stimuli.

Neither of these two schools can be considered as completely independent of, nor as completely unaffected by, the other's activities; but while for the one, an architecture objectively rooted in structure and craftsmanship is an emotional necessity, the other neither finds such objectivity possible, nor perhaps desirable. For the first school, architecture still possessed a certain moral quality, among its purposes was that of imparting a truth; for the second its significance was more exclusively aesthetic, its purpose was to convey a sensation. The architects of this second school saw the possibilities of a rational manner to lie in the expression of the sensuous content common to all phases of art, and in this emphasis they are perhaps more typical of the late nineteenth century.

The great distinction of this period, its insistence on purely physical and visual justification for form, appears to separate its artistic production from that of all previous epochs—from the Renaissance by its failure to represent public ideas, from the later eighteenth and early nineteenth-century Romantic phase, by its elimination of private literary flavour. For although in intention the architecture of the early nineteenth century was romantic, pictorial and literary; in practice, particularly through its Neo-Classical exponents who have with justice been interpreted as the legatees of the Renaissance tradition, it inherited a good deal of earlier academic thought. For the later nineteenth century, the Renaissance is no longer a positive force but an historical fact; and it is by the absence of the Renaissance theoretical tradition, with its emphasis upon other values than the purely visual, that particularly the academic productions of this time are most clearly distinguished.

Just as the Renaissance, in opposition to the eighteenth and nineteenth centuries, conceives Nature as the ideal form of any species, a mathematical and Platonic absolute, whose triumph over matter it is the purpose of art to assist, so in painting it seeks an infallibility of form. Scientific perspective reduces external reality to a mathematical order, and in so far as they can be brought into this scheme, the 'accidental' properties of the physical world acquire significance. The artistic process is not the impressionist record of the thing seen, but rather the informing of observation by a philosophical idea. In its architecture, imagination and the senses function within a corresponding scheme, proportion is the result of scientific deduction, and form by these means becoming a visual aspect of knowledge, typifies a moral state, acquiring the independent right to existence, apart from the sensuous pleasure which it might possibly convey.

It was not until the later eighteenth century that with Romanticism and the empirical philosophy of the Enlightenment, there emerged their corollary, the direct pictorial approach to architecture, and its evaluation according to impact on the eye. When Hume was able to declare that 'all probable knowledge is nothing but a species of sensation', the possibilities of an intellectual order seem to have been demolished; and when he could add that 'Beauty is no quality in the things themselves', but 'exists merely in the mind which contemplates and each mind perceives a different beauty',[4] rationalism, by emancipating the senses, appears to have provided the stimulus and apologetic of the great nineteenth-century free for all. Eclecticism and an individual sensibility emerged as necessary products; and personal liberty was as effectively proclaimed for the world of forms, as in 1789 it was asserted for the political sphere. But just as politically the *ancien régime* lingered on, so with earlier attitudes persisting, the Romantics saw indirectly according to the associational value of their forms; and it was not until the *furore* of the movement had spent itself, that late nineteenth-century 'realism' regularized the situation.

After the mid-nineteenth century, with Liberalism and Romanticism no longer in active and revolutionary association, that moral zeal which had once infused their programme is less frequently found; and in all activities with a spirit of analytical detachment, the attempt now seems to have been made to systematize the Romantic experience, to extract 'scientific' formulae from its subjective enthusiasms. Thus in architecture the Romantic forms and their *sensational* implications are codified. While the earlier phase had been sensible of literary and archaeological overtones, for the later these suggestions tend to be discounted. An eclectic research into elements and principles of architecture arises, which is distinguished from the analyses of the Renaissance theorists by its exclusively functional and visual frames of reference.

The development of the idea of architectural composition might be cited as typical of these generalizations. The conception of architectural composition was never during the Renaissance successfully isolated, and while Reynolds and Soane were alive to the scenic possibilities of architecture, architectural composition as such does not play a large part in their lectures. A developed literature upon the subject is of comparatively recent growth; and as representing the co-ordination of a subjective point of view, the idea seems to be characteristic of the later nineteenth century.[5]

Apart from an expressed antagonism to the exponents of the late nineteenth century, modern architects have still not clarified their relationship to its ideas. Although these ideas now usually called academic have never been effectively replaced, modern architects generally have expressed a decisive but undefined hostility towards them. 'Moi je dis oui, l'académie dit non', Le Corbusier inscribes a drawing; and in the same spirit functional, mechanical, mathematical, sociological arguments have all, as extra-visual architecture sanctions, been introduced to provide counter-irritants to the prevailing theory. But mere reaction from a system of ideas is scarcely sufficient to eradicate that system and it is more than probable that in the sense of providing a matrix, the attitudes of late nineteenth-century analysts were historically effective in the evolution of the Modern Movement.

It is a defect of the pictorial approach, taking account chiefly of masses and relationships in their effect upon the eye, that frequently the object itself and its detail suffer a devaluation. Subjected exclusively to the laws of human sensation, it is seen in an impressionist manner, and its inner substance, whether material or formal, remains undeveloped. It is a defect of a universalized eclecticism that it must inevitably involve a failure to comprehend both historical and individual personality. Its theorists perceive a visual common denominator of form, but are unable to allow the non-visual distinctions of content; indisposed to permit the internal individuality of particular styles, but affirming the idea of stylistic reminiscence, the late nineteenth-century academy destroys the logic of the historical process, while insisting on the value of historical precept.

By all-inclusive tolerance history is neutralized, and eclecticism, which as a principle demands a fundamental prejudice, is seriously weakened. The specialized eclecticism of the early Romantics no longer convinces, and the reduced effects of the eclectic method are rationalized in order to support a more abstract investigation of sensuous properties in mass and proportion. Thus almost by negative action a most powerful solvent of revivalism is provided; and in advanced circles, by the early twentieth century, with the identity of the past destroyed and revivalist motifs reduced to mere suggestion, there is in general circulation a developed and systematic theory of the effects of architecture upon the eye.

With this conception the Art Nouveau, the more expressionist schools of contemporary architecture, and the current of Neo-Georgian taste could certainly be associated, and in their direct sensory appeal, those Mendelsohn sketches[6] representing film studios, sacred buildings, observatories and motor-car chassis factories, might be considered a logical conclusion of the idea of architecture as pictorial composition. Within the terms of this vision it seems probable that advanced architects of the structural tradition came to interpret the formal suggestions of 'the styles', and in Mr Philip Johnson's recent monograph there has been demonstrated the partial dependence of Mies van der Rohe's early designs on the works of Schinkel. Schemes of Gropius have suggested a descent from the same sources; but it should be noticed that this early twentieth-century admiration for Neo-Classicism was not exclusive to the Modern Movement, for so many commercial palaces and domestic monuments betray the same affinity. In these buildings although attempts are made to enforce classical detail, the necessarily increased scale or elaborated function leads either to inflation or a too discreet suggestiveness; and it is in reproducing the blocking, the outline, the *compositional* elements that greatest success seems to have been experienced.   ,

The Edwardian Baroque in fact offers admirable examples of the impressionist eye brought to bear upon the remnants of the classical tradition, and outside the strictly academic limits we find architects functioning within the structural tradition whose point of view remains decisively impressionist. With the early Gropius a *compositional* norm rather broadly derived from Neo-Classicism is actively balanced by the promptings of a mechanized structure.

As arising from such an antithesis between newly clarified conceptions of vision and structure, those early buildings which are rightly considered to belong to the Modern Movement can be understood for by other means it seems difficult to account for the stylistic differences which separate the works of these years from those which appeared in the 1920s. The buildings of Perret, Behrens, Adolf Loos, to name architects illustrated by Professor Pevsner in his *Pioneers of Modern Design*, are not naive, nor primitive; they are evidently precursors of the later development. But comparing for instance the Adolf Loos house of 1910 at Vienna with any typical production of the 20s, it becomes clear that there are differences of formal ideal, which neither nationality, nor the temperament of the architect, nor technical innovation, nor the maturing of an idea, can fully explain.

Loos, with his fanatical attacks on ornament, might possibly from one point of view be considered already as showing Mannerist tendencies; but allowing for an elimination of extraneous detail and a certain mechanical excellence, this house with its extreme severity and 'its unmitigated contrast of receding centre and projecting wings, the unbroken line of the roofs, the small openings in the attic',[7] even in the horizontal windows, is not entirely remote from the more naked types of Neo-Classical villa as projected by Ledoux. Without injustice it can be evaluated by the pictorial criteria which we have discussed; and although a late

4 House at Vienna by Adolf Loos (1910). Although the naked quasi-abstract forms of this house have endeared it to the polemical modernists, its composition is still uncompromisingly Neo-Classical

nineteenth-century academician might not be overjoyed in the contemplation of this façade, there is nothing here to which he could raise theoretical objection.

Such is certainly not the case with the villa at La Chaux-de-Fonds.

A work of art lives according to the laws of the mind, and some form of abstraction must clearly form a basis for all artistic achievement; but it is apparent that over and above this minimum, a work may possess those specifically cerebral qualities to which the term 'abstract' is more conveniently applied, and it has in this sense been commonly employed in the definition of the Cubist and subsequent schools of painting. The Cubist experiment which can now be seen, not as an arbitrary break with tradition, but as the necessary development of an existing situation, is the single most striking artistic event of the early twentieth century. Its influence, and that of abstract painting in general upon the Modern Movement in architecture has been consistently emphasized, and its effects are obvious—simplification and intersection, plane as opposed to mass, the realization of prism-like geometrical forms, in fact the developed manner of the Modern Movement in the 20s. But it is clear, too, that though working with a visual medium, the abstract art of today is working with a not wholly visual purpose, for abstraction presupposes a mental order of which it is the representative.

Here it is important to distinguish between its process in the Renaissance and at the present day. Abstraction occurring in Renaissance art makes reference to a world of ideal forms, asserts what the artist believes to be an objective truth, and typifies what he considers to be the scientific workings of the universe. Abstraction in contemporary art makes reference to a world of personal sensation, and typifies the private workings of the artist's mind.

There is thus in both cases a reluctance merely to report the outward forms of the external world: but, in the one it is related to a world of public, in the other of private, symbolism. That private symbolism might form a basis for art is clearly a point of view inherited from the subjective attitudes of developed Romanticism; and thus, while on the one hand contemporary painting, in abandoning the impressionist programme, denies the value of sensational schemes which had developed since the eighteenth century; on the other it affirms an attitude derived from closely related sources.

This reaction to sensation, at the same time positive and negative, is as characteristic of the output of our own day as it is of certain works of the sixteenth century; and the analogy of the development in painting might conveniently be applied to architecture. Here one might notice how characteristic are Le Corbusier's reactions towards the intellectual atmosphere of 1900. His *Oeuvre Complète* is a production as developed and as theoretically informed as any of the great architectural treatises of the sixteenth century; and his published writings form perhaps the most fertile, suggestive and exact statement of a point of view which has emerged since that time. Contradictions in a work of this scale are inevitable, and they are public property. It is not these which require exposition, but rather those more specific contradictions, which emerge *vis-à-vis* the pictorial, rationalistic, universalized premises of the opening century.

In affirming, through the medium of abstraction, a mental order, Le Corbusier immediately dissents from the theory of rationalized sense-perception which was current in 1900; but disgusted by the inflated insipidity of Beaux Arts practice, he yet inherits its whole rationalized position in connection with the 'styles'; and the notes of travel from his student's sketch book represent an eclectic principle which that institution would have fully endorsed. There is here a fine lack of distinction which only the liberalism of the late nineteenth century could have permitted; and although each example is experienced with a passion of personal discovery, this is still the characteristic theoretical programme of the time. The Venetian Piazzetta, Patte's *Monuments Erigés à la Gloire de Louis XV*, the forum of Pompeii, and the temples of the Acropolis offer the material for a deduction of the bases of civic space; while impressions of Stamboul, Paris, Rome, Pisa, and the temples of Angkor Vat are jostled alongside notes from the plates of Androuet du Cerceau— apart from the late nineteenth century, no other phase in history could, with so magnificent a lack of discrimination, have comprised so wide a field.

If *Towards a New Architecture* is read from time to time, and the reader can avoid being absorbed by its legitimate excitement, a fundamental dilemma becomes evident . . . as an incapacity to define an attitude to sensation. An absolute value is consistently imputed to mathematics, which are 'sure and certain', and order is established as an intellectual concept affirmative of universal and comforting truths; but perhaps even with the word 'comforting' the senses are involved, and it becomes apparent that cubes, sphere, cylinders, cones and their products are demanded as objects governed by and intensifying sensuous appreciation. At one moment, architecture is 'the art above all others which achieves a state of Platonic grandeur'; at the next it becomes clear that this state, far from being changeless and external, is an excitement subsidiary to the personal perception of 'the masterly, correct, and magnificent play of masses brought together in light'. The reader can never be clear to what conception of rightness the word 'correct' refers. Is it an intellectual idea, apart from, but infusing, the object (the theory of the Renaissance); or is it a visual attribute of the object itself (the theory of 1900)? Its definition remains elusive to the end.

Mathematics and geometry are, of course, not the only standards which Le Corbusier erects against the theory of the Beaux Arts and 1900. *Towards a New Architecture* proposes programmes of social realism, within which architecture, generated by function, structure of technique, is to acquire objective significance as symbolizing the processes of society. But it becomes clear that for reasons of the same indecision, the essential 'realism' of these programmes cannot be converted into a system of public symbolism. The attempt to assert an objective order appears fated to result in a kind of inversion of the aestheticism, which was in the first case so much deplored. The mathematical or mechanical symbols of an external reality are no sooner paraded than they are absorbed by the more developed sensuous reaction which they provoke; abstraction, far from making public, confirms the intensification of private significance.

This spectacle of self-division is not peculiar to Le Corbusier. In varying degrees it is a dilemma which the whole Modern Movement appears to share; and in it the mental climate of the sixteenth century receives its clearest parallel at the present day. Internal stylistic causes for sixteenth-century Mannerism seem chiefly to lie in the impossibility of maintaining the majesty balance between clarity and drama, which had marked the mature style of Bramante; but external factors of schism are also represented, and Mannerism's architectural process is to a great extent determined by those religious and political conflicts which devastated contemporary Europe. The Reformation and Counter-Reformation emphasis of religious values opposed to those of the humanists; the threat to the Papacy, and the European schism, which the Reformation itself provoked; the resulting increase of Spanish influence in Italy; all both represent and contribute to the emotional and intellectual disturbance. If, in the sixteenth century, Mannerism is the visual index of an acute spiritual crisis, the recurrence of similar attitudes at the present day should not be unexpected, and corresponding conflicts should scarcely require indication.

In an architectural context, the theory of 1900 might be interpreted as a reflection of the tolerant liberalism of that period; and in our own inability to define our position towards it, we might observe our contempt for the nineteenth-century liberal's too facile simplifications. Eclecticism is essentially the liberal style, and it was eclecticism which created that characteristic product, the detached and sophisticated observer. He is a personality who seems to be in fairly constant demand by the Modern Movement—the Ville Radieuse exists for him to enjoy—but this town also embodies a society in which it seems likely that his detached observation could have no place.

It is by conflicts such as these that the drama of Le Corbusier's architecture is promoted, and while the villa at La Chaux-de-Fonds might be presented as a first step in such a process of inversion, it would perhaps be more apt to return to the distinctions between the Modern Movement before 1914 and the Modern Movement in the 1920s.

In his *Space, Time and Architecture*, Dr Giedion makes a comparison between Gropius's Bauhaus building of 1926 and a Cubist head, Picasso's *l'Arlésienne* of 1911–12.[8] From it he draws an inference of which the correctness cannot be denied. In the Bauhaus, 'the extensive transparent areas, by dematerializing the corners, permit the hovering relations of planes and the kind of overlapping which appears in contemporary painting'. But if, as has already been suggested, the programme of Cubism is not wholly a visual one, are we to assume that these works, apart from a similarity of form, are animated by a deeper similarity of content? If so we shall be obliged to admit that Gropius's aims are partly independent of visual justification; and if not we shall be obliged to deduce that either the comparison is superficial, or that Gropius himself had not fully understood the significance of Cubism. Of these conclusions it is surely the first which demands our assent.

A professed lack of interest in formal experiment, and the possibility of extracting an architectural lyricism from the application of rational techniques to the demands of society, appear to form the bases of Gropius's system. Yet Dr Giedion's successful comparison between the Bauhaus and Picasso shows that in Gropius's work of 1926 abstraction is not wholly denied, and it is this 'abstract'

5 Gropius's Haus am Horn (1928) and his building at the Deutscher Werkbund Exhibition of 1914 (illustrated on p. 44) still exhibit, if only in composition, the elements of academic theory. The space-time factor has not emerged

element which most clearly separates the Bauhaus from the productions previous to the 1914 war.

Apart from Gropius's Alfeld factory, the Fabrik for the Deutscher Werkbund Exhibition represents the most advanced attempt before 1914 to extract architectural feeling from a building's structural skeleton. Specific architectural effects of the past make the slightest contribution, and detail is reduced to the simplest geometrical form; but, although in this building, mass is contracted to an ultimate limit, there appears to be no decisive break with the pictorial ideals of 1900. The motif of the famous staircases, a corner cylindrical element, which appears as wrapping round or bursting through flat façades, can be paralleled in academic architecture before this date; and although the transparent masses of this building represent the supreme affirmation of a mechanistic idealism, they contain in themselves no single element which appears to contradict the dominant academic theory. The famous element of space-time does not enter into this building, and unlike the Bauhaus its complex can be summed up from two single positions.

Even as late as 1923, the experimental Haus am Horn at Weimar, a simple pyramidal composition of geometrical masses, can be interpreted in these terms, and a parallel with a Neo-Classical monument, Goethe's garden house, could still be maintained.[9] But in the previous year certain schemes suggest that approach, which has come to be considered as characteristic of modern architecture. We notice in these an abandoning of the idea of mass and masses, a substitution of plane, an emphasis upon the prismatic quality of the cube, and at the same time an attack on the cube, which by disrupting the coherence of its internal volume, intensifies our appreciation of both its planar and its geometrical qualities. These are projects which appear as complete illustrations of that Giedionesque concept of space-time for which the Bauhaus is so justly famous. They are compositions which 'the eye cannot sum up . . . at one view'; which 'it is necessary to go around on all sides, to see . . . from above as well as from below'.

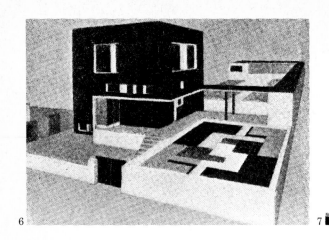

6

7

8

9

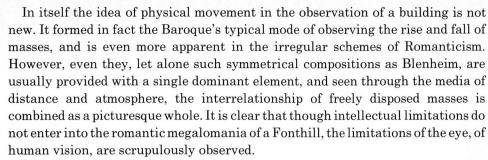

6 Ferenc Molnar's design for a house: the Red Cube (1922)

7 A project by Van Doesburg (1923). In this and the Red Cube, the theory of composition based on picturesque viewpoint has entered into a definite conflict with a system of personal abstraction deriving from Cubism

8 and 9 The Bauhaus: elements of the strictly functional programme are given unity in a Cubist composition

10 Cappella Sforza

In itself the idea of physical movement in the observation of a building is not new. It formed in fact the Baroque's typical mode of observing the rise and fall of masses, and is even more apparent in the irregular schemes of Romanticism. However, even they, let alone such symmetrical compositions as Blenheim, are usually provided with a single dominant element, and seen through the media of distance and atmosphere, the interrelationship of freely disposed masses is combined as a picturesque whole. It is clear that though intellectual limitations do not enter into the romantic megalomania of a Fonthill, the limitations of the eye, of human vision, are scrupulously observed.

At the Bauhaus one registers mental appreciation of both plan and structure, but the eye is faced with the disturbing problems of simultaneous impact from widely discrepant elements. A dominating central element is eliminated, subsidiary units are thus *unable* to play a supporting role; and in a state of visual autonomy they are disposed around the void of the central bridge, which neither provides visual explanation for them as a consistent scheme, nor allows them to assume independence as separate units. Clearly the activities of this bridge as the functional core of the conception, and as the negation of the visual function of a central element, are closely related to those of the blank panel at La Chaux-de-Fonds. In a similar way, it is both central and peripheral; and it is significant that only from a non-visual angle, the 'abstract' view from the air, can the Bauhaus composition become intelligible to the eye.

In this idea of disturbing rather than giving pleasure to the eye, the element of delight in modern architecture appears chiefly to lie. An intense precision or an exaggerated rusticity of detail is presented within the bounds of an overall complex of planned obscurity; and an intellectual scheme is offered, frustrating the eye by intensifying the visual pleasure of individual episodes, which in themselves can only become coherent as the result of a mental act.

Sixteenth-century Mannerism is characterized by similar exaggerations—a deliberate and insoluble spatial complexity is, for instance, offered equally by Michelangelo's Cappella Sforza,[10] and a project of Mies van der Rohe's, the brick country house of 1923.

Michelangelo, working in the tradition of the centralized building, establishes an apparently centralized space, but within its limits every effort is made to destroy the idea of focus which such a space demands. It is invaded by columns set on the diagonal, supported by apses of a form both indefinite and tense; and, with the central space in actual competition with the plan space of the sanctuary, distraction rather than ideal harmony is the necessary and intended result. Mies by comparison appears to invert the irregular and freely disposed space of the Romantic plan, but once more there is neither conclusion nor focus. The disintegration of a prototype is as complete as with Michelangelo, and here again form is both precise and undefined. Visual incoherence is apparently an ideal in both schemes, but, where Michelangelo in his use of the orders offers a statement of conventional intelligibility, the recognizable clarity of Mies seems to lie in the private abstraction of his plan.

Similar correspondences could be found between two such widely differing schemes as the Mies project of 1935 for the Hubbe House, and the Villa Giulia of Vignola and Ammanati. Both are developed within the bounds of a tightly defined courtyard scheme; and although in neither is there the exaggerated complexity of the last two examples, in both, elements are neither clearly separated, nor is an unimpeded flow of space permitted. The general layout of the Villa Giulia is axial, emphasizing the hemicycle of its *corps-de-logis*, but the unifying quality of the axis is not allowed to appear. As an agent of organization it is constantly interrupted by light screens and small changes of level, which are sufficient to create ambiguity, without making its sources in any way too obvious. At the Hubbe House, Mies imposes a T-shaped building upon his courtyard, but like the axis at the Villa Giulia its role is passive. It is both subordinate and contradictory to the rigid organization of the bounding wall; and while the idea of the T-shape suggests a

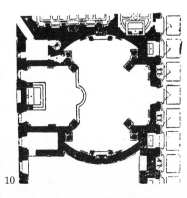
10

187

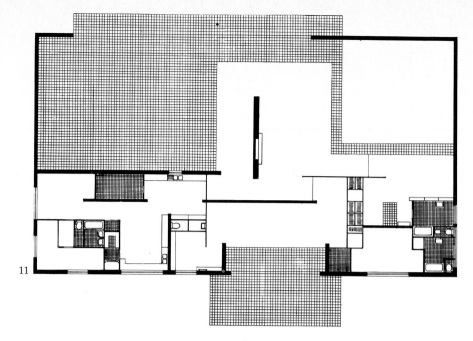

11 Mies van der Rohe: the Hubbe House (1935). A plan of the brick house appears on p. 61

12 Villa Giulia

11

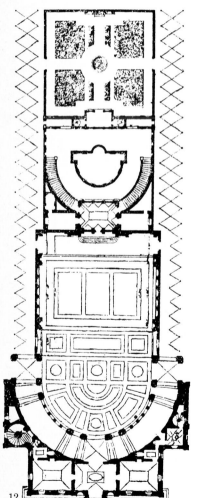

12

geometrical form, by an unaccountable advance and interception of planes, the purely logical consequences of the form are studiously avoided. Thus in both schemes, precise compositions of apparently undeniable clarity offer an overall intellectual satisfaction, within which it seems neither to be desired nor expected that any single element should be visually complete.

It is particularly the space arrangements of the present day which will bear comparison with those of the sixteenth century; in the arrangement of façades Mannerist parallels must be both harder to find and less valuable to prove. The Mannerist architect, working within the classical system, inverts the natural logic of its implied structural function; modern architecture makes no overt reference to the classical system. In more general terms the Mannerist architect works towards the visual elimination of the idea of mass, the denial of the ideas of load, or apparent stability. He exploits contradictory elements in a façade, employs harshly rectilinear forms, and emphasizes a type of arrested movement. All these are characteristic occurrences in the vertical surfaces of contemporary architecture; but comparison here is perhaps of a superficial, a more general than clearly demonstrable order.

In the choice of texture, surface and detail, aims general to Mannerism can also be detected. The surface of the Mannerist wall is either primitive or over-refined, and a brutally direct rustication frequently occurs in combination with an excess of attenuated and rigid delicacy. In this context it would certainly be frivolous to compare the preciosity of Serlio's restlessly modelled, quoined designs with our own random rubble; but the frigid architecture which appears as background to Bronzino's portraits is balanced by the chill of many interiors of our own day, and the linear delicacy of much contemporary detail surely finds a sixteenth-century correspondence.

A further Mannerist device, the discord between elements of different scale placed in immediate juxtaposition, offers a more valuable parallel. It is familiar as the overscaled entrance door; and it is employed alike by Michelangelo in the apses of St Peter's, and with different elements, by Le Corbusier in the Cité de Refuge. The apses of St Peter's alternate with large and small bays, extracting the utmost poignancy and elegance from the movement of mass and the dramatic definition of plane. They are of a perfection beyond the ordinary, and side by side with the gaping, overscaled voids of window and niche in the large bays, there appears the violent discord of the smaller and dissimilar niches, which seem to be crushed but not extinguished by the minor intercolumniations.

In comparing the apses of St Peter's with the building for the Salvation Army perhaps we really measure the production of our own day. In a composition of aggressive and profound sophistication, plastic elements of a major scale are foiled against the comparatively minor regulations of the glazed wall. Here again the complete identity of discordant objects is affirmed; and, as at St Peter's, in this intricate and monumental conceit, there is no release and no permanent satisfaction for the eye. Disturbance is complete, and although in this mechanized composition there is no element which replaces the purely human poetry of the sixteenth century organization, there is a savage delicacy which makes explicable Le Corbusier's *éloge* upon Michelangelo and St Peter's, which 'grouped together the square shapes, the drum, the dome,' and whose 'mouldings are of an intensely passionate character, harsh and pathetic'.

The quality of this appreciation penetrates beyond the mere externals of appearance. Even in his choice of adjectives Le Corbusier involves the observer on a plane other than that of visual discrimination; and, although such discrimination may assist the appreciation of Mannerist and Modern architecture, through the standards of the eye neither can be fully understood. St Peter's as conceived by Michelangelo, Le Corbusier finds the embodiment of 'a passion, an intelligence beyond normal, it was the everlasting Yea'; an eternal scheme, which is beyond the limitations of any time. But it is surely not accidental that it is the Mannerist excess and conflict of this building by which he is most deeply moved; nor presumably is it by accident that this capacity of a modern architect to perceive stridently incompatible details should so closely coincide with the beginning of their investigation by historians of art.

For Burckhardt in the nineteenth century, Michelangelo's Laurenziana, embodying some of his earliest Mannerist experiments, was 'evidently a joke of the great master'. For a subsequent generation the joke became less clear, and although for a time it was only a proto-Baroque sixteenth century which was visible, for the 1920s an epoch curiously reproducing contemporary patterns of disturbance became apparent. At this time it is as though the eye received a decisive twist, by which, since it demanded visual ambiguity, it could produce it in contemporary works, and to discover it in a previous age, even in works of apparently unimpeachable correctness. Thus, at one time the classicism of the whole Renaissance movement seemed completely clear; and at another the impressionist eye of the Edwardians was everywhere enabled to see the comforting qualities of their own baroque; so the present day seems to be particularly susceptible to the uneasy violence of Mannerism, which marks both its own productions and its historical admirations. It is perhaps inevitable that Mannerism should come to be isolated and defined by historians, during those same years of the 1920s, when modern architecture feels most strongly the demand for inverted spatial effects.

NOTES

[1] In the *Vers une Architecture*. According to the English translation 'This villa of small dimensions, seen in the midst of other buildings erected without a rule, gives the effect of being more monumental, and of another order'.

[2] See Serlio, *Tutte l'Opera d'Architettura*. The panel alternating with windows occurs in Book IV, pages 15, 23, 25, 27, 29, 33, 43, 45, 49, 53, 151, 159, 187, 221, 229. The example in Book VII, p. 187, suggests itself as a possible source for Palladio's scheme. It was perhaps through the influence of Serlio that this motif penetrated France, where for instance, alternating with a range of attic windows, it is to be seen in such a scheme as Lescot's Louvre.

[3] Nikolaus Pevsner, *The Architecture of Mannerism*, The Mint, 1946. Anthony Blunt, Mannerism in Architecture, *RIBA Journal*, March 1949.

[4] Hume, *Of the Standard of Taste*, 1757. For this quotation I am indebted to Professor Wittkower's Principles of Palladio's Architecture, *Journal of the Warburg and Courtauld Institutes*, vols VII and VIII.

[5] See the bibliography to Howard Robertson's *Principles of Architectural Composition*.

[6] See Arnold Whittick, *Eric Mendelsohn*, 1940.

[7] Nikolaus Pevsner, *Pioneers of the Modern Movement*, 1937, p. 192.

[8] Sigfried Giedion, *Space, Time and Architecture*, p. 402.

[9] Herbert Bayer, Walter Gropius, Ise Gropius, *Bauhaus*, 1919–28, p. 85.

[10] This Cappella was designed by Michelangelo very late in his life, at the request of Cardinal Ascanio Sforza, and finished after his death by Giacomo Della Porta in 1573.

A master plan
for London

by Arthur Korn and Felix J. Samuely

The MARS plan for London was produced by the MARS (Modern Architectural Research) Group's Town Planning Committee in 1938. Arthur Korn was Chairman of that committee and a sub-committee dealing with transport and economics was led by the consulting engineer Felix J. Samuely. The purpose of this article (originally published in The Architectural Review, *June 1942) was, according to Korn, to indicate a rational concept for the future of the great metropolis hoping that 'interpretations, might follow. Inevitably it seems these aims were misinterpreted and most conservative British critics dismissed it as a 'fantasy' that bore little relation to the needs and aspirations of people. Be that as it may, the mis-titled 'master' plan was a bold attempt, indeed the only British-inspired attempt, to translate the CIAM ideas of the rationalized city into an inspirational project.*

1 Factors involved

The fact that during the last 20 years before the war as many as 900,000 houses were built in Greater London, rehousing over four million people, is sufficient proof of the scale on which a modern metropolis develops. To study methodically the component forces which, although unrecognizable to the perspective of the single individual, determine the very existence of such a community, to draw the conclusions they indicate and to allow himself to be guided to a logical conclusion are the main tasks of the town-planner. The fact that a workable plan has been arrived at in this way—one which is technically and economically capable of being carried out—bears witness to the efficiency of this method. The three basic forces can be defined as social, geographical and economic. Even the effect of the second greatly depends on the state of society and of technical progress.

The town is primarily a social phenomenon. Even if the general social structure in a country were assumed to be more or less invariable for a certain period and its influence upon the town therefore considered as 'static', there would still be influences or dynamic forces of a social nature at work depending to a large extent upon the change of background and its economical influence, of the kind that govern the birth of a town, its growth and decay. London is a unique and, at the same time, a typical metropolis. It shares with other capitals all the typical features: the general chaotic conditions, the spoiled countryside, the slums, the dreary suburbs. These are all witnesses to a rapid and unorganized growth. Its individual problems are unparalleled, due to the insular position of England which has allowed her inhabitants to develop their own habits independent of the continent, and because of England's role as financier of an Empire, London representing the 'City' and the chief port. This particular function, together with the country's great colliery development, is the reason why, after many centuries of indifferent growth and even stagnation, the nineteenth century saw the evolution which, with ever-increasing speed, created both enormous wealth and mass poverty. The analysis of contemporary social influences uncovers many problems which can be solved only by considering the nation as a whole, and not from the point of view of a single town, even London. The question of concentration versus deconcentration, the location not only of production but also of consumption, etc, can be answered only by national planning. For the time being any plan must be sufficiently flexible to allow the results of any national investigations to be made use of whenever they become available.

The chief geographical feature of London is still the Thames Valley and the

Thames estuary. The two areas of high ground to the north and south—Hampstead Heath and Sydenham Hill—the tributaries of the Thames—the Lea, the Brent and the Colne—and the large parks, are all geographical elements that cannot be ignored. But it is more than anything else, the Port of London, the largest importing centre in the world, which is responsible for the prosperity of the town, and which provides the reason why the City stands for what it does. The City, in turn, has had the effect of attracting further shipping to the Port of London. Table I, giving the import and export values for Britain's five principal ports (average of the year 1935–6) shows that, while Liverpool was but little behind London with exports, London was 200 per cent ahead with imports. The fact that Liverpool, in its turn, outdistances all the remaining ports in Britain, and that both Liverpool and London act as sources of supply for raw material, explains why the London–Liverpool line is an ever-growing magnet to industry. Along this line there is again a trend towards London, which apart from being the larger port, also represents a vast market.

1 London's commercial situation

Economic considerations remind us that during a time of rapid and unmethodical development a town is apt to get out of control. It can be compared with a factory that is technically deteriorating, and therefore has to be rebuilt. This is exactly what has happened to London, and now is the time when rebuilding should be considered. It is necessary for a moment to look at the town simply as an economic unit, because only by considering it as such will it become clear that all labour and material spent on distribution is unproductive and, therefore, a loss to the community and to each single member of it. This economic unit must be assumed to include the town and its inhabitants, in the sense of institutions as well as individuals. It is the growing distribution costs (mainly represented by transport) and the resultant gap between production and consumption, that is the economic equivalent of those evils which town planning should eradicate.

TABLE I The importance of the Port of London

(Average 1935–6)

	Import value (million £)		Export value including re-export (million £)		Part of British export deficit	Tonnage of shipping Arriving Departing (million tons per year)			
London	337·23	42·1%	151·00	30·7%	60·2%	30·271	17·0%	30·685	17·2%
Liverpool	149·39	18·6%	135·09	27·6%	4·6%	16·863	9·5%	16·883	9·5%
Hull	52·31	6·5%	25·66	5·2%	8·6%	6·075	3·4%	5·931	3·3%
Southampton	27·94	3·5%	31·70	6·4%	1·1%	12·690	7·1%	12·659	7·1%
Manchester	42·65	5·3%	13·37	12·5%	9·4%	3·952	2·2%	3·727	2·1%
Gt Britain	801·90	100%	191·75	100%	100%	177·662	100%	178·125	100%

In value 42·1 per cent of all imports, and 30·7 per cent of all exports go through the Port of London. In addition, 57·1 per cent of goods imported for trans-shipment under bond (15·60 million £) pass through London. Expressed in weight, the imports (about 21 million tons) represent only 33 per cent. The great difference between the percentage of import and export on the one hand, and shipping tonnage on the other, is due mainly to two facts:
(1) Not many vessels, on the voyage from the continent to overseas, put in at London.
(2) At present, passenger traffic is concentrated more at ports like Southampton and Liverpool, than at London.

TABLE II Balance sheet (expressed in weekly working hours)

In London the value of one person's work each year=£275=2/6 per hour, 43 hrs per week.
The number of working people in 1938 was 4,349,000.
From this, the total value of one London ‖working hour per week

$$=4{,}349{,}000 \times \frac{2 \cdot 5}{20} \times 52 = £28{,}267{,}000.$$

To understand the relative importance of various items, they are all expressed in terms of weekly working hours.

	Capital	Annual value	§ Weekly working hours Hrs	§ Weekly working hours Mins
Rateable value of Greater London	—	104,627,000	3	48
Amount required to build London from scratch, as it is (including services, roads, railways)	1,750,000,000	†70,000,000	2	8
London's productive capacity	—	1,196,000,000	43	0
Amount required to carry out MARS Plan	1,200,000,000	‡60,000,000	2	6
Amount required to carry out patchwork improvements (Bressy Plan)*	230,000,000	‡11,500,000	—	13
Administration income of Greater London (rates)	—	62,152,000	2	7
Capacity of London building trade (1937)	—	75,000,000	2	38
London Transport Board (capital)	110,000,000	†4,400,000	—	9.3
All British Railways (capital)	1,100,000,000	40,000,000	1	25
London public traffic receipts (1938)	—	42,120,000	1	30
British export deficit	—	346,379,000	12	17
Saving of ½ hr per person per working day due to improved plan	—	84,802,000	3	0
Total saving expected (distribution costs, freight, etc)	—	239,200,000	8	28

* The alterations suggested in the Bressy Report would be helpful, but by the time they are carried out many of them would already be obsolete. They are on the same lines as the Paris Rebuilding of 1870 (Haussman).

† 4 per cent interest.

‡ Twenty yearly instalments.

§ Number of weekly working hours per working person in London.

‖ If every working person in London works one hour each week.

Compare:

   Cost of carrying out MARS Plan=£60,000,000 per year for 20 years.

   Saving expected in time alone=£84,802,000 per year indefinitely.

   Capacity of London building trade (1938)=£75,000,000 per year.

Compare also:

   Total saving expected=£239,200,000 per year.

   (To be used for increased production).

   British export deficit, 1938=£346,379,000.

Circumstances will undoubtedly make it necessary to decrease this deficit after the war. The rebuilding of London alone would effect a reduction of 70 per cent without reducing the standard of consumption, and with a colossal increase in the standard of living. A similar organization of the conurbations of Manchester—Liverpool—Birmingham—Wolverhampton and Glasgow would most likely wipe out the deficit and provide a much needed surplus.

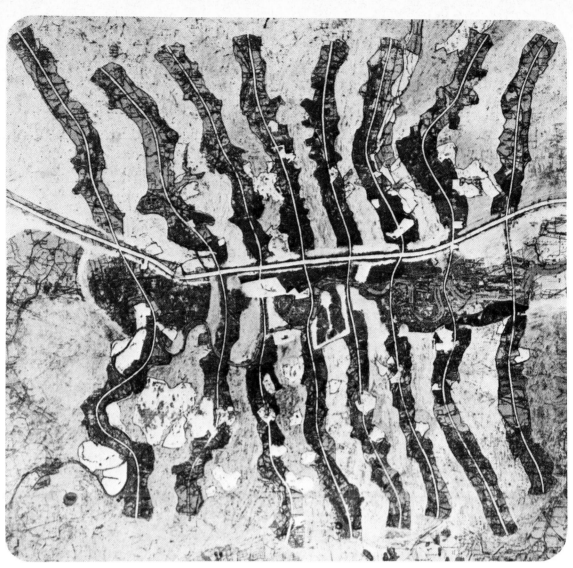

2 Draught plan giving a rough impression of what the map of London would look like after completion of the MARS replanning scheme; ribbons of open country penetrate into the city between the main roads. For improved layout see figs 4, 5 and 16

If a town can be redesigned so that distribution costs are reduced, production and amenities will be correspondingly increased. To compare a town with an industrial plant does not mean that the individual should be considered as a cog in the machine, nor does it signify that the character of a town, its beauty, its buildings, its gardens and its cultural life are of secondary importance. On the contrary, all attempts at improvement are directed solely towards improving the living conditions of the people, the cultural standards, the leisure opportunities and amenities. It should be kept in mind that distribution costs are what the engineer calls 'loss in efficiency' or 'internal friction' in a machine. To say that these losses are the most important factor of an engine would be incorrect. What is important is to reduce these losses to a minimum.

Nowhere in the British Isles is the comparative number of people engaged in distribution as great as in London where, according to the census of 1931, 25 per cent were so occupied. Nor is that the full figure, as people employed by private industries, but actually working for distribution, like lorry drivers, packers and agents, are not included, nor does it include people engaged in commerce, etc. Also any person travelling must be considered as temporarily engaged in distribution, so that the actual proportion becomes much greater (more than 40 per cent). Distribution costs are partly commercial and partly dictated by transport, but even the former can be greatly reduced if the transport is simplified.

These considerations bring transport to the fore, but it would be wrong to believe that decisive results can be obtained merely by reorganizing transport. It is the town which must be organized and planned so that a suitable transport system can be developed.

The above considerations show that it is necessary to be radical, ie to adjust the

194

town to its needs. Any purely local planning is doomed to failure. It is necessary to have a master plan, a grid on which the town can be developed. This master plan must take into account the 'backbone' consisting of the Port, the City and the West End, and the industries which mainly converge upon the London–Liverpool line. It has also to allow for the organization of the vast population (eight and a half million people in 1937) which at present straggles untidily over the whole London area.

The idea of such a superimposed grid may appear somewhat Utopian, but this is of little consequence provided a schedule is worked out by which London can gradually be converted to its new plan. A glance at Table II will show that the number of people working in London is so colossal that the total capital investments represent but a few hours' labour for each person; or, in other words, looked at from the point of view of national economy, only a fraction of the time proper planning could save is necessary to rebuild the whole of London from scratch. It is worth while to appreciate this fact thoroughly, even though the realization of the aims set out here does not require quite such radical measures.

2 Development of a plan

The final aim of all town planning is to provide the maximum number of amenities for the population. These amenities can be grouped under the following headings: Public Health, Culture[1] and Leisure. It has been found that the provision of the maximum benefits depends on three other items: Housing,[2] Work and Transport. Housing and transport are an integral part of town-planning. Work, the combined labour of the community, is affected only with regard to location. The study of work is a study of statistics, directed towards achieving the best possible location.

The various investigations, therefore, have to be subdivided under the following headings:

A Amenities
Compared with country and small towns, large towns have the advantage of more efficient health services. They are at a disadvantage, however, if the air is polluted and if the natural mode of living is hindered. These effects approximately cancel each other in the present LCC area.

The outer suburbs of London show a great improvement (for infant mortality and death rate see Table III). This table also shows how much more can, and must, be done until the present health standard of, say, Amsterdam, a continental town of comparable wealth, is reached and, it is hoped, surpassed.

The essential health requirements in a plan (and they do not allow of any compromise) are:
1 Green spaces, sufficient for long continuous walks, combined with sports grounds, should not be more than ten minutes' walk from any dwelling.[3]
2 Pollution of the air due to industry, steam, etc, is to be avoided (which means complete separation of industry and living quarters).
3 Transport between home and work should be as simple and as short as possible, and not underground.
4 Density should be so controlled that the vegetation in each area is sufficient to constantly and completely regenerate the foul air produced by human beings.
5 Low-lying districts should not be used for human habitation.
6 Overcrowding must be eliminated.
7 There must be a sufficient number of medical centres, hospitals, etc, entirely separated from the noise of traffic, and situated in green surroundings.

The present inadequate disposition of open-air recreation space is the result of unco-ordinated purchases and bequests of isolated parks, and is unrelated to the housing areas, the most densely populated areas being almost unprovided for. The majority of schools, and even new flat developments, provide only asphalt playgrounds, and the children have to travel considerable distances to reach adequate open space. The provision of allotments and gardens is negligible in the areas where the need is greatest. While in recent years efforts have been made to reduce overcrowding and to improve the hospital position, practically nothing has been done about the other requirements, and there is little chance of anything being achieved within the framework of present-day London.

While the requirements for public health are of a general nature, the cultural necessities are more specific. Education has, for many years, been on such a low level, particularly in its technical and economic aspects, that it has even hampered international competition. The situation has improved during the last two decades, but much scope for further improvement remains. To convert elementary, secondary and other schools, libraries, etc, into real centres of community interest is mainly a housing problem. The same applies to other public buildings like theatres, cinemas, concert and lecture halls, etc. Well-organized leisure serves either health or culture.[4]

Leisure may be sub-divided first into indoor leisure, which includes that intimately related to the design of the home and dependent on privacy, quietness and a direct contact with nature, but also includes cinemas, museums, etc; and, secondly, open-air leisure, which can itself be divided into the following categories:

1 Horticultural pursuits.
2 Organized recreation.
3 Unorganized recreation.

Provision must be made for the first nearer to houses or flats. The second can be organized at home, at school or elsewhere. For people have different requirements according to their age or occupation. The young children require play space near their homes, the school children at school, and the adults either near their factory or office or within their housing district.

On the basis of present leisure habits, 14 acres per 1,000 persons would be required. This area does not include for playing fields for those workers who find organized recreation locally rather than at their centre of employment. Nor does it include for civic open space, such as aerodromes, stadia, race tracks, etc.

B Housing

At present the people of London live in a vast urban agglomeration which sprawls for more than twenty miles from its centre—without organization either of the housing or the social amenities which should accompany it. An administrative panelling into boroughs has little meaning while it is impossible to differentiate where one begins or another ends. London as a whole is the only social unit which conveys anything to its people, but it conveys a social life which is read about rather than lived. An organic social structure in which the individual can take an active part is a vital necessity, for at the moment there is more individual isolation in this mass of $8\frac{1}{2}$ millions than in the smaller towns and villages of the country.

Such isolation will continue unless there is some organization of social life and its expression in architectural and town-planning form; for the visual effect on the mind is considerable. The vast crowds must be split up into groups in which the individual does not feel so overwhelmed that he is forced to retire to his own home almost entirely for his social life.

Only by forming clearly defined units, which in turn are part of larger units, can social life be organized. These units should not be chosen at random, and much investigation is necessary before their nature will become clear. Only the general trend of such investigation can be given here.

Each unit must have a centre about which its life pivots, and which, at the same time, is expressed architecturally and in plan. In the Middle Ages, life centred only around the church and the market, and this is why the towns of that time were so satisfactory, from a town-planning point of view. Life today is not so simple, and focuses about many things. Theoretically, churches, shopping centres, schools, railway stations, etc, could all serve as focal centres, but in fact, life would be very limited if such purely commercial elements as shopping centres or railway stations

3 System of housing units (diagrammatic)
(1) Residential unit (not shown here) (approximately 1,050 people). Comprising nursery school for 70 children—small shopping street for everyday needs
(2) Neighbourhood unit (6 residential units). Elementary school for 600 children between 5 and 11 and 150 between 11 and 15—health centre—church—branch of public library
(3) Borough unit (4 to 8 neighbourhood units). Secondary and central schools—civic, cultural, and entertainment centre—hospital—main shopping street—local railway station—building yards, coal depots and other local industry with the necessary administration
(4) District (12 borough units). Technical school and educational offices—exhibition hall and galleries, market hall—special hospitals—goods station and secondary industry
(5) The City (14 districts.) University, museums—administration of London, United Kingdom and Empire—main shopping and amusement centre—Port of London—centralized industry—main railway station and railway system—aerodrome

4 Borough (50,000 inhabitants)
(1) Secondary artery—station in centre
(2) Shopping street
(3) Town hall, library, etc
(4) Cinema
(5) Open-air theatre
(6) Boys' secondary school
(7) Girls' secondary school
(8) Hospital
(9) Sport fields
(10) Swimming bath
(11) Intermediate road, for private car traffic
All the area to the left of the secondary schools is common. A similar unit is arranged on the other side of the artery

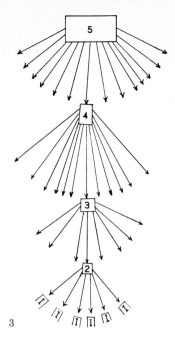

3

were to become the acknowledged centre of any domestic unit. For this reason, the educational structure has been taken as the primary unit-forming constituent. Itself comprising small units which are gradually built up, it lends itself very well to the purpose from an organic point of view (figure 3). It is important that the commercial and technical elements (shopping streets, railway stations, etc) should adapt themselves to the same units.

Two or more units, added together, do not make a new unit (two small towns are not one large one), but if something is added—a centre—that is of common interest to the small units and gives their life a new aspect, they, together with the new centre, do form a larger unit. For instance, fourteen towns each of 600,000 people do not equal London, but if the administration, universities, museums, theatres, special shopping facilities and the Port are added, then we have the capital of the British Empire. These considerations have led to the arrangement of units as shown in figures 4 and 5.

5 District (600,000 inhabitants). This particular drawing shows a flat development, but the principles remain the same with dwelling houses. The district shown has been assumed six miles long, allowing about 100 persons per acre, while generally a strip of eight miles length was taken as a basis (see also fig 13). The sample district shown here would stretch from the area at present occupied by Shoreditch and Hackney towards Edmonton (west of the Lea Valley). Observe the main station, approximately where King's Cross now is, and the parks extending down to it, combining Finsbury Park, Alexandra Park and Hampstead Heath with other existing open spaces and replacing the present sidings and slums of Camden Town, etc. The railway on the right would be the main line to Yorkshire and eastern Scotland (see fig 16). The intermediate road (see fig 4) is omitted here

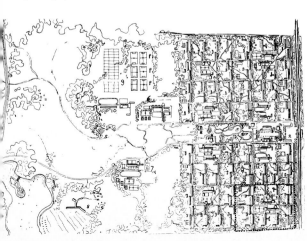

4

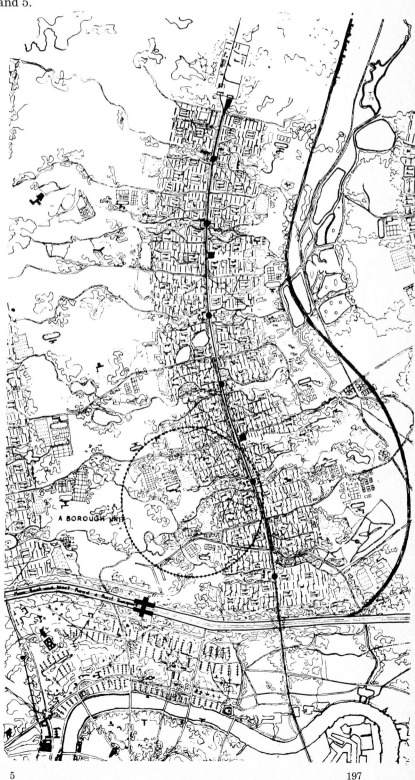

A BOROUGH UNIT

5

C Work

To achieve proper location, an analysis must be made of the place of work of the 4·3 million breadwinners in London. The latest census is that of 1931, but many changes have taken place during the last decade: more light industry has sprung up in London, and at the same time small local traders have given place to combines and chain stores. A continuous movement in this direction is to be expected after the war. Work might be sub-divided into:

1 Local and country administration.
2 Industrial and commercial administration.
3 Industry.
4 Services.
5 Distribution.
6 Miscellaneous.

A different sub-division is, however, necessary from a town-planning point of view, as it is only to a certain extent that work can be grouped geographically in accordance with the above headings. The suggested sub-division is:

(*a*) Deconcentrated work which is necessarily spread over the whole town, including most of the retail shops, the professions, most of the building trade, stores of vital materials, a certain proportion of transport and administration and all domestic work.

(*b*) Work which is dependent upon certain centres about which it is concentrated, including harbour industries, docks, wharves, depots, etc.

(*c*) Concentrated work which is independent and can be arranged according to general town-planning needs, including central administration and the light industries such as are at present located in the north-west of London.

The relationship of all these groups is not constant and good planning will allow a reduction to be made in the number of people required for distribution and administration, but the following considerations lead to preliminary results.

The annual value of work in 1937 was 1,200 million pounds in London (out of 4,900 million in the United Kingdom). Of this, administration represented approximately 100 millions, distribution and transport 520 millions and production of goods 580 millions. Transport and distribution belong mainly to part *a* (deconcentrated work), while administration and production are to be divided between all three groups. Administration is most easily dealt with as it is quite obvious that, apart from local administration, the maximum concentration leads to the best co-operation between departments. The production of goods depends mainly on raw materials, available markets and labour, in varying proportions. Within an organized town the problem of accessible labour supply should disappear so that raw materials and markets will be the deciding factors. Raw materials are derived from outside sources in every instance, while the market is either London itself (200 million pounds expenditure—34·5 per cent) or the United Kingdom (310 million pounds—53·5 per cent) or overseas (70 million pounds—12 per cent).

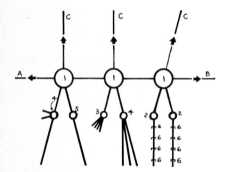

6 System of goods transport (diagrammatic)
(1) Main goods station
(2) Secondary goods station to serve local consumption
(3) Secondary goods station for harbour traffic
(4) Secondary goods station for industrial area
(5) Secondary goods station for main shopping centre
(6) Local shopping street
A-B goods ring (connecting to other main goods stations)
C Long distance goods traffic

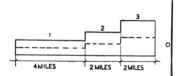

7 Housing density
(1) 55 people per acre (12 houses per acre—no flats)
(2) 85 people per acre (houses and some flats)
(3) 110 people per acre (mainly flats)
O Main artery

TABLE III Mortality rate

	Infant mortality per 1,000 born	Crude death rate per 1,000 living
England and Wales	59	12·1
LCC area	66	12·3
Outer London	49	9·7
Amsterdam	29	8·6

The adjusted death rate, taking into account the age distribution of the population, would reduce the difference between Outer London and the LCC area by about 15 per cent. (10·5 against 12·5). If the death rate of Amsterdam is adjusted in the same way the difference would again be reduced by a similar amount. It should be noted, however, that the better age distribution in Amsterdam is partly due to the reduced infant mortality in former years.

The present infant mortality in Greater London (56) is 93 per cent higher than that in Amsterdam.

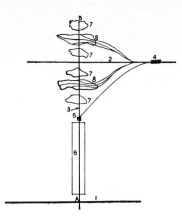

8 Satellite towns
(1) Main artery
(2) Goods ring
(3) Secondary artery
(4) Main goods station
(5) Secondary goods station
(6) District for 600,000 people
(7) Satellite towns
(8) Satellite industry
A Intersection of arteries
B End of secondary artery
Length A–B=19.5 miles

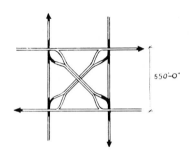

9 The fly-over. This system is preferable to the clover-leaf. The internal cross avoids the crossing of traffic lanes

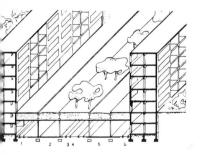

10 Shopping street of borough. The two internal tracks (3, 4) and two goods lanes (2, 5) connect to market hall and secondary goods station. No stationary vehicles allowed on 3, 4, 2, 5. The outer lanes along the loading dock (1, 6) serve for road and rail vehicles, loading and unloading. The rail tracks are frequently connected to the tracks 3 and 4. The upper level serves persons and local traffic. The shopping street is not a thoroughfare

It is obviously most reasonable to concentrate those industries with widespread markets outside London, in order to reduce the cost of goods transport, but the industries which mainly serve London itself must be further investigated. This is done in Tables IV and V, although the figures are largely estimated. A final plan would have to be based on a much more detailed analysis than is possible at present.

D Transport

There are two types of transport—goods and passenger. Economically, goods transport is the more important (see Table VI), and great saving could be made by proper planning. The average citizen, when speaking of transport, usually means passenger traffic, and every often it is road traffic only to which he refers.

Goods traffic must be analysed in accordance with its origin and destination (figure 6):

1 Raw materials and semi-manufactures arriving for the local industry; semi-manufactures and manufactures leaving the industry (industrial goods).
2 Transit goods.
3 Goods manufactured elsewhere, destined for local consumption (entering the town).
4 Goods for consumption (produced inside the town).
5 Erratically moving goods.

Group 1. The ideal arrangement for these goods is for them to come from an exterior point to a main goods station, thence possibly to a secondary one, and thence to the industry, and vice versa. If the passage of these goods is not to interfere with interior traffic, industry must be so located that it is separated from the residential as well as from the administration district. The more compact the grouping of the industry, the smaller the capital outlay and running costs. For reasons given later, main and secondary goods stations have to serve road as well as rail traffic, although for the former the station is merely a clearing point.

Group 2. Goods in transit should arrive at the main goods stations and depart from there. Most transit goods will either come from, or go to, the Port. A special clearing station is required for these goods. It is essential that this traffic should not pass through the residential, industrial or business districts, nor touch even the secondary goods stations.

Group 3. Incoming goods for local consumption should arrive at secondary goods stations (by road or rail), each situated in the immediate neighbourhood of the district for which they are destined. From there, the goods must be conveyed to the place of consumption (usually the main shopping street) by the shortest possible route.

At present, all suburbs in London could not be provided with a suitable goods station, but in a planned town arrangements could be made by which goods were delivered by rail or road, either at night or (better still) underground (see figure 10). A main shopping centre like the West End of London must have a properly devised goods delivery system.

Group 4. Goods produced by industry within the town and used in the town itself, would, with small communities, be delivered direct. In a city the size of London it is best to let them pass via the secondary goods station, ie by the same route as outgoing traffic for industry and the same as incoming traffic for consumers. The increase in distance involved is more than compensated for by the improved organization and the complete separation of goods and passenger traffic (see figure 13).

Group 5. Erratically moving goods (mainly parcel post) is a comparatively small item (which is already better organized than the rest of the traffic). An underground post collection could easily be combined with the above-mentioned goods delivery.

Passenger traffic can be sub-divided into the following four groups:

	%
1 Pendulum traffic—comprising traffic of any working member of the community from home to work and back	60
2 Point traffic—comprising travel from home to any other points, such as theatres, shops, railway stations, etc	12
3 Circle traffic—comprising traffic of any member of the community between several working points, such as commercial travellers	20
4 Local traffic—comprising travel between several homes, generally for pleasure or social reasons	8

The percentages may be altered to a certain extent with the reorganization of the town. It is obvious, however, that (1) is the most important. Any replanning that is done for the sake of transport must aim at making pendulum traffic as simple and rapid as possible.

Instead of the usual distinction that is drawn between road and rail traffic, distinction should be made between completely organized transport on the one hand and flexible transport, which is partly organized or not organized at all, on the other. In the general way this coincides with road and rail traffic, but if, for instance, public transport had its own thoroughfares, was absolutely timed to schedule and had no crossings, it would come under organized traffic, although some of the vehicles would run on roads.

While it has not been possible to fix definite scales it is established that, other circumstances being equal, flexible transport is cheaper over short distances and organized transport over long distances.

These 'other circumstances', however, play a very important part. They are entirely different in the USA where there is a population of 36 persons per square mile, from those in England, where there are 766 per square mile. Also, the better planned or concentrated a town, the greater the volume of traffic taken by the organized transport system. If many people are to be carried from one fixed point to another, a completely organized transport system can do so with the minimum expense and time. If, on the other hand, these people are to be collected from many different points, frequent stops and branches will reduce their efficiency considerably. Flexible traffic could still keep up with such conditions.

The change from rail to road traffic during the fifteen years before the war was mainly due to the excessive charges of the former, resulting from a lack of organization on the part of the railways. Under average conditions in this country, the economic road limit for goods should be about 80 miles, and for passengers between 100 and 120 miles.

Time is the criterion for traffic, not distance. Ten miles means not more than twelve minutes for a vehicle travelling at 50 mph, but ten miles across London takes more than an hour. Of the cost of buses running in London 15 per cent is spent on fuel, and the other 85 per cent on time. If the same buses were capable of travelling twice the distance in a working day, the overhead expenses per mile would be only 68·5 per cent of what they are. This also holds good for railways. Even the number of vehicles required depends on time, and if each bus could do twice the present number of journeys, only half the number would be necessary for the same amount of traffic, also relieving congestion in the streets.

Thus, in planning a town, it is not at all necessary to reduce distances, and if a better traffic system and better living conditions can be obtained by dispersal, there should be no hesitation in doing this. On the other hand, if the traffic system is complicated by a certain type of dispersal, this should not be tolerated. Both the grouping of industry as well as living quarters in the neighbourhood of arteries simplifies the traffic. A well-organized artery, with no level crossings, may imply increased distances, but it will provide a steady flow for the traffic and travelling time and cost will be reduced. High average speeds can be attained if the artery does not, as the same time, serve as a local road or main shopping street. This grouping along arteries does not mean ribbon development. On the contrary, it suggests the complete separation of the artery from industrial and domestic districts, possibly by wooded strips (see figure 11).

TABLE IV   Location of industry

The following groups allow further insight into the suitable location of industry. The areas referred to are selected to fit the transport grid.

Table V gives a more detailed account of Group X.

Group I   Personal services, laundries, domestic services, etc.
Group II   Entertainment, sports, hotels
Group III Professions
Group IV   Government (local)
Group V   Government (central)
Group VI   Commerce, banks
Group VII Distributors, transport
Group VIII Harbour works
Group IX   Services—gas, water, electricity
Group X   Industries, largely for local consumption
Group XI   Industries, mainly for export and UK

Group	Industrial Area west	east	Adminis- tration area	Shop- ping area	Cultural centre	Industrial area near goods stations	Decon- centrated	Total
I	25,000	25,000	25,000	20,000	15,000	5,000	301,000	416,000
II	2,000	22,000	31,000	2,000	100,000	1,000	112,000	270,000
III	2,000	2,000	127,000	1,000	1,000	1,000	45,000	179,000
IV	2,000	5,000	134,000	2,000	1,000	1,000	42,000	187,000
V	—	—	172,000	—	—	—	—	172,000
VI	4,000	6,000	121,000	4,000	2,000	2,000	24,000	163,000
VII	84,000	110,000	140,000	230,000	10,000	82,000	461,000	1,117,000
VIII	—	64,000	3,000	—	—	—	—	67,000
IX	50,000	68,000	6,000	—	—	1,000	1,000	126,000
X	69,000	105,000	40,000	23,000	—	93,000	209,000	539,000
XI	442,000	352,000	65,000	18,000	—	5,000	6,000	888,000
	680,000	759,000	864,000	300,000	129,000	191,000	1,201,100	4,124,000
	16·49%	18·39%	20·9%	7·26%	3·12%	4·65%	29·19%	100%

In addition to the industry in the east and west, further industry might be located near the goods ring (north and south) where satisfactory transport facilities would be available. They would be arranged in small groups (satellite towns). They could accommodate up to 300,000 working people and any additional light industry might allow a further 400,000 workers to be settled in such districts. All numbers refer to working population and are based on the 1931 census.

TABLE V   Suitable location of industries largely for local consumption

Items in accordance with census of 1931	Total no. of working people	Admin- istration	Concen- trated	Near goods stations	Decon- centrated	Shopping area
Linoleum	2,520	200	—	2,300	—	—
Building industry	279,910	28,000	56,000	42,000	153,910	—
Shopfitters	13,410	540	3,700	8,770	—	400
Cabinet makers	49,200	1,000	25,000	1,200	21,400	600
Other woodwork	8,320	150	4,200	200	3,670	100
Mineral waters	4,790	150	—	4,640	—	—
Brewing	19,920	1,000	18,920	—	—	—
Bakers	45,690	2,000	—	20,000	19,690	4,000
Tailors	88,320	4,500	57,820	5,600	2,400	18,000
Constructional engineers	9,250	2,000	5,750	1,000	500	—
Cycle and motor accessories	5,900	300	2,500	1,500	1,600	—
Glass bottles	4,900	—	—	4,900	—	—
Gardening	6,370	—	—	770	5,600	—

It must be appreciated that the number of workers in every industry may be completely altered, either due to incidental reasons, or to any national location scheme which might be put into operation.

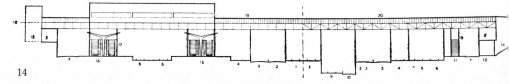

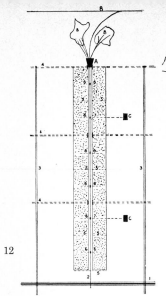

11 Relation between traffic artery and housing
(1) Artery, 265 ft wide
(2) Wooded strip, not less than 240 ft wide
(3) Residential area, 1,000 yards wide
(4) Common land

12 Traffic plan for district
(1) Main artery (see fig 15)
(2) Secondary artery (public traffic and cyclists only) (see fig 14)
(3) Intermediate road (private vehicles)
(4) Private car road, crossing artery on viaduct
(5) Local road, crossing artery on viaduct
(6) Main borough shopping street, two storey traffic (See fig 10)
(7) As 6, but with market hall at the end
A Secondary goods station
B Local industry
C Market hall
Intermediate roads are connected to 1 and 4 by internal crosses. No heavy goods traffic on 1, 3, 4, 5

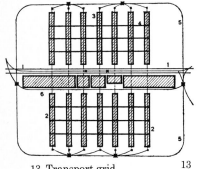

13 Transport grid
(1) Main artery; (2) Secondary artery; (3) Intermediate road; (4) Parallel connection; (5) Goods ring; (6) Goods artery
Secondary arteries for public vehicles only, the corresponding private traffic takes the intermediate roads and parallel connections. The main artery has lanes for private as well as public traffic. The former are connected to the intermediate roads. Long distance traffic is not shown on the plan

It is necessary to face the fact that the present-day street system, which is not more advanced than that of old Babylon, cannot cope with twentieth-century traffic. This street system causes those obstacles which prevent steady flow, eg level crossings and forks, and the presence on the same road of vehicles of all speeds, the slowest of which, naturally, sets the pace.

For a time, the type of organization exemplified by traffic lights has been considered the best remedy. These had an important influence on the prevention of accidents, but they have slowed up the traffic even further. Their installation on main roads induced motorists to take to the side streets, and this in turn made more lights necessary and slowed up traffic even more.

Nowadays, two-level crossings of the 'clover leaf' or 'internal cross' type are advocated (figure 9). They can solve the problem better as long as no line of traffic depends on another. Unfortunately, a large number of fly-overs cannot be arranged because they take up too much space and are structurally expensive. Fly-overs are of advantage only if there is very little diverging traffic, as stagnation can easily occur at the separation points, particularly where there are several lanes.[5]

There is one real solution. Let the street serve the purpose for which it was invented, namely, as access to buildings, and for slow traffic, but provide highways for fast, through traffic. In order to keep a steady flow, the number of vehicles changing direction must be reduced to the bare minimum.

3 The master plan

On the basis of the considerations set out above it is possible to arrive at a grid which would suit the transport of twentieth-century London, and which, at the same time, would provide the amenities required. The grid (see figure 13) is based on the following assumptions:

Population

Since the simplest system, one long strip, is obviously impossible for London, a number of parallel arteries, connected by a main artery, are suggested. The population could be settled along the secondary arteries, with industry, administration, culture, etc, near the main artery.[6]

Housing should extend for about half a mile on either side of the secondary arteries (ten minutes' walk at most) so that no public vehicles need be provided to bring people to the artery. Housing considerations support the adoption of eight-mile strips, each for 600,000 people. On this assumption, for a population of $8\frac{1}{2}$ millions, seven secondary arteries, together with fourteen housing strips, would be required (see figure 7).

The secondary artery is intended to serve public traffic and cyclists only. Private cars are to use an intermediate road traversing the green spaces, which separate two settlements. Traffic along the artery, apart from the cycle tracks, can then be fully organized, both road and rail, and the very density of the traffic makes the arrangement of separate tracks for long distance trains and coaches economical (see figure 14).

No public traffic is to turn off the artery and the number of tracks and traffic lanes on either side need not cause any complications. Figure 14 gives a section through a secondary artery. In the centre is the goods lane (rail and road) flanked by the fastest passenger traffic, then medium traffic and so on to the slowest (cycle track) on the outside. Pedestrian crossings are to be accommodated, in

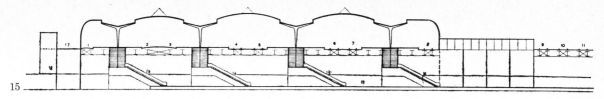

15

14 Cross section of secondary artery. The left-hand part shows a section through the station, the right-hand part between stations. (1) Goods track (secondary goods station to market halls and shopping streets); (2) Goods road for same purpose; (3) Road for fast coaches, stopping only at the end of secondary and at intersection with main artery; (4) Track for fast trains (same stops); (5) Track for intermediate trains, stopping every third station; (6) Track for trains stopping at every station (L miles); (7) Road for buses; (8) Cycle track, raised 8 ft; (9) Branch of track a, leading downward to a cross tunnel into a shopping street; (10) Branch of road b, as track 9; (11) Pedestrian way connecting platforms 16 for emergency, serves also as intermediate entry to buses; (12) Alternative entry to buses under cycle track; (13) Staircase to pedestrian bridge at intermediate bus stop; (14) Stairway to local street from bus stop; (15) Platform for tracks 4 and 5, every third stop only; (16) Platform for buses and ordinary trains, every mile; (17) Escalators; (18) Cycle lift (where required for difference of level); (19) Access road to station (no through traffic); (20) Intermediate pedestrian bridge (about 300 yards apart)

15 Cross section of main artery. Only half the centre part (public vehicles) is shown. (1) Fast coaches, stopping at main stations only; (2) Slow coaches, stopping at every arterial crossing; (3) Buses stopping frequently; (4 and 5) Trains stopping at every station; (6 and 7) Trains stopping at crossings only (every 3 miles); (8) Trains stopping at main stations only (9, 10, 11) Long distance trains; (12) Platform of secondary artery (crossing); (13, 14, 15, 16) Escalators; (17) Cycle track; (18) Crossing cycle track and lift

conjunction with cyclist lifts, by bridges and tunnels. Private cars will have to cross the arteries only on rare occasions, and a viaduct every mile will be ample.

With an excellently organized public traffic system, the number of people going to and from town in private cars will be few, being confined mainly to certain professions. Other private cars would serve merely for pleasure. Cars will reach the intermediate roads by six double roads crossing the secondary arteries on either side of the main artery, and parallel to it. The lanes carrying traffic going in the opposite directions are about 170 yards apart. These roads would be connected to the intermediate roads (those parallel to the secondary arteries) by an arrangement similar to an 'internal cross' situated entirely in the open. The separation of roads into one-way lanes simplifies the arrangement. The main artery (figure 15) is similar to the secondary arteries. It has, of course, more tracks, and in addition, has facilities for long distance traffic, and two parallel, one-way, lanes for private cars.

The crossing of main and secondary arteries would occur at two-level interchange stations, but if the majority of the people live in the housing unit opposite their work, these interchange stations would not be congested. There should be direct escalator connection between the two levels. The intermediate roads cross the main artery by viaducts and would be connected to the private traffic lanes parallel to the main artery.

The administration district and the central shopping area are both served from the main artery, and as they must have a certain depth a number of one-way streets, at right angles to the main artery, must be provided to ensure internal connections. Public vehicles will serve them, running on short routes.

Long-distance passenger traffic is to converge to one or several main stations[7] situated on the main artery so that the interchange facilities to secondary lines are simple. The main artery itself is to carry one line of long distance traffic and all trains should run right through the town to sidings beyond the outer circle. The enormous amount of space taken up by sidings in London would then be available for other uses: green spaces, housing or, in suitable areas, for industry.

Goods (figure 13)

By arranging a ring system for goods traffic, connecting all main goods stations and far enough away from the centre of the town not to hinder growth, goods traffic is completely separated from the passenger traffic. This ring must have one diametrical connection parallel to the main artery, but for practical reasons separated from it, forming a goods artery.

Main goods stations are to be at points where a main railway line crosses the outer circle. From the main goods stations, east and west, shopping centres, etc, are served from secondary goods stations. There would also be a secondary goods station at the end of each secondary artery, serving the needs of the 600,000 people living in that section. Each of these stations is connected with two market halls and with six local shopping centres, coal depots, etc, by road and rail along the secondary arteries (see figure 12). In this way a continuous stream of goods can be delivered, even during the day, without hindering passenger traffic. Even goods arriving by road must pass through the secondary stations in order that an organized traffic between goods stations is maintained, and from there to the shopping centres. Road-borne goods would not be unloaded at the stations, nor should rail-borne goods, the entire waggon loads being delivered, where possible, direct to their destination.

In industrial areas, goods traffic will run at right angles to the passenger and pedestrian traffic. It would be possible to look upon each block (about six square

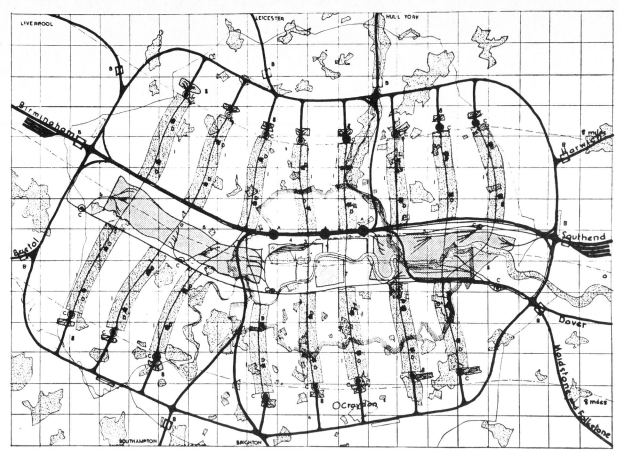

16 The MARS plan. Area of
Greater London, 443,450 acres.
With average density of 75 per
acre, for 8,655,000 people 115,500
acres are required; for industry,
20,480 acres; for administration,
shopping, etc, 3,840 acres. The
remainder, 303,630 acres or 68·4
per cent of the total, can be made
to serve leisure and become an
inestimable resource of public
health and culture.
(1) Residential districts
(2) Commercial administration
(City)
(3) Political administration
(4) Shopping centre (the goods
rails shown are underground)
(5) Cultural centre and park
(6) Western industries
(7) Eastern industries and Port of
London
(8) Local industries, possibly
combined with satellite towns.
A Main passenger station
B Main goods stations
C Secondary goods stations
D Market halls
The map shows railway
connections, but all roads are
omitted

miles), bounded by main and secondary arteries, as an industrial estate similar to
Trafford Park, Manchester. The traffic systems in these estates can be improved
upon by arranging two different levels, one for goods (east-west) and one for
passengers (north-south). A number of roads will be required leading to the main
artery, similar to the administrative district, but half a mile apart.

So far a purely theoretical traffic grid has been evolved, but in fact the
geographical and commercial structure of London lends itself particularly well to
this arrangement (see figure 16). The suggested east-west line is already
established by the Port, the Thames and the main connections to Liverpool, which
form the industrial life-line of the country. Administration (the City), main
shopping centre (the West End) and the cultural centre of the Empire are already
near the centre of this line. Also industry is, to a certain extent, already located as
required: in the east, near the port, and in the west, in the triangle between the
Great West Road, the Grand Junction Canal and the River Colne. Moreover, it is
an established fact that the areas north and south of the river are better adapted
for residential districts, and healthier, than the immediate neighbourhood of the
river. At present, fourteen districts, each of 600,000 inhabitants, have been
assumed, but the number could be varied. For the purpose of arriving at a plan it
has been taken that 70 per cent of the people live in houses and 30 per cent in
flats. The outer half of each district strip would consist mainly of houses, and the
density of 55 people to the acre (twelve houses) recommended by the Ministry of
Health would be kept. A higher density can be allowed for the areas where flats
predominate. In this way a strip $1\frac{1}{2}$ miles wide and eight miles long has been arrived
at. Figure 7 is a density diagram, but owing to the continuous green spaces never
farther than half a mile from any house, the real density is nowhere more than half.

The same layout could be adhered to if the density were to be varied, for example,
if the length of the district were reduced to six miles, or increased to twelve miles,
or split into several parts. From figure 1, in which the general layout is shown, it is
evident that the extreme point of every district is much nearer the centre of the
town, in time and distance, than the outer suburbs are today.

The health and leisure requirements are fulfilled by the character of the layout

204

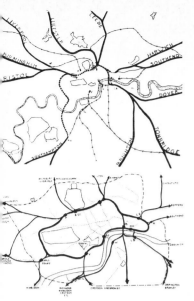

A Aldwych
BSt Baker Street
B Blackfriars
CC Charing Cross
E Euston
LS Liverpool Street
LB London Bridge
MH Mansion House
P Paddington
V Victoria
W Waterloo
–·–·–·– Outer Circle

17 Unified railway system (first stage of reconstruction). Long distance.
Main stations:
P=Paddington
K=City (King's Cross and St Pancras)
To be kept in use:
B=Blackfriars
L=Liverpool Street and Broad Street
LB=London Bridge
Wi=Willesden Junction
Fi=Finsbury Park
To be used for suburban traffic only (connected to Metropolitan):
W=Waterloo
V=Victoria
Cl=Clapham Junction
M=Cannon Street and Mansion House
To be abolished altogether:
M=Marylebone
SP=St Pancras
F=Fenchurch Street
E=Euston
Ch=Charing Cross
All trains pass Paddington and City. The thin dotted lines show the only portions specially built

18 Suburban traffic connected to Inner Circle (first stage of reconstruction). By running all suburban trains over part of the Inner Circle, traffic is dispersed

(continuous green spaces between the districts, supplemented by large garden areas within the strips), and the full consideration of cultural requirements is guaranteed by the organization of the districts, based, as already described, on the educational structure.

Work is distributed in accordance with Table IV. If it should prove economically possible to deconcentrate part of the industry further, the arrangement of a certain number of 'Garden Cities' or 'Satellite Towns' situated on the extensions of the secondary arteries could be considered. Their industries would be connected to the goods ring, and with units of 25,000 people each an additional population of up to 1·4 millions could be settled in this way within the London traffic area, and have the benefit of excellent connections to the centre, while the main grid would not be affected (figure 8).

Although such a colossal increase in the population is neither desirable nor likely, it is worth mentioning that the number of secondary arteries could easily be increased to twelve, so that the maximum capacity of the present London traffic area would be approximately 16 millions.

4 Realization

The best plan is of no value unless it is possible to visualize the stages of its execution. Two aspects are important—economic and technical.

Table II shows that the total building cost of domestic and other buildings, services, transport, etc, is much less than the saving that would be effected in time alone. Additional savings would be: decreased freight charges owing to simplified distribution costs, decreased fuel, land value and running costs of transport and services, not to mention the expected increase of trade due to reduced overhead expenses. The immense saving in land value by proper arrangement is a much more important item than is generally realized. In particular, the transfer of railway sidings from expensive central sites to cheaper outside districts would make available areas which can only be estimated, but which might be appreciated when it is mentioned that sidings in the LCC area represent 3,422 acres (more than the City, Holborn and St Marylebone). The execution of the plan could be so arranged that it is possible to effect sufficient saving during the first few years to pay for the remainder of the work.

Space permits only a rough tracing of the process of realization. Twenty years have been taken as the basis, assuming that 80 per cent of the pre-war London building industry is employed on the task, but the amount of destruction during, and the temporary depopulation to be expected after the war may reduce the building time considerably. Coupled with this is the fact that we have become accustomed to astronomical budgets. Consider: the total cost of rebuilding equals the amount spent by Great Britain on three months of the war. Also an enormous building programme might be the only thing which will keep our economy alive after the war. The extensive attempts at standardization and the introduction of prefabrication are likely to increase the capacity of the building trade by 30 to 50 per cent.

The following stages have been assumed, allowing in each case for new buildings to be erected before the old ones are abandoned. As a preliminary, an exact plan would have to be drawn up, showing how to fit into the new scheme the parts of London which are to be retained. Historic monuments, other valuable buildings and places which deserve survival will be retained, most of them being already correctly situated for incorporation in the new cultural centre. A pooling system for land would also have to be arranged, and this would be facilitated by the present rating system for which all ground is valued.

Stage 1: Years 1–4

To be cleared—Little wholesale demolition of existing buildings during this period.

To be rebuilt—All railways to be brought under one control and into one system, with every train passing two main stations (figure 17)—City (King's Cross) and West (Paddington), and all suburban trains travelling over at least part of the inner circle. Comparatively little construction work would be necessary to bring this about as all the necessary tracks are already in existence. All sidings must disappear from inner London. Suburban traffic is simplified as on figure 18.

Building programme for houses for 1·5 million people on sites now open and in accordance with the plan; 70 per cent of the administration district to be rebuilt.

Provisional arrangement of main artery by using the Oxford Street–Cheapside and Marylebone–City Road traffic lanes as one-way streets, with crossing only at certain points. No turnings to the right.

Stage 2.   Years 5–8

To be cleared—An east-west strip, one mile wide for main artery (north of Euston Road—mostly slums) and two half-mile wide strips in north–south direction for secondary artery.

Cleared railway sites to be used for new buildings or green spaces, according to master plan. All slum areas to be cleared. Sites to be used as above.

To be rebuilt—Administration section to be finished. Houses for 1·5 million people to be erected on cleared sites. The internal traffic is not affected during this stage.

Stage 3.   Years 9–12

To be cleared—All redundant buildings near secondary artery mentioned in Stage 2. Two other arteries to be cut, and five further north–south strips to be cleared, each half a mile wide.

To be rebuilt—Main artery, two secondary arteries and goods ring. Houses to be erected for 1·5 million people (this includes the finishing of four town units each for 600,000 people).

There will be some of the old traffic system still in use at the end of this period, as well as the main and two secondary arteries.

Stage 4:   Years 13–16

To be cleared—All redundant buildings near remaining secondary arteries and in the industrial areas.

TABLE VI Calculation of relative income from goods and passenger transport (March 1939)

	Receipts	% of total	% of total excluding London suburban traffic
Passenger Traffic:			
(a) LPTB	578,813	4·15	—
(b) Other suburban traffic in the London area	1,049,262	7·5	—
(c) Passenger traffic, excluding London suburban traffic	2,770,494	19·92	22·43
	4,398,569	31·57	22·43
Goods Traffic:*			
(a) Parcels and misc. traffic	1,091,327	7·82	8·85
(b) Freight	8,445,375	61·61	68·72
	9,536,702	69·43	77·57
Grand total	13,945,271	100·0	100·0

The actual proportion of the cost of goods transport is much higher than shown by this table because passengers assist in defraying the costs of goods transport.

* Excluding postal service.

To be rebuilt—Shopping centre, housing for one million people; new industries in the west of London. All secondary goods stations and goods artery.

By the end of this period all traffic will be running to the new system. No underground line need be abandoned unless the fall in passenger traffic on these lines is so great that further running is uneconomical.

Stage 5:   Years 17–20

To be cleared—All derelict buildings.

To be rebuilt—The Port of London, warehouses, etc. Finish green spaces, reconstruct cultural centre, theatres, hotels, etc.

Additional steps might become necessary, and allowance has been made in Stages 4 and 5 for extra dwellings, should the population increase during this time.

It should finally be said that the Town Planning Committee of the MARS Group does not maintain that every feature of this plan is original. On the contrary, much use has been made of other material available. Ideas suggested by famous town-planners, like Le Corbusier and others, the experience gained at various places where town planning has been put into practice, notions borrowed from the supporters of Garden Cities and Satellite Towns, have all been used, but because of different analytical methods, the final conclusions have been new, and different. The Group does not dispute that an entirely different grid might be developed which served the purpose better than the one proposed, but it is convinced of two things: that London can and must be rebuilt on organized lines, and that the methods employed to find the most suitable solutions must be scientific investigation into every mode of life, involving preliminary analysis, followed by imaginative and unprejudiced composition of the results.

NOTES

Sources: The following official publications provide valuable statistical material and have been used as sources of reference:

London Statistics. Vols 39–41 (1936–8)

Report of the Royal Commission on the Distribution of the Industrial Population

Report of the Location of Industry, PEP, 1939

Chisholm's Handbook of Commercial Geography (Dudley Stamp, 1939)

D. Stamp and Beaver, *The British Isles. A Geographical Economic Survey*

Report of the Land Utilization Survey of Britain, Part 79. 1937

Annual Reports of the LPTB, 1934–8, 1940

Port of London Authority Handbook and Diary

Annual Report, Metropolitan Water Board

City of London Corporation Market Report

Publications of Ministry of Transport and Board of Trade

Broadsheets of Association for Planning and Regional Reconstruction

New Survey of London Life and Labour, Vols 1–9 (P. S. King & Son)

[1] 'Culture' means education, training, development of mental and bodily faculties, intellect and judgement.

[2] 'Housing' means, primarily, the grouping of peoples in units and is a social question. The word also refers, of course, to research into the needs and design of dwellings. These aspects have been dealt with in many publications, and there is much scope for research. They are omitted here as they are a detail and not a primary consideration.

[3] The much-vaunted idea of a green belt loses much of its value when applied to large towns with such a low density as is prevalent in this country. With the high density of continental towns a green belt is usually within reasonable distance of all the inhabitants, except in the case of a metropolis. In order to bring the open space within reach of everybody, it is necessary to amplify the green belt into strips reaching to the heart of the city, and the belt itself is, therefore, of little significance.

[4] There has never been a large demand for 'fun-fairs' in the districts near St James's Park and Hyde Park, but between Tottenham Court Road and the Bank, where there are no parks, there is a fabulous number of places providing such useless entertainment.

[5] Two-level streets have also been often suggested. These are structurally expensive and make crossings more difficult than if traffic lanes are kept on the same level. Two-level streets are, however, worth considering where it is required to separate two types of traffic, such as goods and passenger traffic on a shopping street.

[6] A grid with radial arteries either coming together at a central point, or to an inner ring similar to the main artery, was considered; but it was rejected because:

(a) It makes the solution of the organization of the traffic more difficult;

(b) it does not fit the geographical position of London;

(c) it does not lend itself to future extensions.

[7] The green spaces being carried to the heart of the city makes it possible to arrange a central aerodrome, of any size, in the immediate neighbourhood of the main station.

Irrational Rationalism:
the Rats since 1960

by Charles Jencks

In this final chapter of the book, Charles Jencks summarizes developments in Rational architecture and examines the recent work and theories of the so-called neo-rationalists. He looks at various manifestations of the rational attitude to architectural design and discusses the work of Mies, Kahn, Rossi, the Krier Brothers, Isozaki, Bofill, Koolhaas and Aida as well as the New York Five.

Philosophical Antecedents

The philosophical problems with rationalism have long been known, especially in the Anglo-Saxon world. Hence its recent re-emergence as an architectural movement is apt to raise eyebrows. Can these designers really propose a return to principles we know to be questionable and furthermore ones which have had such a deleterious effect in this century? (Abstract form, endless right angles, and architectural 'truths' which are supposedly universal.)

The answer to this question is by no means clear. On the one hand, the architects (known affectionately as 'Rats' since at least 1975) share some of the defects of the rationalist philosophy—dogmatism, élitism, reductivism—but, on the other hand, they have given this philosophy a new twist so that it often appears ambiguous, surreal and sensible by turns. Like any architectural movement it is made from a heterogeneous corpus of styles and ideas which are only loosely grouped around a common banner. No doubt some of these architects wish the movement had a different slogan and pennant under which they could fight. A name, a tag, influences the way people look at architecture, which is why I propose, half ironically, the prefix 'irrational'. This rationalism has always been, in part.

As a philosophy, stemming from Plato, Descartes in his more Jesuitical moments and Kant, rationalism emphasizes truths known intuitively to the mind, without any reliance on experience. The a priori truths of mathematics, the categorical truths of space, time and causality don't, it was argued, depend on knowing anything about the external world. These self-evident propositions (2+2=4, the laws of geometry and logic) could generate a whole series of deductive truths as long as correct reasoning was followed.

By the same token, Rationalist architects would generate wholly consistent and 'true' buildings if they followed certain general principles in a rational way. The Abbé Laugier said 'if the problem is well stated, the solution will be indicated', a slogan Le Corbusier and other French architects liked to quote. Laugier hoped to generate truthful architecture from the elements of a primitive hut built out of wood. 'Let us never lose sight of our little hut.' He needn't have argued. The next 150 years were spent looking at primitivist construction, designing primitive huts in first year studies at the Bauhaus and in woodlands away from the city.

'An architect must be able to justify by reason everything he does', Laugier also averred, and it was this proposition which really proved so fatal to the rationalists. Their assumed truths, like the primitive hut or the grid used for all planning, have always seemed embarrassingly absurd. How could one possibly base a sophisticated urban architecture on such simplistic notions? The successive attempts by rationalists to find new, indubitable propositions were equally bizarre. An eighteenth-century architect wrote 'Gothic architecture improved' and tried to do just that by rationally turning the Gothic pier into a Classical order. Another eighteenth century rationalist sought the natural model for architecture and inevitably came up with man's ancestor, monkey-man, living in caves. In the

Sir Thomas Tresham: the Triangular Lodge, Rushton (1595). With certain historical licence, this essay in Catholic symbolism is illustrated as a Rationalist building. Like other buildings of its time, it is an absolutely clear geometric expression of a single idea, in this case the Trinity. Rationalist architecture makes a virtue of reducing form to the expression of a powerful idea which is held dogmatically. Boullée, Ledoux and Le Corbusier established this reductive poetry, Aldo Rossi and the Krier brothers are now its most effective proponents

twentieth century the same pursuit continued as architecture would be indubitably founded on the firm rock of function, logic, economy and structural determinants. All these vain attempts were motivated by the search for *certainty*. And here we have a deep, underlying psychological motive which runs through all the rationalists, no matter what their particular truth happens to be.

Before discussing the Rats, I should like to mention the pitfalls of the basic philosophy. In architecture, as indeed most science, it is clear rationalism won't take us very far, since a large part of its creation and realization consists in endless empirical data. Interviewing clients, using material at hand, modifying design endlessly according to ad hoc, contingent requirements—Rationalist architects have always proved themselves weak on these things. In general they are hostile towards public opinion and contemptuous of anything that would disprove their basic assumption. In short they are 'fact-proof', hermetically sealed off from the pollution of reality like a good air-conditioned building. These architects might be called 'reinforced dogmatists'; their ideology continually reinforces the evidence to which they attend thus strengthening their original belief, much the way reinforced concrete gets stronger and stronger if heated and battered.

Admitting all this quite candidly, and the Rats are disarmingly frank unlike their twentieth-century predecessors, they might point out the following virtues in their position. It is clear, consistent and unlike other architecture, quite passionate and convincing. If architecture is an art that should move and persuade us, then Rationalism is the best style. It is not botched and bungled by petty requirements, it can be quick and decisive, cutting through all the indecision and fog of more democratic design. Finally, in a rationalist age, the age of science, when all positions are unprovable, it becomes the most credible. People, especially leaders of a field and academics, are most credulous towards anything offered up as rational.

This last argument however pragmatic, is tasteless and needn't be dwelt upon. The devastating critique of Rationalism is quite enough, and it has been made by Karl Popper.[1] Basically the critique shows that no propositions are self-evident and unquestionable. Contrary to what the Rationalists contend, science develops by subjecting its 'truths', or hypotheses to constant criticism, or refutation, and it is this continual process of conjecture and refutation which eliminates errors. The Rationalists rarely, if ever, try to refute their own theories; they wouldn't, for instance, conduct market research on one of their housing estates, because its truth lies outside society and everyday experience. They have no use for Popper's Critical Rationalism, or what is now called the 'sophisticated form of falsificationism'. This Rationalism which tries to falsify all its truths and keep only those which stand the test has replaced the previous philosophy.

Hence the Rats are doomed to a kind of beautiful irrationalism, the lyrical and clear expression of propositions which are often as unlikely as Laugier's primitive hut. The beautiful style, which has been going on since at least Boullée and Ledoux appeals particularly to an élite—a small but coherent group of architects and critics. They have, in this century, produced the supreme expressions of organization that appeal to the mind. The sublime idealism of Leonidov's structures, the grand organizational sweep of Tony Garnier's Ideal Industrial City where every function has a logical place, the well-ordered, and well-scrubbed housing blocks of J. J. P. Oud, almost all the work of Le Corbusier and some of that of Nervi—these are the triumphs of *the style that appeals to thought*. If the irrational Rationalists have a justification it isn't in either their truths or their method, but in their ability to make diagrams of ideas exact and exciting (1). This reduction of architecture to a propositional model pleases the mind and delights the spirit, even if we know it rests on an ultimate stupidity (or a falsifiable truth).

Many of the themes, and problems of recent Rationalism were worked out by the Italian architects in the 20s and 30s. Guiseppe Terragni and the MIAR (Movimento Italiano per L'Architettura Razionale) (1927) stated the abstract

SOUTH WEST ELEVATION

NORTH ELEVATION

1 The Triangular Lodge with its symbolism of the Trinity. Three triangular gables on each of three sides surround a central triangular chimney. The windows are built from trefoils, so is the door-head with its inscription announcing the theme *tres testimonium dant*. Three floors, countless plays on the owner's name (*tres*—ham) and various other hermeneutic symbols of the banished Roman Catholic Mass made this a sermon of high treason. Rationalist buildings are often just as symbolic and geometric

qualities to be sought: 'The desire for *sincerity*, *order*, *logic* and *clarity* above all, these are the *true* qualities of the *new* way of *thinking*' (my emphasis). The 'call to order' is a recurrent call: Paul Valéry made it in his dialogue *Eupalinos, or the Architect*, an article which Le Corbusier and other Rationalist architects continually cited. The desire to put architecture 'in order' corresponded quite directly to attempts to order the political universe in the 20s, so it was not surprising that the MIAR often looked to fascism to give the lead. In fact several Rationalist exhibitions and manifestos were explicitly dedicated to Mussolini, and Terragni's best work—the Novecomun and Casa del Fascio—were implicated in reactionary politics. This sad and confusing connection of Italian Rationalism with fascism has been well documented by Giulia Veronesi and Leonardo Benevolo and I will not dwell on it except to point out the psychological connection.[2]

Rationalism has *sometimes* proved weak on totalitarianism because they both emphasize order, certainty and clarity, and they both tend to look to a classical past for inspiration. These common tendencies don't of course mean that Rationalist or Neo-Classical architecture is 'fascist', but it does mean that in our century they have tended to go hand in hand. This connection poses a great semantic problem for architects such as Aldo Rossi, because try as they might to dissociate themselves from fascist architecture of the 30s, their style is historically tied to it. We know that one dimension of architectural meaning is always historical association, and no one can escape this. All the Rationalists try to resemanticize their style, but they are only partly successful. There is always a tinge about it of Mussolini's Third Rome.

Universals and right angles
The Rationalist architecture of the early 60s was carried on by Mies van der Rohe, James Stirling, Louis Kahn and Matthias Ungers and his students in Berlin. At least, in retrospect, these seem to be the major exponents of ideas and a style that were later to be named in the 1973 exhibition 'Architettura Razionale'.[3] This exhibition took place at the 15th Milan Triennale, forty years after the last exhibition with this name.

Mies's work put forward the notion of 'universal space', a neutral, flexible sandwich of space with movable elements that could supposedly incorporate all functions. This ubiquitous right angle, justified in part as the universal element which comes from post and beam construction, became the single most identifiable element of the Rationalist style. It is quite true that all architecture, even Expressionist, has some right angles, but Rationalist works have an excessive amount of these 90° relations. One might properly speak of a fetish for right angles and grids in this work, without meaning anything derogatory, since all architecture highlights and overemphasizes some aspects of its language.

The underlying notion which justifies this, the a priori truth of the right angle, is not just based on constructional truth—or vertical loads and horizontal surfaces. It is also one of the ordering systems most easily grasped by the mind and hence claims a certain psychological universality. Furthermore it is simple. For these sorts of reasons Louis Kahn often started his design with a square plan—what he called the preform or *form*. He would then look for circumstances in the particular brief which distorted this Platonic form—what he called *design*. Thus any of his buildings would be a mixture of Rationalist forms (triangles and circles were added) with empirical twists and kinks. The particular style he used to represent these buildings in model form was very reminiscent of Palladio's drawings, those smooth surfaces punctuated by dark square holes (3). Kahn's models looked like Palladio's farmhouses, and they were so starkly seductive that the style of 'cardboard architecture' was formed, influencing greatly the whole Philadelphia School and the New York Five. Even Robert Venturi, whose later work was in an empirical style, adapting to the local vernacular, practised cardboard architecture.

Another great influence of the early 60s was Hadrian's Villa, an example for

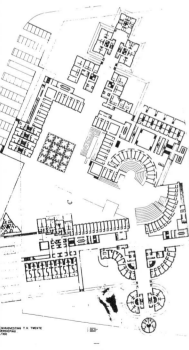

2 O. M. Ungers, J. Savade and J. F. Geist: Student Hostel Competition (1963). Like Hadrian's Villa, a series of different unit shapes are repeated on a series of axes that cross and sometimes collide. Multiple geometries, dissonant angles and a subtle *public* order emerge

211

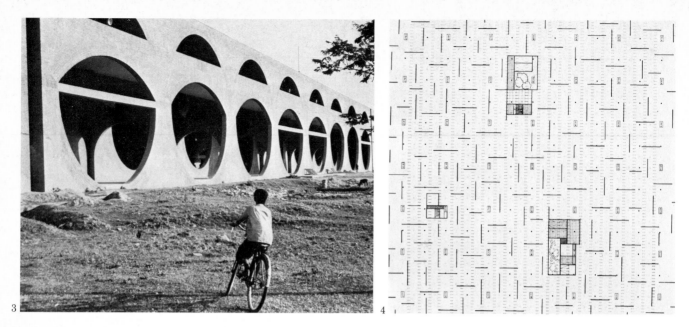

3 Louis Kahn: Dacca Assembly
Building, office corridors, Bangla
Desh (1962–8). 'Cardboard
architecture' stems from the
drawing method of Palladio and
his representation of flat,
masonry surfaces ruptured by
black, geometric holes. A
dramatic style of building,
reminiscent of Roman
massiveness, looks best in sharp
sunlight. Otherwise drab

4 Archizoom: 'Homogeneous
Living Diagram' from *No Stop
City, a Climatic Universal City*
(1970). An endless Cartesian
space with recurrent partitions,
columns and services. The models
of supermarket and parking lot
are used with a mixture of irony
and love. Isotropic space is at
once the death and resurrection
of architecture

urban planning which fascinated not only Kahn, but Colin Rowe, Vincent Scully
and Matthias Ungers. Projects began appearing by 1963, showing the mixture of
varied and clashing geometries of this Roman villa (2). Hadrian had done in the
second century what modern planners could do now: use a limited repertoire of six
or eight geometric units and their extensions and then smash them together in a
'juxtaposed manner' (a favourite phrase of the time). Colin Rowe was later to write
a book around this compelling image and method, which he called Collage City
and Collision City.[4] Part utopian and absolutist and part historical and accidental,
Collage City, like Hadrian's Villa, could incorporate anything into its pattern
without being destroyed, because its pattern was already rich and fragmented, *and*
geometric. It is worth emphasizing that Rowe's approach was much more universal
than Mies's and other Rationalists' because it was made from a richer repertoire of
primary elements and was more open to distortion and accepting new uses.

The work of Archizoom and Superstudio in the late 60s took the collage
approach and streamlined it back in the direction of Mies (4). Back was the
ubiquitous grid; in fact, No Stop City and the Continuous Monument were three-
dimensional gridded space that was to zoom around the whole world, uniting all
activities in a common white rectangle. Superstudio spoke, with barely discernible
irony of the 'sweet tyranny' this would induce in people admiring the grids.
Archizoom spoke about 'isotropic space', homogeneous sandwiched space which
would be well serviced like a supermarket and just about as neutral and boring.
They considered this a subversive proposition to a consumer society, taking its
ultimate building type and the pressures towards conformity to their absurd
extreme. Rationalists have always loved an argument pushed to absurdity,
especially if it starts from a self-evident truth.

Reduction to archetypes

About 1968, Aldo Rossi's projects started to have a great influence in Italy, and
elsewhere in the student design world. In a sense they had a profound impact for
precisely the reason that the schemes of Archizoom, Superstudio and the New
Brutalists did: for pushing the nihilism of consumer society so far that it actually
became poetic. This paradox of meaning through anti-meaning is underlined by all
critics of Rossi whether they praise or attack him. They all respond to the
ambiguity of portraying death, silence, and alienation with such ruthless
consistency and remorseless repetition that these primary meanings are partly
transformed.[5]

The experience of the modern architect in Italy has always been closely
associated with death—several Rationalists were killed in concentration camps,
others designed monuments to patriots—so it is not surprising that mortuary

5 Aldo Rossi: Project for the Modena Cemetery (1971). Along the four massive walls and under them is the Columbaria; in the centre, stepped shapes are the ossuaries; in the green patches the burial ground. The cone represents the common grave while the sacred cube is for the war dead and partisans. The symbolism is as strong in its own way as Thomas Tresham's triangle

6 Aldo Rossi: residential unit in the Gallaretese quarter, Milan (1969–70). A long residence—182 long—has a 'portico' entrance repeated infinitely at its base, and then long corridors above. The stark black and white photos again remind one of Palladio and cardboard architecture—indeed the reality looks like a model

themes and death-camp overtones constantly inform their work. One of Rossi's most important schemes, the project for the Modena Cemetery, 1971, is next to the Lager of Fossoli, a place of commemoration for those who died under fascism, and the cemetery has a sanctuary for the war dead and partisans (5). It's a cube with black square windows opening on to a void—a sort of mass housing for the dead, in a de Chirico style (even with pitch black shadows drawn in the empty piazza). Endless straight lines and repeated arcades enclose this sacred image of stillness. A squat cone juts up on the main axis, reminiscent of death-camp chimneys, but this awkward cone is not for 'the final solution', it's a monument to 'the common grave'. The fury that such ambiguous images can inspire in people should be compared with the anger that Lina Wertmüller's *Seven Beauties* generated. She also used the images of an extermination camp for their ambiguous beauty, and like Rossi is inspired by a kind of metaphysical gloom, a morbid delight in the idea that society is really an infernal machine, and life a horrible game that just manages to survive between its gears.

Rossi's images are not necessarily pessimistic, although they have been compared even by favourable critics such as Vittorio Savi to mental hospitals; Rossi is inspired by galleries, arcades, silos, factories and farmhouses in the Lombard countryside. In his additions to the working-class area in Milan (6) the Gallaretese neighbourhood, he has produced a modern version of the traditional tenement corridor which, he says 'signifies a life-style bathed in everyday occurrences, domestic intimacy, and varied personal relationships'.[6] The only problem with this characterization is that few people would see it; most would compare it with engineering works, tunnels or roadworks, as Rossi has admitted in the same article quoted above. Or they might say it signifies 'barracks', 'social deprivation' and 'l'homme machine'. In point of fact Rossi's language is so reduced in signification that it is read in diametrically opposite ways: by the élite and by critics such as Manfredo Tafuri, as 'emptied sacredness' as 'a discourse on itself', and by the public or hostile critics as 'quasi-fascist' and 'cemeteries and prisons'.

Tafuri answers these critics with a kind of miraculous escape-clause contending that Rossi can rise above historical associations, like an architectural superman, because his architecture is autonomous, free from contamination:

'the sacred precision of his geometric block [the Gallaratese] is held above ideology and above all utopian proposals for "a new lifestyle" ', or
'the accusations of fascism hurled at Rossi mean little, since his attempts at the recovery of an ahistoricizing form exclude verbalizations of its content and any compromise with the real'.[7]

How does Rossi manage this disappearing act, this superhuman feat which has eluded every other architect? By using a 'syntax of empty signs', by 'the law of exclusion', by reducing the classical language of architecture even beyond the purity of fascist-stripped or 'deflowered classicism'.

Such extreme nudity ravages the mind of certain critics and makes them suspend their usual scepticism in a conversion that can only be termed religious: 'emptied sacredness', they avow.

Well, it may be too obvious to mention, but Rossi's forms *are* what may be termed bivalent: sacred and all too real, sublime and prison-like, heaven and the concentration camp, and I don't see any point in denying both aspects since Rossi himself so clearly plays on both sets of meaning. This duality of extremes is slighty titillating, if not provocative, and I personally find his work full of a terrifying loneliness and claustrophobia which is not undesirable in a painting. Some of his best architecture is painting. The same is true of another Rationalist, Massimo Scolari, who also claims the 'autonomy of architecture' from ideology and historical contamination (9).

Such autonomy is possible only under extreme and artificial conditions: when the perceiver abstracts himself in time and space from a building, brackets off its contextual setting and concentrates on the distortions of the language itself. Within these limits he can experience the building as a unique aesthetic act, an act which furthermore just refers to itself, or its own internal relations (void against curved barrel vault etc). It is this kind of meaning towards which Rossi and Scolari aspire, hence their celebration of the monument as the most architectural of building types.

'Distributive indifference belongs to architecture . . . the architecture of maximum precision—ie, that of monuments—offers potentially the maximum freedom'.[8]

We are thus back in the Surrealist world of Mies where any function can be poured into the same semantic form. The Japanese Rationalist Takefumi Aida has pushed this sort of thinking to the same irrational limits in an attempt to induce a kind of metaphysical trance in the spectator or inhabitant.

Aida has designed square, symmetrical, white boxes, one called Nirvana House, another the Annihilation House (this one Rossi chose to illustrate in his Rationalist exhibition), but the most delightful absurdity was his 'House like a Die' (7). This, as you will guess, was a cube with apertures or square marks on all sides: one on the top a skylight, two windows in one side, three on the next . . . and six columns for support. To Einstein's injunction that 'God doesn't play dice with the universe' (suspend its laws from time to time), Aida answers 'since I am not God, I'll play dice with my buildings' (or something like that):

'I intend to make my judgements as autocratic as I can . . . I consciously try to remove functional restrictions from my thinking and to search for a prototypical image. I do this because I want to seal architectural functions within architecture'.[9]

Elsewhere Aida says he wants to see how far he could 'imprison function within innate forms', and here we see the recurrent prison metaphor being tied to the Rationalist pursuit of the archetype. Rem Koolhaas takes this theme, as he does so many others, one step further in his scheme 'Exodus, or the Voluntary Prisoners of Architecture'.

Historicist Rationalism

The one area where the Rationalists aren't altogether irrational is in their treatment of urban form. Several of them, particularly two brothers from Luxembourg, Robert and Leon Krier, have mounted well-observed attacks on the devastation of city fabric. They criticize all the forces, whether economic or ideological, which have destroyed the texture of cities and they have proposed quite elegant alternatives which patch it up or create new wholes (8, 10).

'The debate which both Robert Krier and myself want to raise with our projects is

7 Takefumi Aida: House like a Die, Izu (1973). Aida has made the fortuitous similarity of a die with a house into a Rationalist proposition: 'this house was created according to the system used in dice and says no more than that dice are dice'. Except of course that a die is a house to live in. Conceptually the scheme bears comparison to Tresham's Triangular Lodge

8 Leon Krier: High School at Echternach (1970). Krier takes this mediaeval and Baroque city and accentuates its fabric sympathetically as shown by this tourist perspective. The existing Baroque school is doubled and a glazed corridor is placed between the two halves. Then this Baroque façade is varied to form a main entrance boulevard that focuses on the existing church (which is transformed into a community house). Sportsground, park and a circus are added. Note the quaint 1920s technology, the bi-plane and balloon monument to Leonidov—typical Rat symbols

9 Massimo Scolari: Architectural Landscape (1975?). Like Collage City a set of fragments from utopia. The wall, the nineteenth-century tube bridge, the girder support 'an impossible' cupola in a still landscape. M. C. Escher is just as much an influence here as de Chirico

10 Leon Krier: Royal Mint Square Housing project (1974). A very sympathetic bit of city stitching and patchwork that nevertheless has a grand urban scale reminiscent of Bath. A triangular route bisects the site, saving several existing buildings, keeping the street fabric and creating green triangular courts. A 'public room' with entrance portico on one side and gate to a car park on the other is in the centre of the pedestrian way. Various 'poetic' elements are placed along this route such as the cypress trees and four telephone kiosks

7

9

10

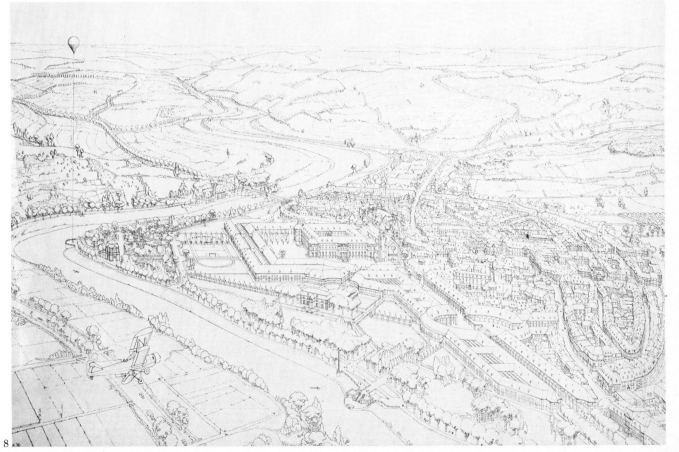

8

215

11

13

12

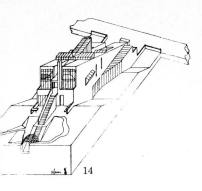

14

that of the urban morphology as against the zoning of the planners. The restoration of precise forms of urban space as against the wasteland which is created by zoning. The design of urban spaces, both traffic and pedestrian, linear and focal, is on the one hand a method which is general enough to allow flexibility and change and on the other hand precise enough to create both spatial and built continuity within the city.'[10]

Basically the Krier brothers follow Camillo Sitte's notions of articulating continuous urban space as a negative volume that flows and pulsates and reaches a crescendo around public buildings. This against functional separation and the forces that tend to make each building a freestanding, embarrassed monument. At Echternach Leon Krier inserts a traditional arcade and circus, using the existing eighteenth-century morphology to create an identifiable spine to the town and a culmination of the entrance route on the existing abbey (9). Height, scale, silhouette, and building material are all compatible with the existing fabric, although accentuated to give a new emphasis to the public realm. Leon Krier uses the traditional aerial perspective, which you find on tourist maps, to stitch these forms together. The image which results is reminiscent of eighteenth-century Bath and it is with such master builders as the Woods that the Krier brothers bear comparison. They are inheritors of a great tradition which was broken in the twentieth century by, among others, the previous Rationalists.

Leon Krier's competition entry for the Royal Mint Square Housing, 1974, is, in my view, the most sympathetic urban scheme of the Rationalists (10). It preserves old London street patterns and a few existing buildings, but incorporates those elements in a new pattern which cuts diagonally through the block. Thus two triangular courts and a central avenue are created which remain free from motor traffic; and the public realm is very subtly introduced in the form of arcades and a public square in the centre. Krier introduces several touches reminiscent of Le Corbusier and his 'objets à réaction poétique': a set of four telephone boxes grouped together as a raised altar, existing trees, a gate and portico entrance to the 'public room' and a row of cypress trees. These elements are set along the avenue to punctuate its otherwise rather repetitive syntax.

Both Kriers extend their historicism to all periods including the recent past, so their buildings tend to be ironic juxtapositions of various references rather like the collage cities already discussed. The work of Le Corbusier, James Stirling, Palladio, Leonidov and de Chirico is incorporated or transformed in fragments to provide hermeneutic texts for the other Rats to decipher. In-group jokes (a head-waiter serving up Le Corbusier's head, like Holofernes, while James Stirling scratches his head in consternation) as well as barely disguised communist slogans decorate their public realms. Robert Krier, in his Siemer House near Stuttgart (13, 14), plays with Expressionism and the black and white architecture of the 20s. Black-edged skylights and black voids punctuate white stucco cubes with a nearly complete symmetry. The Rats have reintroduced symmetry ironically, along with the white International Style that had previously banished it.

The most successful historicist, at least in terms of public recognition, is Ricardo Bofill and his group from Barcelona (Giscard d'Estaing described him as 'the finest architect in the world' and Bofill is not even French). They have produced housing in a variety of historical styles varying from neo-Gaudiesque through neo-vernacular to neo-Gothic (housing in the shape of a cathedral—what occupies the high altar? Nothing). Bofill and his partners have consciously embraced the Rationalist position, so that now one can speak of a Paris–Rome axis to the movement that includes peripheral centres in Berlin, Barcelona, London and New York.

For Bofill the Rationalist historicism means the free use of endless Roman arches, peppered with a few columns, gothic windows and cypresses (12). At Walden 7 (a hill of housing satirizing the dystopia of B. F. Skinner), Bofill has used an intricate geometry on a vast scale to induce true basic responses: claustro-

11 Ricardo Bofill: Walden 7, Barcelona (1972–5). A man-made hill of twenty stories with twelve storey holes punched through it and precipitous bridges across the open courts within. The red tile and repeated curves set up a very sensual rhythm

12 Ricardo Bofill and Taler: concrete factory converted into architects' office, Barcelona (1972–6). Grand vistas of space opening out to the horizon, the sea, the mountains and architecture! This is that nineteenth-century theme *The Architect's Dream* finally realized

13–14 Robert Krier: Siemer House, Warmbronn near Stuttgart (1968–73). Near symmetry and the black/white stucco style of the 20s is given an Expressionist twist. Skylights and geometry interplay very nicely with the slanted groundform

phobia on the inside and agoraphobia on the outside (11). When one is on the eighteenth floor, on one of the bridges overlooking a fountain at ground level, and the wind is whistling through a twelve-storey opening cut into the hill, then vertigo is the proper response. Bofill has proved popular because he makes picturesque use of the Rationalist style, always varying the surface and usually painting it a strong colour, so his work contrasts strongly with the grey mass-housing it is meant to supplant.

Very often Piranesi's prison sketches are invoked as a source of Rationalist poetics, and with Bofill more than the others, you feel you are back in this delightful madhouse of the eighteenth century. Appropriately his office is moving into one of these phobic buildings, a converted concrete factory that already is *The Architect's Dream* come true (endless vistas of pure form, grand space and cypresses, cypresses, cypresses on the *roof!* (12))

In America, Rationalist historicism got a champagne breakfast with Arthur Drexler's exhibition at the Museum of Modern Art entitled 'The Architecture of the Ecole des Beaux Arts' (October 1975–January 1976). Here was MOMA, the mother of the International Style in the USA, almost polemicizing a return to all the bad old virtues of the nineteenth century: ornament instead of pseudo-functionalism; urbanism and public buildings instead of mass housing; axes and heavy arcades and even heavier cornices against airy transparencies; a love of detail, colour and history instead of the eternal, black and white present. Such were the implied alternatives. Unfortunately as a coherent polemic Drexler's exhibition never finally took a stand and engaged the present as it might have done if put on by a European Rat. But it gave a good indication of which way the wind was blowing up Fifth Avenue, from the IAUS to the MOMA.

Architecture about itself

The acronym IAUS refers to the Institute for Architecture and Urban Studies, an institute run more or less by Peter Eisenman which has been a centre for Rat study for five years. Not only do many of the New York Five meet there, but Rem Koolhaas, Mario Gandelsonas and Kenneth Frampton, all sometime Rats, also work there. The house magazine *Oppositions* always carries one or two articles on international Rationalism by Manfredo Tafuri, Colin Rowe and others.

Eisenman's work, when it is not called Rationalist, is termed 'White' (which it almost always is when not black); 'Structuralist' (concerned with the relation between deep structural grids and surface structural representation); 'cardboard' (not only looking like this homogeneous cardboard, but also like a model); 'virtual' (in the sense of conceptual rather than just perceptual); and 'Corbusian' (actually more like Terragni). There are many labels under which a discussion of Eisenman's work can proceed and all of them are esoteric. He claims to be an élitist, indeed an anti-populist, making architecture more complicated than it has to be in order to engage the mind (and torture it into submission).

His logical diagrams of the way the building is 'generated' (a key word borrowed from Chomsky) would please any scholastic; they're more complex than the generation of rib mouldings from fan vaulting. And he presents the finished building as an illustration of the generation! Yes, the buildings are *about* the making of architecture, a process not a result. That is, they represent on the surface very hard to perceive transformations which the interior geometry has undergone (15, 16).

Ideally speaking, Eisenman would like to show the several arbitrary rules which have determined the building: the moving of volumes about on the diagonal, the rotation and inversion of lines and planes, the layering of space and so forth. In short only the syntactical elements are represented (or 'marked' in Eisenmanese). The basic marking is that of the surface structure which represents two or three different deep structures (grids, rotated and sheered grids). The basic problem is that no one, even Colin Rowe who has greatly influenced this process, can actually understand the markings. They are too ambiguous, and coded with too many

16

possible referents to choose between several readings. Thus the glass bead game, which is seductive to play, ultimately has no outcome.

Rationalism pushed into a reductive corner proves once again irrational. To say this, however, is not to condemn it as expression. Eisenman's houses actually absorb a lot of semantic content—they are experienced as elaborate structural symphonies, as the white, light-filled architecture of Le Corbusier and Mykonos, as playful games of nonsense poetry. One client fell in love with his structuralist game even though a transformation in the rules drove a column smack through his marital bed. Another client hated the transformations and lived in the basement before he moved out (a mathematician who understood Chomsky). No matter, Eisenman goes on and on with his logical convolutions until they dazzle the mind through sheer excess. As William Blake said of methodologists 'if the fool would persist in his folly he would become wise' (this is from *Proverbs from Hell*, incidentally).

On this score, Richard Meier isn't quite as wise, or excessive, as Eisenman and his buildings are really just 'about' some schemes Le Corbusier left unfinished or never bothered to work out fully (17). Meier, one of the Five (with Michael Graves, John Hejduk, Charles Gwathmy and Eisenman) confines himself to the early 20s syntax of Le Corbusier before it became more curvilinear and Brutalist. As he says of his Smith house, it is Le Corbusier's Citrohan on one side, Maison Domino on the other, and, one might add, a collage of what's left over in between. The emphasis, again, is on layered space, and distorting syntax, or architecture which is making a comment on previous architecture, and the surprising fact is that, given the rarity of this game, it is neither pastiche nor uncreative. Meier actually continues the Corb tradition, even if he bends it in the direction of *House Beautiful* and the Jet Set. Like many of the Five he has found clients among the

17a

17b

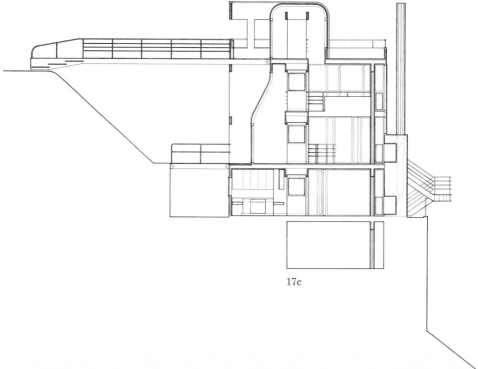

17c

17a, b, and c Richard Meier:
Douglas House, Harbour Springs,
Michigan (1971–3). Using a
Corbusian syntax of independent
structural frame, entrance ramp,
and double height space, this
building like Eisenman's
represents layered space on its
façade. Mullion lines take up, for
instance, balcony points and
column lines. Meier has given a
bent wall on the entrance side
which allows space to flow
vertically and sideways across
four levels—outdoing Corb at his
own game

nouveaux riches; White Rationalist architecture in America is, semantically speaking, the counterpart of the Neo-Classical style. You don't ask for a Palladian villa now, but a Corbusian one.

Meier has recounted, apparently with a straight face, how the Douglasses wanted another Smith House like the one they saw in *House Beautiful*. After persuading them to have a new improved model, Meier found the local citizenry wouldn't accept anything but wood finish. He tried 'thirty different shades of white-grey and buff coloured paint—in an effort to resolve this issue'. But the answer was no. The Douglasses built their white jewel elsewhere.[11]

If Eisenman's architecture is about a logical design process, then Michael Graves's is about certain architectural elements, particularly doors and points of entry.[12] He 'foregrounds' these elements, calling attention to them by dislocating them from their habitual context. For instance, in the Hanselmann House, the public entrance is raised, pulled away from the main body of the house and given an extra articulation of columns, creating a screen, or billboard effect (19). The key to Graves is the opposition between 'sacred and profane' space and the transition between them, particularly pronounced in Baroque church architecture. The Hanselmann House has some of this quality.

You approach directly on axis the frontal planes, and the procession towards the more private areas is articulated by a series of implied and real planes set at right angles to your movement (18). This layering of tight space was a theme of Le Corbusier's Garches as Rowe pointed out in an essay that influenced all the Five's buildings.[13] Graves, however, plays the game quite differently. By pulling away the entrance and making it ceremonial, he creates a big outdoor room, a public space which is in fact a cube of empty space identical to the positive volume of the private space. Thus a certain drama and significance of entry is created, so potent that the house could be more appropriately used as a shrine.

18 Michael Graves: Hanselmann House, actual state. The layering of space, set at right angles to the approach, becomes tighter and tighter as you reach the entrance. You have to cross a series of 'marked' frontal planes which increase in density by the entrance balcony and interior stairway

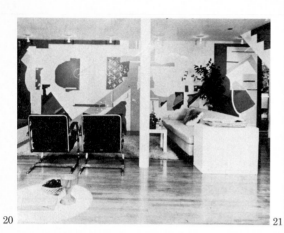

20

21

22

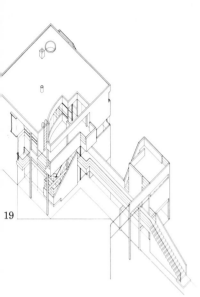

After you reach the ceremonial bridge, you head straight at the centre of the cube noticing such distinctive features as a diagonal to the left (indicating the stairs down to the children's level) and a balcony overhead (articulating the second entry). Certain Corbusian elements are exaggerated. Steel tubing and white picture windows framing the sky, a slight curve recalling the ever-obsessive guitar shape of Cubist paintings. Even the underlying Corbusian order of columns detached from white planes is emphasized.

You open the front door, arrive at the public level, and are confronted by stairways at right angles to each other and an idealized, Cubist mural of the house, a kind of totemistic representation of the whole thing (20). The mural is then a transformation in two dimensions of your experience in three, rather like an Eisenman drawing, except that elements are even further fragmented and made more complex than the architecture. Another notation is set up in terms of colour—blue for sky, green for nature—thus, if you are aware of it, underscoring the views out of the house. (Graves has written on the 'celestial soffit' and he often curves this element, making a visual pun on clouds in the sky.) In all of his buildings, there is a heightening of the vertical dimension: the sky is always brought in by frames, by columns and beams reaching out into space.

In fact there is always an ambiguity of space, best seen in his Gunwyn office conversion (21) where elements are so tightly packed that you have trouble distinguishing foreground from background. Essentially space is collapsed in two dimensions to appear as a Juan Gris still life (the Cubist Graves most admires). The movement through portal frames is so rich that it foreshortens the experience into a single flat plane. Everywhere you look mechanical, structural and wall elements compose into a two-dimensional collage. The trick, like all great architecture, calls attention to itself and takes time to experience.

Obvious doubts arise. Why should Graves confine himself to 1920s semantics? Clearly his emphasis on the significant points of architecture—doors, windows, walls—is valid and exemplary at this time, but he refuses to perform an essentially traditional role with a traditional syntax. No mouldings, capitals and pediments, no popular signs which would have a wider resonance of meaning. Furthermore the symbolic cues necessary for an understanding are essentially esoteric. For instance, in his Benacerraf House, you need a reader's guide to understand that a blue balustrade is really a 'column lying on its side'. There is an infinitude of such hermeneutic meanings in the Five's work.

Influence of the Rats

The work of the Five and the Italian Rationalists has had an enormous influence on architects who aren't directly in the tradition. Arata Isozaki has, since 1970, been producing variations on cubes, grids and Palladian plans (22). His Gunma Museum is a sequence through an implied deep structure of large cubes, which is everywhere articulated by a surface structure of small grids. Isozaki even elaborates the Rationalist style: the non-joint joint, the window or door opening as 'absence of wall', the smash together of grids without any mouldings or visual junctions.

Cesar Pelli and the 'Silvers of Los Angeles' have been developing their own version of spatial ambiguity based on refinements of the curtain wall which bring transparency, reflectivity, and translucency in a sequence of views.[14] The Silvers also reify the grid.

In England, Alan Colquhoun and John Miller use a restrained form of Rationalist style reminiscent of the work of Max Bill, while James Gowan produced a kind of Neo-Neo-Palladianism and James Stirling, slightly influenced by his former draughtsman Leon Krier, practises a kind of modern Neo-Classicism.

Stirling's shift in this direction, noticeable since the Derby scheme of 1970, is interesting because it indicates a general move of many architects toward urban and historicist meanings. A building as a part of the historical fabric, rather than as a discontinuous monument, becomes a prime focus. His museum scheme for

19 Michael Graves: Hanselmann House, Fort Wayne, Indiana (1967–8); axonometric. The entrance from the south-east is up some stairs, over a bridge to the middle of the house. The gate of columns and entablature, if built, would have given a pronounced sacred feeling to entry—in effect a double doorway—the first one a public symbol of the second

20 Michael Graves: Hanselmann House, mural representing layered space and diagonals, green earth and blue sky

21 Michael Graves: Gunwyn office conversion, Princeton, New Jersey (1973). Curved tubes, portals, frames, steel trusses, lighting fixtures, glass block and various colours all focus into a Gris still life and then go out of focus. The experience of space is rich and ambiguous again, being a movement against a series of real and implied planes

22 Arata Isozaki: Gunma Museum (1974). Here the Rationalist grids actually appear represented on the outside and throughout all the surfaces, being suitably rendered in a religious, polished aluminium. This main exhibition hall is turned at an angle to the rest of the grid, thus gaining importance as the 'head'. The space beneath is a mirror image of the volume—cube and anti-cube

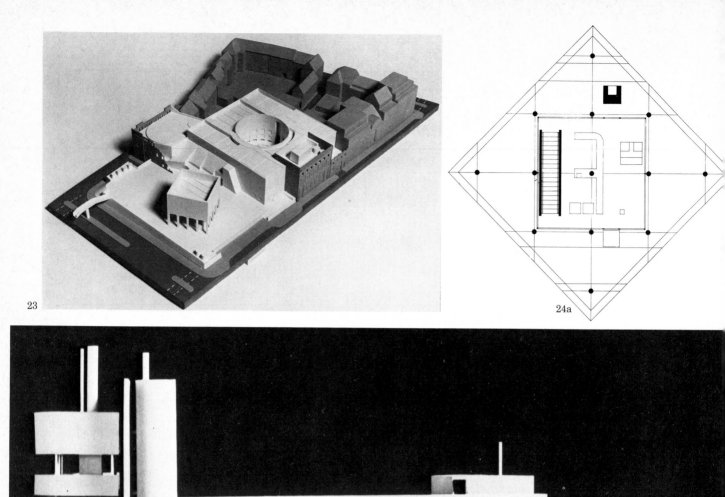

23

24a

25

23 James Stirling: Düsseldorf
museum project (1975). The open
circle becomes the covered
square. Like Kahn and Rossi, the
architect is fascinated by these
basic primitive forms conveyed
with a stripped classicism. The
building fits, on one side, very
neatly into the city fabric taking
up the street façades and cornice
line. Then the square element,
raised on a podium, is turned to
the side picking up major site
lines and acting as a symbolic
entrance

Düsseldorf shows much of the Rationalist historicism I have already mentioned (23).

On the level of details, he uses the German flattened arch common to public
buildings in this area, as well as masonry and the classical grammar of Schinkel.
The base of Schinkel's Altes Museum in Berlin becomes the elevation for a good
part of Stirling's scheme, which also has a facsimile façade on one side (to carry on
the nineteenth-century street façade) and even a real pediment on top of two
columns! (But of course, no mouldings, as the Rats haven't yet gone this far back to
the past.)

In volume, Stirling's museum scheme fits into the city fabric and gives a very
enjoyable twist to the existing pedestrian street: it becomes first an open outdoor
room to the sky, a circle, and then a glass-roofed portico, a square. Positive square,
negative circle, conceptually one tries to square the circle. The same opposition
can be found in Aldo Rossi's urban projects, although made with less tension and
irony. In fact the ironies of this Düsseldorf scheme become a bit black when one
reflects on certain references. The windows of the open circle recall the Nazi work
of Albert Speer and they seem to sink into the ground. They are placed way below
the roof line and emerge half above the ground implying that Nazism is still
present, but that it is sinking (or is it rising?). The only remains of the old Stirling,
the Futurist, are in the ramps and curved, patent glazing. All in all it shows how

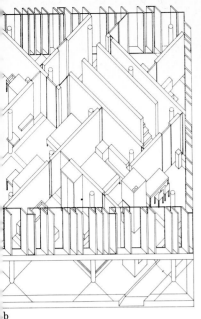

b

24a, and b John Hejduk: House 8, Diamond Series (1962–66). Two squares rotated at 45 degrees create the major opposition between frontal layered space and whirling, centrifugal space. Everywhere you feel the opposition between the two systems because every element of structure and furniture takes up one or another of the themes

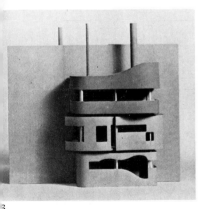

25, 26 John Hejduk: Bye Residence (1972–74). Basically living space on one side of the wall and functional space on the hall side of the wall, periscopes over the top. The guitar and stomach-shaped rooms are painted in muted primary colour. At one point Hejduk was considering that these rooms should be rendered like an architectural drawing with scratchy shadows. 'Everybuddy asks me how we gonna doh dat, but a house can be rendered. Ed Bye, like me is a cunsuvative and said what I want ta hear—I like it.' It took Hejduk two years to make working drawings for this house which may be built

strong the Rationalist influence has become (although of course Stirling has always been something of a Neo-Classicist).

King Rats or Rat Killers?—Surrationalism

We have seen that Rationalism taken to an extreme becomes absurd and that practised as a half measure it's simply irrational. Of course its twin, Functionalism, was never functional and there are few movements that live up, or down, to their slogans. This is not altogether a bad thing since any doctrine is bound to be simplistic and its followers will therefore spend much of their time trying to balance if not altogether refute it. Thus it is appropriate that from within the movement come two supreme ironists whose Rationalism is so explicitly extreme and thorough-going as to make all the pitfalls and beauty of the approach abundantly and deliciously clear. They push Rationalism so far it becomes surreal or Surrationalism; they are the King Rats or Rat Killers, depending on where their extremity leaves the movement. Either way it can't go on anymore pretending to be straightforward and sensible. Either it evolves towards an empirical base and becomes *Critical* Rationalism, or it evolves in more absolutist directions towards the Surrationalism of these two Kings.[15] Both have been influenced greatly by Surrealism and both, not surprisingly, haven't built anything, but their projects are no less persuasive for that.

Big John Hejduk, who must be over six foot six and who speaks like a John Wayne from the Bronx, likes to build little, tiny, miniscule models of his unbuilt houses (some are $1\frac{1}{2}$ inches small). I'm not sure why he likes this massive disjunction in scale (he does of course carry the models in his pockets) but it is entirely fitting to the rest of his message which thrives on absurdity and paradox. Magritte is one of his exemplars.

Hejduk will take an essentially prosaic and normal idea and then belabour it so long that it becomes extraordinary and abnormal. First, in 1954, he worked over Palladio, planning houses based on nine squares until he had exhausted much of the magical potential for filling these squares with columns and chimneys. This research on pure geometric relations and a trabeated, caged system of space lasted until 1962 when, miraculously like Van Doesburg, he rotated his geometry by 45 degrees. The result? 'Diamond Houses' (24). For the next four years diamonds, diagonals or hypoteneuses were to be explored, and I mean mined, dug up. All sorts of diagonal properties were discovered which Mondrian and Van Doesburg only just touched on: the meshing of two grids produced endlessly nice collisions, space seemed to whirl about like a centrifuge, stairways and chimneys went into 'three-dimensional torque', the edges or corners became 'charged and filled with maximum tension'.[16] The effect was so mesmerizing that Ken Frampton used this formal twist as the second theme of his justification of the Five, in an article he called 'Frontality and Rotation'.[17] This was rotation all right, every corner of the room reminded you of the fact. For initiates into the hermeneutic code of the Five, there were also other cues. Whenever you see a round column you are meant to think 'rotation'. When you see a square column you think 'frontality'. As Hejduk said of Le Corbusier's Carpenter Centre, 'The shape of the structural columns is round, indicating a centrifugal force and multi-directional whirl'. Or, as Frampton said of Eisenman's House 1 (Rats number their houses like mathematical propositions), 'the unresolved tension between frontalization and rotation [is created by] the presence and/or absence of stainless steel cylindrical columns.'[18]

Oh those *absent square* columns are just so . . . frontalized! This is all very interesting and it reminds one of the traditional Japanese, indeed Shinto, distinction between round, untreated cypress columns symbolizing tree (nature) and squared-up wooden beams symbolizing man-made (culture). But of course this code was not so esoteric, nor based on missing cues for its interpretation.

Anyway, Hejduk moved on from his diamond fixation to concentrate on what he really came to love: walls. He designed one project, somewhat racist in overtones, which consisted of two houses, one black, the other white, which were separated by a high wall. Then he provided holes and periscopes so these opposite neighbours could surreptitiously monitor each other, the wall uniting them in a mutual obsession. Hejduk then looked at Philip Johnson's wall houses and the canonical Rationalist building Hadrian's Villa, with all its types of wall, and of course Hadrian's Wall itself.[19]

By 1964 he was really into the wall in a big way and he started designing houses whose drama consisted in constantly penetrating through an outside wall to find yourself—outside. ('You goh truh da waal ta make yah way back to da house'.)

For instance, on one side of the Bye Residence (25–26) there are three superimposed rooms of living, sleeping and dining which are separated by a flat ('frontalized') wall plane from bathroom, stairs, study and long linear hall. A periscope is thoughtfully provided 'so Ed can come intuh his house and luk ovah his waal'. Putting a large, structured wall, a shield between these two types of room (rendered in Cubist shapes and pale primaries) gives them a felicitous kind of schizophrenia, as if they belonged to two different families (one horizontal, one vertical). It also increases the drama of transition and, a functional point Hejduk might not like to make, is very sensible if there is a lot of traffic and noise on the garage side.

The fascination for walls ('Wallism'—a well-known disease of bad neighbours)[20] reached a pinnacle (if that is the right architectural word) with his project for the Venice Biennale in 1974. This was called a 'Cemetery for the Ashes of Thought', a kind of museum or mausoleum for thoughts that weren't quite dead, or at least ones that he wished to commemorate (27). Hejduk made it an explicit commentary on Rationalism, since it was a project for Italy, a 'commentary on and answer to the architecture of death', those schemes of Aldo Rossi which appear so quiescent and necrophiliac. His answer was a lot of wall. Many (it's hard to count because of optical vibration) walls to be twelve feet high, to be placed four feet apart and run straight for six hundred feet. Six hundred feet of wall, one side black, the other white, holes every two or three feet! You'd feel like a termite lost in a straightened Bridget Riley.

What was the point? Hejduk said that various plaques and cubic gravestones would be placed throughout giving the titles of old thoughts (eg *Remembrance of Things Past*, *The Counterfeiters*, various titles to books he admires). The main house, an abandoned factory, would be painted deep black, would have more plaques now with the authors' names, and it would be inhabited from time to time by a visiting dignitary (who presumably would spend his time recalling those precious moments of time past, *Death in Venice* etc).

Hejduk spent a whole month colouring in the spaces between the walls. Such projects starting from a Rationalist concern with first principles, and architecture about itself, renders the principles authoritarian. They grow to consume everything else. Like a traditional Surrealist, Hejduk focuses on everyday aspects of reality, but then gives them an independent life of their own, cut off from their original function. Doors, walls, triangles, chimneys, linear halls dominate everything, like Magritte's apple that expanded so much that the inhabitants were forced to flee their room. This impossible likelihood, like magic, forces us to reconsider the prosaic, and the assumption of what really is rational.

The other Rat killer, or King Rat, Rem Koolhaas and his team of metropolitan enthusiasts, is also very influenced by Surrealism, particularly the 'paranoid-critical method' of creativity practised by Salvador Dali.[21] Central to this method is the projection of dreams, phobias, ideologies and obsessions, on to the real world, until they become true by sheer force of repetition and willpower. The history of civilization, and particularly that of New York City, looks from this angle like a sequence of such projections. Koolhaas says of Manhattan (and he quickly turns this *aperçu* into a philosophy, Manhattanism), that it was 'a compression of all the best of Europe'. It was a successful paranoid projection of the Dutch phobia, 'New Amsterdam'; its history has suffered successive projections, those of endless ethnic groups and paranoid Rationalists such as Le

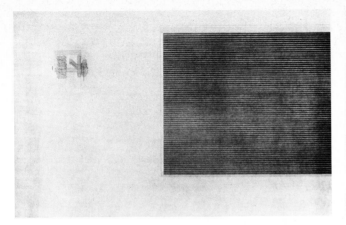

27a and b John Hejduk:
Cemetery for the Ashes of
Thought, Venice Biennale project
(1976). An old factory (section) is
kept empty and many walls, 600 ft
long, 4 ft apart with black and
white sides, are placed at right
angles (plan). Various
transparent cubes and plaques
commemorate dead authors such
as Marcel Proust. 'Most
Rationalists I hold in high regard,
but day are dealing in an
architecture of death. This is a
commentary and answer to them.'
Visiting dignitaries would
inhabit the memorial for a limited
time

Corbusier, until each part of it represents the distillation of some ideal dream. To take this tendency even further, and bring it to self-consciousness, Koolhaas has designed 'the City of the Captive Globe' (28).

This project gives to each city block a self-consistent and self-referring style and ideology—or 'mania'. Thus Le Corbusier's serrated towers stand next to Expressionist pointed arches, Malevitch near Superstudio, the ever-present globe and needle (1939 World's Fair) is next to what looks to be the Plaza Hotel and Mass Housing. Other Rationalist icons are strewn about; the World Trade Center looks down on 'the captive globe' at the centre.

The point of these blocks, like the paranoid-critical method, is to banish any reality which does not serve the original mania. What could be a better critique of Rationalism. In Koolhaas's words (and he is the son of a Dutch poet):

'Each science or mania has its own plot. On each plot stands an identical base, built from heavy polished stone. These bases, ideological laboratories are equipped to suspend unwelcome laws, undeniable truths (sic), to create non-existent physical conditions to facilitate and provoke speculative activity . . .
The changes of this ideological skyline will be rapid and continuous, a rich spectacle of ethical joy, moral fever or intellectual masturbation'.[22]

In a sense this is just real New York intensified.

Koohaas and OMA developed their theories in 1972 with a study of the Berlin Wall (walls again), and their scheme for London called 'Exodus, or the Voluntary Prisoners of Architecture'. Is it true that people, not only designers, love to be 'voluntary prisoners of architecture'? Can the history of architecture really be seen as their self-imposed incarceration into walls, skyscrapers, globes and needles? In a dream-sense, yes, and it is this unwritten dream which Koolhaas wishes to record and reinforce.

'Every skyscraper in New York wanted to be a sphere and every sphere secretly wanted to be a needle . . .'. The drama of 'delirious New York' unfolds like an illuminated nightmare, with the protagonists, the Chrysler Building and the Empire State in bed with each other (29). There they lie, the feminine Chrysler curving over to meet the larger Empire State, while the Statue of Liberty holds a flaming lamp above them. Their tryst is over, symbolized by the spent rubber balloon of the Good Year Tyre Blimp. But then suddenly the jealous RCA building intrudes, and casts its search-light on them. The best of New York skyscraperdom looks on aghast (or is it with an interest in morals?)

What is the message of this 'in flagrante delecto'? Out from underneath the bed is born the magical New York Grid, Central Park and the spaghetti of roads, tubes and services (the underground, deep collective unconscious). Manhattan is being killed (by recent architects) and in the next set of drawings we see that the only hope is for more spaghetti, more fanatical obsessions which produced these two former 'largest needles in the world'.

In many such drawings and water colours Koolhaas and Vriesendorp portray what they call 'the secret life of buildings':

28

28 Rem Koolhaas and OMA: *The City of the Captive Globe* (1975). What New York City is trying to be, a distillation of ideologies which have been 'inflicted' on the world. Each block is a complete and pure expression of 'a certain form of madness'—notice the Rationalist block of ice-cool cubes, lower right. The captivity of the globe in the centre is the final subjugation of the reality principle by the 'paranoid—critical method'. All blocks are isolated on rectangular podia which carefully exclude unwelcome truth—the censorship practised in every nation. Incidentally, of all nations, South Africa has the highest level of paranoia; West Germany is second

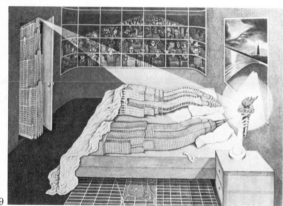

29

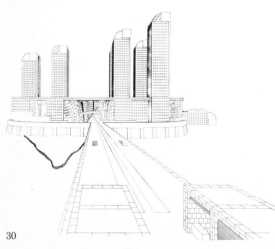

30

31

29 Rem Koolhaas and Madelon Vriesendorp: *In Flagrante Delecto* (1975). The Chrysler Building, female and the tallest until 1933, curls up to the Empire State, while other skyscrapers sprout heads and watch. The print-out under the bed is the offspring of this illicit encounter—the neutral grid of New York which absorbs all paranoid projections equally. This gouache is part of a series 'The Secret Life of Buildings' and the drama continues

30 Rem Koolhaas and OMA: *Welfare Palace Hotel* (1975). This hotel of towers faces Harrison's RCA building and New York with its glass walls and seven heads. A fault runs through the hotel and one tower has fallen over on its back. The site is 'a graveyard for discarded schemes, an architectural parking lot' full of Rat beauty and monotony

31 Rem Koolhaas and OMA: *The Raft of the Medusa* (1975). If New York is an architectural shipwreck which is sinking, then the buildings, like the survivors on Medusa's raft, will have to eat each other. Welfare Island proceeds to eat New York City. All of a sudden everything is saved—'They had recaptured a lost paradise: the ability to love, not so much each other, but themselves'

'To introduce explicit figurative, symbolic elements in the urban realm, OMA is developing a quasi-Freudian language to identify and analyse the psychological characteristics and properties which could be ascribed to architecture'.[23]

With a kind of remorseless, surrealist wit Koolhaas shows what psychological characteristics have existed; the evolving globe and needle became more and more sick and finally degenerate into the awful slab blocks. Wallace Harrison, who has been instrumental in this evolution with his RCA and United Nation slabs, still feels a throb of the Manhattan blood in his clotted arteries, so he is capable of utterly inexplicable gestures, such as the slight curve. Koolhaas finds these curves becoming more and more obsessive after the RCA building (he studied Harrison's curves for three years) until they reach a spasmic crescendo in the UN building. The weak curve of Harrison recurs here fifty times! Whatever can it mean? Koolhaas decodes it: 'That means there's something the matter with it. It's the *limp curve of humanism* which betrays the perpetual representation of guilt feelings'. The same limp curve of humanism disciplines Harrison's Opera House at the Lincoln Centre which is a 'marble cyclotron that twists and turns people until they lose reality'.

This psychoanalysis of architecture is then turned into a utopian paranoid conjecture, a scheme for Welfare Island (30). The grid of Manhattan and Harrison's limp curve are there as well as other recognizable manias: in fact Koolhaas calls his scheme 'an architectural parking lot, a graveyard for discarded schemes', tinged with the 'humiliating setbacks' he prefigures in his future. The skyscrapers are there with their 'heads' looking at Manhattan and the RCA, while one of them has collapsed on its side as a 'groundscraper'. The Rat emphasis on repetition is there, brought to a new pitch of boredom. So is the Rat jumble of buildings, a collision to rival New York which is also a 'shipwreck of architecture'. To 'take the temperature of this shipwreck', Koolhaas has devised his 'architectural dipstick' in the form of Géricault's *Raft of the Medusa* (31). This he inserts at various points to see how healthy is the paranoia. The raft is in a sense the perfect image of Manhattanism, a group of survivors from a shipwreck, who cannibalize each other in order to survive.

'According to the Classic Chronicle, their parachute dropped the castaways of the Medusa and their raft on the rescue-ship "The City". It appeared like a serene monument bursting with the ornamental frenzy that its inner life provoked. It was an unknown, a new form of life, inside a timeless architecture: an innumerable mixture of activities generated by the ship's hedonistic daily program. It was a spontaneous Planning Centre governed by the continuous satisfaction and shameless application of human passions. Amongst the protagonists of this inspired state of anarchy, Jesus Christ and the Marquis de Sade were engaged in a mutant form of behaviour which was echoed by the splendid order of the architecture . . .'[24].

And so Rationalism, born in the paranoid conjectures of an eighteenth-century monk dreaming about the lesson of the Primitive Hut, ends two hundred years later on a wooden raft of Surrationalism, with the Rats unable to leave their sinking ship and eating each other to save their lives.

NOTES
[1] See Karl Popper, *Conjectures and Refutations: the growth of scientific knowledge*, London 1963, particularly the entries under 'Intellectualism' which correspond to Rationalism. Popper's *Critical* Rationalism should not be confused with this intellectualism, because it is rooted in refutation, in criticism.
[2] See Giulia Veronesi, *Difficoltá politiche dell'architettura in Italia 1920–40*, Milan 1953.

Leonardo Benevolo, *History of Modern Architecture*, Vol 2, London 1971, pp. 561–76.
[3] See Also Rossi, Franco Raggi, Massimo Scolari, Rosaldo Bonicalzi, Gianni Braghieri and Daniele Vitale, *Architettura Razionale, XV di Milano*, Milan, Franco Angeli Editore, 1973.
[4] Colin Rowe, Collage City, *The Architectural Review*, August 1975 and following letters.
[5] The main criticisms in English are: Alan

Colquhoun, Rational Architecture, *Architectural Design*, June 1975, pp 365–6; Manfredo Tafuri, L'Architecture dans le boudoir, *Oppositions 3*, May 1974, pp 42–8; Vittorio Savi, Aldo Rossi, *Lotus 11*, 1976, pp 42–52; Vittorio Savi, David Stewart in *A + U* No 5, 1976, issue devoted to Rossi, with bibliography.

[6] Aldo Rossi, *A + U op. cit.*, p 74.

[7] Manfredo Tafuri, *Oppositions 3, op. cit.*, p 45. See also his *Architecture and Utopia, Design and Capitalist Development*, Cambridge, Mass, MIT Press 1976, pp 170–82.

[8] Massimo Scolari, Avanguardia Nuova Architettura, in *Architettura Razionale*, quoted from Alan Colquhoun's translation, *op. cit.*, p 366.

[9] Takefumi Aida, *The Japan Architect*, November 1972, p 101.

[10] Leon Krier, Projects in the City, in *Lotus, op. cit.*, p 73.

[11] Richard Meier, 'My Statement' is an issue devoted to his work of *A + U*, No 4, 1976, p 76.

[12] Susan Whittig pointed out the 'foregrounding' of certain themes in Eisenman, Graves and Venturi in her paper 'Architecture about Architecture' delivered at the Semiotics Conference in Milan, June 1974.

[13] Colin Rowe and Robert Slutzky, 'Transparency: Literal and Phenomenal', *Perspecta*, No 8, New Haven 1963, pp 45–6.

[14] I have written on the 'Los Angeles Silvers', *A + U*, October 1976; *Progressive Architecture*, December 1976.

[15] My own guess is that the movement will split evenly in two directions.

[16] These quotes from John Hejduk actually refer to a discussion of Mondrian, Van Doesburg, Le Corbusier's Carpenter Centre and the paintings of Juan Gris, but they apply equally to his Diamond series. See his 'Out of Time and into Space' in an issue of *A + U* devoted to his work 1975, No 5, pp 3–24.

[17] Ken Frampton, Frontality vs Rotation, *Five Architects*, New York 1972, 1975, pp 9–13. See also his John Hejduk and the Cult of Humanism in the *A + U* cited, note 16. Frampton isn't altogether supportive of the Five and Hejduk, but he confines his analysis to formal concerns and then jumps a mile to pure iconological interpretation.

[18] The Hejduk quotation from *A + U*, p 4; the Frampton one from *The Five, op. cit.*, p. 10.

[19] This chronology Hejduk outlined in a lecture at UCLA in April 1976.

[20] Robert Frost, in *Mending Wall*: 'Something there is that doesn't love a wall, That wants it down'. Of course, as Hejduk shows, walls unite neighbours on a line and are therefore basically ambiguous, half bringing together, half dividing.

[21] Rem Koolhaas formed OMA, the Office for Metropolitan Architecture, on January 1, 1975. This office includes his wife Madelon Vriesendorp, and Elia and Zoe Zenghelis and sometimes O. M. Ungers: two Dutch, two Greeks and an occasional German. Their work has been published in *Lotus 11, op. cit.*, and Koolhaas is working on a book *Delirious New York*, to be published shortly.

[22] Rem Koolhaas, *Lotus 11, op. cit.*, p 36.

[23] *ibid.*, p 34.

[24] *ibid.*, p 36.

Index

232